D0065734

EARLY ECONOMIC THOUGHT

EARLY
ECONOMIC THOUGHT

SELECTIONS FROM
ECONOMIC LITERATURE PRIOR TO
ADAM SMITH

EDITED BY

ARTHUR ELI MONROE, Ph.D.

CAMBRIDGE

HARVARD UNIVERSITY PRESS

1965

PRINTED IN UNITED STATES OF AMERICA

PREFACE

THE history of economic thought is a study at once chastening and heartening; chastening, because it furnishes such abundant evidence of the difficulty of intellectual progress; heartening, because each groping generation does seem to make a real contribution to that progress. Some acquaintance with it is therefore a most valuable background for the student of modern economic theory; indeed, I am inclined to think that it is almost indispensable, if economics is to remain a part of our liberal training.

For the general outlines of this history, and for most of the details, all but specialists will have to depend upon manuals and lectures. With no more than this, however, not only does the student lose the critical practice afforded by reading the early writers, but there is great danger that such important terms as Scholasticism and Mercantilism will remain mere abstractions for those who have never read a chapter of Mun's classic, or perhaps even turned the pages of Saint Thomas. The general outline must be supplemented by an adequate sample of the thing described, if a correct impression is to be obtained.

For the period since Adam Smith this has presented little difficulty, but for the earlier period the barriers of language and inaccessibility have been almost insuperable. To meet this need is the object of the present collection of extracts. It is neither an anthology of all that is important, nor even a gallery of all who are worthy, but only a few representative extracts, sufficiently varied, I hope, to give some idea of the wealth of material available. Against the difficulty inherent in such collections — that the individuality of the selections tends to become merged in that of the collection itself — I have tried to guard in several ways: by making the extracts long enough to insure a lasting impression, by various mechanical devices designed to suggest the independence of the different selections, and by keeping my own contribution as small as possible. In the translations I have tried to keep to the English idiom, without departing too much from the author's own style.

I wish to thank Professor C. J. Bullock of Harvard for help on several matters, Professor D. N. Robinson of Ohio Wesleyan for advice concerning some of the translations, and the several publishers who generously allowed me to reprint portions of works published by them.

A. E. M.

HARVARD UNIVERSITY
July, 1923

CONTENTS

CONTENTS

I

ARISTOTLE

POLITICS · ETHICS

NOTE

ARISTOTLE (384–322 B.C.) was born at Stagira in Thrace, son of a physician. In early youth he went to Athens to study with Plato, and remained there till the great teacher's death twenty years later. After some years of travel he went to Macedonia to act as tutor to the king's son, later Alexander the Great. In 335 he returned to Athens, where he conducted a school of philosophy for the next twelve years. He was forced into exile by a prosecution for impiety, and died at Chalcis the following year. He was a thinker of extraordinary range and power, having left important works on logic, metaphysics, ethics, politics, rhetoric, poetry, history, psychology, and the natural sciences. Unlike the works of his master, Plato, these are often uneven and obscure in style, and it has been suggested that this indicates slow composition and much revision. All are characterized, however, by an impressive respect for facts and a striving for scientific precision which mark a distinct advance. None of the authentic works is devoted to purely economic questions, but he was fully alive to the relation between economic considerations and other aspects of life, and discussed many economic questions from this point of view. His great prestige among the Schoolmen gave these views wide currency, and greatly influenced the development of economic thought.

THE POLITICS[1]

BOOK I

E VERY state is a community of some kind, and every
community is established with a view to some good;
for mankind always act in order to obtain that which they
think good. But, if all communities aim at some good, the
state or political community, which is the highest of all, and
which embraces all the rest, aims, and in a greater degree
than any other, at the highest good.

Now there is an erroneous opinion that a statesman, king,
householder, and master are the same, and that they differ,
not in kind, but only in the number of their subjects. For
example, the ruler over a few is called a master; over more,
the manager of a household; over a still larger number, a
statesman or king, as if there were no difference between a
great household and a small state. The distinction which
is made between the king and the statesman is as follows:
When the government is personal, the ruler is a king; when,
according to the principles of the political science, the citizens rule and are ruled in turn, then he is called a statesman.

But all this is a mistake; for governments differ in kind,
as will be evident to any one who considers the matter according to the method which has hitherto guided us. As in
other departments of science, so in politics, the compound
should always be resolved into the simple elements or least
parts of the whole. We must therefore look at the elements
of which the state is composed, in order that we may see in
what they differ from one another, and whether any scien-

[1] Translated by Benjamin Jowett. Reprinted with the consent of the Master
and Fellows of Balliol College and the Delegates of the Oxford University
Press.

tific distinction can be drawn between the different kinds
of rule.

He who thus considers things in their first growth and
origin, whether a state or anything else, will obtain the
clearest view of them. In the first place (1) there must be a
union of those who cannot exist without each other; for
example, of male and female, that the race may continue;
and this is a union which is formed, not of deliberate purpose, but because, in common with other animals and with
plants, mankind have a natural desire to leave behind them
an image of themselves. And (2) there must be a union of
natural ruler and subject, that both may be preserved. For
he who can foresee with his mind is by nature intended to
be lord and master, and he who can work with his body is a
subject, and by nature a slave; hence master and slave
have the same interest. Nature, however, has distinguished
between the female and the slave. For she is not niggardly,
like the smith who fashions the Delphian knife for many
uses; she makes each thing for a single use, and every instrument is best made when intended for one and not for many
uses. But among barbarians no distinction is made between
women and slaves, because there is no natural ruler among
them: they are a community of slaves, male and female.
Wherefore the poets say, —

> It is meet that Hellenes should rule over barbarians;

as if they thought that the barbarian and the slave were by
nature one.

Out of these two relationships between man and woman,
master and slave, the family first arises, and Hesiod is right
when he says, —

> First house and wife and an ox for the plough,

for the ox is the poor man's slave. The family is the association established by nature for the supply of men's every-day
wants, and the members of it are called by Charondas
'companions of the cupboard,' and by Epimenides the

Cretan, 'companions of the manger.' But when several families are united, and the association aims at something more than the supply of daily needs, then comes into existence the village. And the most natural form of the village appears to be that of a colony from the family, composed of the children and grandchildren, who are said to be 'suckled with the same milk.' And this is the reason why Hellenic states were originally governed by kings; because the Hellenes were under royal rule before they came together, as the barbarians still are. Every family is ruled by the eldest, and therefore in the colonies of the family the kingly form of government prevailed because they were of the same blood. As Homer says [of the Cyclopes], —

> Each one gives law to his children and to his wives.

For they lived dispersedly, as was the manner in ancient times. Wherefore men say that the Gods have a king, because they themselves either are or were in ancient times under the rule of a king. For they imagine, not only the forms of the Gods, but their ways of life to be like their own.

When several villages are united in a single community, perfect and large enough to be nearly or quite self-sufficing, the state comes into existence, originating in the bare needs of life, and continuing in existence for the sake of a good life. And therefore, if the earlier forms of society are natural, so is the state, for it is the end of them, and the [completed] nature is the end. For what each thing is when fully developed, we call its nature, whether we are speaking of a man, a horse, or a family. Besides, the final cause and end of a thing is the best, and to be self-sufficing is the end and the best.

Hence it is evident that the state is a creation of nature, and that man is by nature a political animal. And he who by nature and not by mere accident is without a state, is either above humanity, or below it; he is the

> tribeless, lawless, hearthless one,

6   EARLY ECONOMIC THOUGHT

whom Homer denounces — the outcast who is a lover of war; he may be compared to an unprotected piece in the game of draughts.

Now the reason why man is more of a political animal than bees or any other gregarious animals is evident. Nature, as we often say, makes nothing in vain, and man is the only animal whom she has endowed with the gift of speech. And whereas mere sound is but an indication of pleasure or pain, and is therefore found in other animals (for their nature attains to the perception of pleasure and pain and the intimation of them to one another, and no further), the power of speech is intended to set forth the expedient and inexpedient, and likewise the just and the unjust. And it is a characteristic of man that he alone has any sense of good and evil, of just and unjust, and the association of living beings who have this sense makes a family and a state.

Thus the state is by nature clearly prior to the family and to the individual, since the whole is of necessity prior to the part; for example, if the whole body be destroyed, there will be no foot or hand, except in an equivocal sense, as we might speak of a stone hand; for when destroyed the hand will be no better. But things are defined by their working and power; and we ought not to say that they are the same when they are no longer the same, but only that they have the same name. The proof that the state is a creation of nature and prior to the individual is that the individual, when isolated, is not self-sufficing; and therefore he is like a part in relation to the whole. But he who is unable to live in society, or who has no need because he is sufficient for himself, must be either a beast or a god: he is no part of a state. A social instinct is implanted in all men by nature, and yet he who first founded the state was the greatest of benefactors. For man, when perfected, is the best of animals, but, when separated from law and justice, he is the worst of all; since armed injustice is the more dangerous, and he is equipped at birth with the arms of intelligence and with moral qualities which he may use for the worst ends.

Wherefore, if he have not virtue, he is the most unholy and the most savage of animals, and the most full of lust and gluttony. But justice is the bond of men in states, and the administration of justice, which is the determination of what is just, is the principle of order in political society.

Seeing then that the state is made up of households, before speaking of the state we must speak of the management of the household. The parts of the household are the persons who compose it, and a complete household consists of slaves and freemen. Now we should begin by examining everything in its least elements; and the first and least parts of a family are master and slave, husband and wife, father and children. We have therefore to consider what each of these three relations is and ought to be: — I mean the relation of master and servant, of husband and wife, and thirdly of parent and child. And there is another element of a household, the so-called art of money-making, which, according to some, is identical with household management, according to others, a principal part of it; the nature of this art will also have to be considered by us.

Let us first speak of master and slave, looking to the needs of practical life and also seeking to attain some better theory of their relation than exists at present. For some are of opinion that the rule of a master is a science, and that the management of a household, and the mastership of slaves, and the political and royal rule, as I was saying at the outset, are all the same. Others affirm that the rule of a master over slaves is contrary to nature, and that the distinction between slave and freeman exists by law only, and not by nature; and being an interference with nature is therefore unjust.

Property is a part of the household, and therefore the art of acquiring property is a part of the art of managing the household; for no man can live well, or indeed live at all, unless he be provided with necessaries. And as in the arts which have a definite sphere the workers must have their own proper instruments for the accomplishment of their work, so it is in the management of a household. Now, instruments are of various sorts; some are living, others lifeless; in the rudder, the pilot of a ship has a lifeless, in the look-out man, a living instrument; for in the arts the servant is a kind of instrument. Thus, too, a possession is an instrument for maintaining life. And so, in the arrangement of the family, a slave is a living possession, and property a number of such instruments; and the servant is himself an instrument, which takes precedence of all other instruments. For if every instrument could accomplish its own work, obeying or anticipating the will of others, like the statues of Daedalus, or the tripods of Hephaestus, which, says the poet,

of their own accord entered the assembly of the Gods;

if, in like manner, the shuttle would weave and the plectrum touch the lyre without a hand to guide them, chief workmen would not want servants, nor masters slaves. Here, however, another distinction must be drawn: the instruments commonly so called are instruments of production, whilst a possession is an instrument of action. The shuttle, for example, is not only of use, but something else is made by it, whereas of a garment or of a bed there is only the use. Further, as production and action are different in kind, and both require instruments, the instruments which they employ must likewise differ in kind. But life is action and not production, and therefore the slave is the minister of action [for he ministers to his master's life]. Again, a possession is spoken of as a part is spoken of; for the part is not only a part of something else, but wholly belongs to it; and this is also true of a possession. The master is only the master of the slave; he does not belong to him, whereas the slave is not only the slave of his master, but wholly belongs to him. Hence we see what is the nature and office of a slave; he who is by nature not his own but another's and yet a man, is by nature a slave; and he may be said to belong to another who, being a human being, is also a possession. And a possession may be defined as an instrument of action, separable from the possessor.

But is there any one thus intended by nature to be a slave, and for whom such a condition is expedient and right, or rather is not all slavery a violation of nature?

There is no difficulty in answering this question, on grounds both of reason and of fact. For that some should rule and others be ruled is a thing, not only necessary, but expedient; from the hour of their birth, some are marked out for subjection, others for rule.

And whereas there are many kinds both of rulers and subjects, that rule is the better which is exercised over better subjects — for example, to rule over men is better than to rule over wild beasts. The work is better which is executed by better workmen; and where one man rules and another is ruled, they may be said to have a work. In all things which form a composite whole and which are made up of parts, whether continuous or discrete, a distinction between the ruling and the subject element comes to light. Such a duality exists in living creatures, but not in them only; it originates in the constitution of the universe; even in things which have no life, there is a ruling principle, as in musical harmony. But we are wandering from the subject. We will, therefore, restrict ourselves to the living creature which, in the first place, consists of soul and body; and of these two, the one is by nature the ruler, and the other the subject. But then we must look for the intentions of nature in things which retain their nature, and not in things which are corrupted. And therefore we must study the man who is in the most perfect state both of body and soul, for in him we shall see the true relation of the two; although in bad or corrupted natures the body will often appear to rule over the soul, because they are in an evil and unnatural condition. First then we may observe in living creatures both a despotical and a constitutional rule; for the soul rules the body with a despotical rule, whereas the intellect rules the appetites with a constitutional and royal rule. And it is clear that the rule of the soul over the body, and of the mind and the rational element over the passionate is natural and expedient; whereas the equality of the two or the rule of the inferior is always hurtful. The same holds good of animals as well as of men; for tame animals have a better nature than wild, and all tame animals are better off when they are ruled by man; for then they are preserved. Again, the male is by nature superior, and the female inferior; and the one rules, and the other is ruled; this principle, of necessity, extends to all mankind. Where then there is such a difference as that between soul and body, or between men and animals (as in the case of those whose business is to use their body, and who can do nothing better), the lower sort are by nature slaves, and it is better for them as for all inferiors that they should be under the rule of a master. For he who can be, and therefore is another's, and he who participates in reason enough to apprehend, but not to have, reason, is a slave by nature. Whereas the lower animals cannot even apprehend reason; they obey their instincts. And indeed the use made of slaves and of tame animals is not very different; for both with their bodies minister to the needs of life. Nature would like to distinguish between the bodies of freemen and slaves, making the one strong for servile labour, the other upright, and although useless for such services, useful for political life in the arts both of war and peace. But this does not hold universally: for some slaves have the souls and others have the bodies of freemen. And doubtless if men differed from one another in the mere forms of their bodies as much as the statues of the Gods do from men, all would acknowledge that the inferior class should be slaves of the superior. And if there is a difference in the body, how much more in the soul! But the beauty of the body is seen, whereas the beauty of the soul is not seen. It is clear, then, that some men are by nature free, and others slaves, and that for these latter slavery is both expedient and right.

But that those who take the opposite view have in a certain way right on their side, may be easily seen. For the words slavery and slave are used in two senses. There is a slave or slavery by law as well as by nature. The law of which I speak is a sort of convention, according to which whatever is taken in war is supposed to belong to the victors. But this right many jurists impeach, as they would an orator who brought forward an unconstitutional measure: they detest the notion that, because one man has the power of doing violence and is superior in brute strength, another shall be his slave and subject. Even among philosophers there is a difference of opinion. The origin of the dispute, and the reason why the arguments cross, is as follows: Virtue, when furnished with means, may be deemed to have the greatest power of doing violence: and as superior power is only found where there is superior excellence of some kind, power is thought to imply virtue. But does it likewise imply justice? — that is the question. And, in order to make a distinction between them, some assert that justice is benevolence: to which others reply that justice is nothing more than the rule of a superior. If the two views are regarded as antagonistic and exclusive [i. e., if the notion that justice is benevolence excludes the idea of a just rule of a superior], the alternative [viz., that no one should rule over others] has no force or plausibility, because it implies that not even the superior in virtue ought to rule, or be master. Some, clinging, as they think, to a principle of justice (for law and custom are a sort of justice), assume that slavery in war is justified by law, but they are not consistent. For what if the cause of the war be unjust? No one would ever say that he is a slave who is unworthy to be a slave. Were this the case, men of the highest rank would be slaves and the children of slaves, if they or their parents chance to have been taken captive and sold. Wherefore Hellenes do not like to call themselves slaves, but confine the term to barbarians. Yet, in using this language, they really mean the natural slave of whom we spoke at first; for it must be admitted that some are slaves everywhere, others nowhere. The same principle applies to nobility. Hellenes regard themselves as noble everywhere, and not only in their own country, but they deem the barbarians noble only when at home, thereby implying that there are two sorts of nobility and freedom, the one absolute, the other relative. The Helen of Theodectes says, —

> Who would presume to call me servant who am on both
> sides sprung from the stem of the Gods?

What does this mean but that they distinguish freedom and slavery, noble and humble birth, by the two principles of good and evil? They think that as men and animals beget men and animals, so from good men a good man springs. But this is what nature, though she may intend it, often fails to accomplish.

We see then that there is some foundation for this difference of opinion, and that some actual slaves and freemen are not so by nature, and also that there is in some cases a marked distinction between the two classes, rendering it expedient and right for the one to be slaves and the others to be masters: the one practising obedience, the others exercising the authority which nature intended them to have. The abuse of this authority is injurious to both; for the interests of part and whole, of body and soul, are the same, and the slave is a part of the master, a living but separated part of his bodily frame. Where the relation between them is natural they are friends and have a common interest, but where it rests merely on law and force the reverse is true.

The previous remarks are quite enough to show that the rule of a master is not a constitutional rule, and therefore that all the different kinds of rule are not, as some affirm, the same with each other. For there is one rule exercised over subjects who are by nature free, another over subjects who are by nature slaves. The rule of a household is a monarchy, for every house is under one head: whereas constitutional rule is a government of freemen and equals. The master is not called a master because he has science, but because he is of a certain character, and the same remark applies to the slave and the freeman. Still there may be a science for the master and a science for the slave. The science of the slave would be such as the man of Syracuse taught, who made money by instructing slaves in their ordinary duties. And such a knowledge may be carried further, so as to include cookery and similar menial arts. For some duties are of the more necessary, others of the more honourable sort; as the proverb says, 'slave before slave, master before master.' But all such branches of knowledge are servile. There is likewise a science of the master, which teaches the use of slaves; for the master as such is concerned, not with the acquisition, but with the use of them. Yet this so-called science is not anything great or wonderful; for the master need only know how to order that which the slave must know how to execute. Hence those who are in a position which places them above toil, have stewards who attend to their households while they occupy themselves with philosophy or with politics. But the art of acquiring slaves, I mean of justly acquiring them, differs both from the art of the master and the art of the slave, being a species of hunting or war. Enough of the distinction between master and slave.

Let us now enquire into property generally, and into the art of money-making, in accordance with our usual method [of resolving a whole into its parts], for a slave has been shown to be a part of property. The first question is whether the art of money-making is the same with the art of managing a household or a part of it, or instrumental to it; and if the last, whether in the way that the art of making shuttles is instrumental to the art of weaving, or in the way that the casting of bronze is instrumental to the art of the statuary, for they are not instrumental in the same way, but the one provides tools and the other material; and by material I mean the substratum out of which any work is made; thus wool is the material of the weaver, bronze of the statuary. Now it is easy to see that the art of household management is not identical with the art of money-making, for the one uses the material which the other provides. And the art which uses household stores can be no other than the art of household management. There is, however, a doubt whether the art of money-making is a part of household management or a distinct art. [They appear to be connected]; for the money-maker has to consider whence money and property can be procured; but there are many sorts of property and wealth: — there is husbandry and the care and provision of food in general; are these parts of the money-making art or distinct arts? Again, there are many sorts of food, and therefore there are many kinds of lives, both of animals and men; they must all have food, and the differences in their food have made differences in their ways of life. For of beasts, some are gregarious, others are solitary; they live in the way which is best adapted to sustain them, accordingly as they are carnivorous or herbivorous or omnivorous: and their habits are determined for them by nature in such a manner that they may obtain with greater facility the food of their choice. But, as different individuals have different tastes, the same things are not naturally pleasant to all of them; and therefore the lives of carnivorous or herbivorous animals further differ among themselves. In the lives of men too there is a great difference. The laziest are shepherds, who lead an idle life, and get their subsistence without trouble from tame animals; their flocks having to wander from place to place in search of pasture, they are compelled to follow them, cultivating a sort of living farm. Others support themselves by hunting, which is of different kinds. Some, for example, are pirates, others, who dwell near lakes or marshes or rivers or a sea in which there are fish, are fishermen, and others live by the pursuit of birds or wild beasts. The greater number obtain a living from the fruits of the soil. Such are the modes of subsistence which prevail among those whose industry is employed immediately upon the products of nature, and whose food is not acquired by exchange and retail trade —

there is the shepherd, the husbandman, the pirate, the fisherman, the hunter. Some gain a comfortable maintenance out of two employments, eking out the deficiencies of one of them by another: thus the life of a shepherd may be combined with that of a brigand, the life of a farmer with that of a hunter. Other modes of life are similarly combined in any way which the needs of men may require. Property, in the sense of a bare livelihood, seems to be given by nature herself to all, both when they are first born, and when they are grown up. For some animals bring forth, together with their offspring, so much food as will last until they are able to supply themselves; of this the vermiparous or oviparous animals are an instance; and the viviparous animals have up to a certain time a supply of food for their young in themselves, which is called milk. In like manner we may infer that, after the birth of animals, plants exist for their sake, and that the other animals exist for the sake of man, the tame for use and food, the wild, if not all, at least the greater part of them, for food, and for the provision of clothing and various instruments. Now if nature makes nothing incomplete, and nothing in vain, the inference must be that she has made all animals and plants for the sake of man. And so, in one point of view, the art of war is a natural art of acquisition, for it includes hunting, an art which we ought to practise against wild beasts, and against men who, though intended by nature to be governed, will not submit; for war of such a kind is naturally just.

Of the art of acquisition then there is one kind which is natural and is a part of the management of a household. Either we must suppose the necessaries of life to exist previously, or the art of household management must provide a store of them for the common use of the family or state. They are the elements of true wealth; for the amount of property which is needed for a good life is not unlimited, although Solon in one of his poems says that,—

No bound to riches has been fixed for man.

But there is a boundary fixed, just as there is in the arts; for the instruments of any art are never unlimited, either in number or size, and wealth may be defined as a number of instruments to be used in a household or in a state. And so we see that there is a natural art of acquisition which is practised by managers of households and by statesmen, and what is the reason of this.

There is another variety of the art of acquisition which is commonly and rightly called the art of making money, and has in fact suggested the notion that wealth and property have no limit. Being nearly connected with the preceding, it is often identified with it. But though they are not very different, neither are they the same. The kind already described is given by nature, the other is gained by experience and art.

Let us begin our discussion of the question with the following considerations:

Of everything which we possess there are two uses: both belong to the thing as such, but not in the same manner, for one is the proper, and the other the improper or secondary use of it. For example, a shoe is used for wear, and is used for exchange; both are uses of the shoe. He who gives a shoe in exchange for money or food to him who wants one, does indeed use the shoe as a shoe, but this is not its proper or primary purpose, for a shoe is not made to be an object of barter. The same may be said of all possessions, for the art of exchange extends to all of them, and it arises at first in a natural manner from the circumstance that some have too little, others too much. Hence we may infer that retail trade is not a natural part of the art of money-making; had it been so, men would have ceased to exchange when they had enough. And in the first community, which is the family, this art is obviously of no use, but only begins to be useful when the society increases. For the members of the family originally had all things in common; in a more divided state of society they still shared in many things, but they were different things which they had to give in exchange for what they wanted, a kind of barter which is still practised among barbarous nations who exchange with one another the necessaries of life and nothing more; giving and receiving wine, for example, in exchange for corn and the like. This sort of barter is not part of the money-making art and is not contrary to nature, but is needed for the satisfaction of men's natural wants. The other or more complex form of exchange grew out of the simpler. When the inhabitants of one country became more dependent on those of another, and they imported what they needed, and exported the surplus, money necessarily came into use. For the various necessaries of life are not easily carried about, and hence men agreed to employ in their dealings with each other something which was intrinsically useful and easily applicable to the purposes of life, for example, iron, silver, and the like. Of this the value was at first measured by size and weight, but in process of time they put a stamp upon it, to save the trouble of weighing and to mark the value.

When the use of coin had once been discovered, out of the barter of necessary articles arose the other art of money-making, namely, retail trade; which was at first probably a simple matter, but became more complicated as soon as men learned by experience whence and by what exchanges the greatest profit might be made. Originating in the use of coin, the art of money-making is generally thought to be chiefly concerned with it, and to be the art which produces wealth and money; having to consider how they may be accumulated. Indeed, wealth is assumed by many to be only a quantity of coin, because the art of money-making and retail trade are concerned with coin. Others maintain that coined money is a mere sham, a thing not natural, but conventional only, which would have no value or use for any of the purposes of daily life, if another commodity were substituted by the users. And, indeed, he who is rich in coin may often be in want of necessary food. But how can that be wealth of which a man may have a great abundance and yet perish with hunger, like Midas in the fable, whose insatiable prayer turned everything that was set before him into gold?

Men seek after a better notion of wealth and of the art of making money than the mere acquisition of coin, and they are right. For natural wealth and the natural art of money-making are a different thing; in their true form they are part of the management of a household; whereas retail trade is the art of producing wealth, not in every way, but by exchange. And it seems to be concerned with coin; for coin is the starting-point and the goal of exchange. And there is no bound to the wealth which springs from this art of money-making. As in the art of medicine there is no limit to the pursuit of health, and as in the other arts there is no limit to the pursuit of their several ends, for they aim at accomplishing their ends to the uttermost; (but of the means there is a limit, for the end is always the limit), so, too, in this art of money-making there is no limit of the end, which is wealth of the spurious kind, and the acquisition of money. But the art of household management has a limit; the unlimited acquisition of money is not its business. And, therefore, in one point of view, all wealth must have a limit; nevertheless, as a matter of fact, we find the opposite to be the case; for all money-makers increase their hoard of coin without limit. The source of the confusion is the near connexion between the two kinds of money-making; in either, the instrument [i. e., wealth] is the same, although the use is different, and so they pass into one another; for each is a use of the same property, but with a difference: accumulation is the end in the one case, but there is a further end in the other. Hence some persons are led to believe that making money is the object of household management, and the whole idea of their lives is that they ought either to increase their money without limit, or at any rate not to lose it. The origin of this disposition in men is that they are intent upon living only, and not upon living well; and, as their desires are unlimited, they also desire that the means of gratifying them should be without limit. Even those who aim at a good life seek the means of obtaining bodily pleasures; and, since the enjoyment of these appears to depend on property, they are absorbed in making money: and so there arises the second species of money-making. For, as their enjoyment is in excess, they seek an art which produces the excess of enjoyment; and, if they are not able to supply their pleasures by the art of money-making, they try other arts, using in turn every faculty in a manner contrary to nature. The quality of courage, for example, is not intended to make money, but to inspire confidence; neither is this the aim of the general's or of the physician's art; but the one aims at victory and the other at health. Nevertheless, some men turn every quality or art into a means of making money; this they conceive to be the end, and to the promotion of the end all things must contribute.

Thus, then, we have considered the art of money-making, which is unnecessary, and why men want it; and also the necessary art of money-making, which we have seen to be different from the other, and to be a natural part of the art of managing a household, concerned with the provision of food, not, however, like the former kind, unlimited, but having a limit.

And we have found the answer to our original question, Whether the art of money-making is the business of the manager of a household and of the statesman or not their business? — viz., that it is an art which is presupposed by them. For political science does not make men, but takes them from nature and uses them; and nature provides them with food from the element of earth, air, or sea. At this stage begins the duty of the manager of a household, who has to order the things which nature supplies; — he may be compared to the weaver who has not to make but to use wool, and to know what sort of wool is good and serviceable or bad and unserviceable. Were this otherwise, it would be difficult to see why the art of money-making is a part of the management of a household and the art of medicine not; for surely the members of a household must have health just as they must have life or any other necessary. And as from one point of view the master of the house and the ruler of the state have to consider about health, from another point of view not'they but the physician; so in one way the art of household management, in another way the subordinate art, has to consider about money. But strictly speaking, as I have already said, the means of life must be provided beforehand by nature; for the business of nature is to furnish food to that which is born, and the food of the offspring always remains over in the parent. Wherefore the art of making money out of fruits and animals is always natural.

Of the two sorts of money-making one, as I have just said, is a part of household management, the other is retail trade: the former necessary and honourable, the latter a kind of exchange which is justly censured; for it is unnatural, and a mode by which men gain from one another. The most hated sort, and with the greatest reason, is usury, which makes a gain out of money itself, and not from the natural use of it. For money was intended to be used in exchange, but not to increase at interest. And this term usury (τόκος), which means the birth of money from money, is applied to the breeding of money because the offspring resembles the parent. Wherefore of all modes of making money this is the most unnatural.

Enough has been said about the theory of money-making; we will now proceed to the practical part. The discussion of such matters is not unworthy of philosophy, but to be engaged in them practically is illiberal and irksome. The useful parts of money-making are, first, the knowledge of live stock, — which are most profitable, and where, and how, — as, for example, what sort of horses or sheep or oxen or any other animals are most likely to give a return. A man ought to know which of these pay better than others, and which pay best in particular places, for some do better in one place and some in another. Secondly, husbandry, which may be either tillage or planting, and the keeping of bees, and of fish, or fowl, or of any animals which may be useful to man. These are the divisions of the true or proper art of money-making and come first. Of the other, which consists in exchange, the first and most important division is commerce (of which there are three kinds — commerce by sea, commerce by land, selling in shops — these again differing as they are safer or more profitable), the second is usury, the third, service for hire — of this, one kind is employed in the mechanical arts, the other in unskilled and bodily labour. There is still a third sort of money-making intermediate between this and the first or natural mode which is partly natural, but is also concerned with exchange of the fruits and other products of the earth. Some of these latter, although they bear no fruit, are nevertheless profitable; for example, wood and minerals. The art of mining, by which minerals are obtained, has many branches, for there are various kinds of things dug out of the earth. Of the several divisions of money-making I now speak generally; a minute consideration of them might be useful in practice, but it would be tiresome to dwell upon them at greater length now.

Those occupations are most truly arts in which there is the least element of chance; they are the meanest in which the body is most deteriorated, the most servile in which there is the greatest use of the body, and the illiberal in which there is the least need of excellence.

Works have been written upon these subjects by various persons; for example, by Chares the Parian, and Apollodorus the Lemnian, who have treated of Tillage and Planting, while others have treated of other branches; any one who cares for such matters may refer to their writings. It would be well also to collect the scattered stories of the ways in which individuals have succeeded in amassing a fortune; for all this is useful to persons who value the art of making money. There is the anecdote of Thales the Milesian and his financial device, which involves a principle of universal application, but is attributed to him on account of his reputation for wisdom. He was reproached for his poverty, which was supposed to show that philosophy was of no use. According to the story, he knew by his skill in the stars while it was yet winter that there would be a great harvest of olives in the coming year; so, having a little capital, he gave earnest-money for the use of all the olive-presses in Chios and Miletus, which he hired at a low price because no one bid against him. When the harvest-time came, and many wanted them all at once and of a sudden, he let them out at any rate which he pleased, and made a quantity of money. Thus he showed the world that philosophers can easily be rich if they like, but that their ambition is of another sort. He is supposed to have given a striking proof of his wisdom, but, as I was saying, his device for getting money is of universal application, and is nothing but the creation of a monopoly. It is an art often practised by cities when they are in want of money; they make a monopoly of provisions.

There was a man of Sicily, who, having money deposited with him, bought up all the iron from the iron mines; afterwards, when the merchants from their various markets came to buy, he was the only seller, and without much increasing the price he gained 200 per cent. Which when Dionysius heard, he told him that he might take away his money, but that he must not remain at Syracuse, for he thought that the man had discovered a way of making money which was injurious to his own interests. He had the same idea as Thales; they both contrived to create a monopoly for themselves. And statesmen ought to know these things; for a state is often as much in want of money and of such devices for obtaining it as a household, or even more so; hence some public men devote themselves entirely to finance.

BOOK II

OUR purpose is to consider what form of political community is best of all for those who are most able to realize their ideal of life. We must therefore examine not only this but other constitutions, both such as actually exist in well-governed states, and any theoretical forms which are held in esteem; that what is good and useful may be brought to light. And let no one suppose that in seeking for something beyond them we at all want to philosophize at the expense of truth; we only undertake this enquiry because all the constitutions with which we are acquainted are faulty.

We will begin with the natural beginning of the subject. Three alternatives are conceivable: The members of a state must have either (1) all things or (2) nothing in common, or (3) some things in common and some not. That they should have nothing in common is clearly impossible, for the state is a community, and must at any rate have a common place — one city will be in one place, and the citizens are those who share in that one city. But should a well-ordered state have all things, as far as may be, in common, or some only and not others? For the citizens might conceivably have wives and children and property in common, as Socrates proposes in the Republic of Plato. Which is better, our present condition, or the proposed new order of society?

. . . .

Next let us consider what should be our arrangements about property: should the citizens of the perfect state have their possessions in common or not? This question may be discussed separately from the enactments about women and children. Even supposing that the women and children belong to individuals, according to the custom which is at present universal, may there not be an advantage in having and using possessions in common? Three cases are possible: (1) the soil may be appropriated, but the produce may be thrown for consumption into the common stock; and this is the practice of some nations. Or (2), the soil may be common, and may be cultivated in common, but the produce divided among individuals for their private use; this is a form of common property which is said to exist among certain barbarians. Or (3), the soil and the produce may be alike common.

When the husbandmen are not the citizens, the case will be different and easier to deal with; but when the citizens till the ground themselves the question of ownership will give a world of trouble. If they do not share equally in enjoyments and toils, those who labour much and get little will necessarily complain of those who labour little and receive or consume much. There is always a difficulty in men living together and having things in common, but especially in their having common property. The partnerships of fellow-travellers are an example to the point; for they generally fall out by the way and quarrel about any trifle which turns up. So with servants: we are most liable to take offence at those with whom we most frequently come into contact in daily life.

These are only some of the disadvantages which attend the community of property; the present arrangement, if improved as it might be by good customs and laws, would be far better, and would have the advantages of both systems. Property should be in a certain sense common, but, as a general rule, private; for, when every one has a distinct interest, men will not complain of one another, and they will make more progress, because every one will be attending to his own business. And yet among the good, and in respect of use, ' Friends,' as the proverb says, ' will have all things common.' Even now there are traces of such a principle, showing that it is not impracticable, but, in well-ordered states, exists already to a certain extent and may be carried further. For, although every man has his own property, some things he will place at the disposal of his friends, while of others he shares the use with them. The Lacedaemonians, for example, use one another's slaves, and horses and dogs, as if they were their own; and when they happen to be in the country, they appropriate in the fields whatever provisions they want. It is clearly better that property should be private, but the use of it common; and the special business of the legislator is to create in men this benevolent disposition. Again, how immeasurably greater is the pleasure, when a man feels a thing to be his own; for the love of self is a feeling implanted by nature and not given in vain, although selfishness is rightly censured; this, however, is not the mere love of self, but the love of self in excess, like the miser's love of money; for all, or almost all, men love money, and other such objects in a measure. And further, there is the greatest pleasure in doing a kindness or service to friends or guests or companions, which can only be rendered when a man has private property. The advantage is lost by the excessive unification of the state. Two virtues are annihilated in such a state: first, temperance towards women (for it is an honourable action to abstain from another's wife for temperance sake); secondly, liberality in the matter of property. No one, when men have all things in common, will any longer set an example of liberality or do any liberal action; for liberality consists in the use which is made of property.

Such legislation may have a specious appearance of benevolence; men readily listen to it, and are easily induced to believe that in some wonderful manner everybody will become everybody's friend, especially when some one is heard denouncing the evils now existing in states, suits about contracts, convictions for perjury, flatteries of rich men and the like, which are said to arise out of the possession of private property. These evils, however, are due to a very different cause — the wickedness of human nature. Indeed, we see that there is much more quarrelling among those who have all things in common, though there are not many of them when compared with the vast numbers who have private property.

THE NICOMACHEAN ETHICS[1]

BOOK V

THERE are some people who hold that retaliation is absolutely just. This was the doctrine of the Pythagoreans, who defined justice absolutely as retaliation on one's neighbour.

But retaliation does not accord with the conception of either distributive or corrective justice, although corrective justice is certainly what is intended by the Rhadamanthine rule:

> As a man's action, such his fate;
> Then justice shall be true and straight.

The law of retaliation and the law of corrective justice in many cases do not agree. For instance, if a person who strikes another is a magistrate, he ought not to be struck in return, and if a person strikes a magistrate, he ought not only to be struck but to be punished. Again, it makes a great difference whether what is done to a person is done with his consent or against it, *and the law of retaliation takes no account of this difference.* Still in such associations as depend upon exchange it is this kind of justice, viz., retaliation, which is the bond of union; but it is proportionate, and not equal retaliation; for it is proportionate requital which holds a state together.

People seek to requite either evil or good. It looks like slavery not to requite evil; and if they do not requite good, no interchange *of services* takes place, and it is this interchange which holds society together. It is thus that men build a temple of the Graces in their streets to ensure reciprocity, as being the peculiar characteristic of grace; for it is our duty to return the service of one who has been

---

[1] Translated by J. E. Welldon. Reprinted with the consent of the publishers, Macmillan & Co., London.

gracious to us, and to take the initiative in showing grace ourselves.

Now, proportionate requital is produced by cross-conjunction. Thus let A represent a builder, B a cobbler, C a house, and D a shoe. Then the builder ought to receive from the cobbler some part of his work, and to give him his own work in return. If then there is proportionate equality in the first instance, and retaliation or *reciprocity* follows, the result of which we are speaking will be attained. Otherwise the exchange will not be equal or permanent. For there is no reason why the work of the one should not be superior to that of the other, and therefore they ought to be equalized. (This is equally the case with all the arts; they would be destroyed, if the effect upon the patient were not, in kind, quantity and quality, the same as the effort of the agent.) For association is formed, not by two doctors, but by a doctor and a husbandman, and generally by people who are different, and not equal, and who need to be equalized. It follows that such things as are the subjects of exchange must in some sense be comparable. This is the reason for the invention of money. Money is a sort of medium or mean; for it measures everything and consequently measures among other things excess or defect, e. g., the number of shoes which are equivalent to a house or a meal. As a builder then is to a cobbler, so must so many shoes be to a house or a meal; for otherwise there would be no exchange or association. But this will be impossible, unless the shoes and the house or meal are in some sense equalized. Hence arises the necessity of a single universal standard of measurement, as was said before. This standard is in truth the demand for mutual services, which holds society together; for if people had no wants, or their wants were dissimilar, there would be either no exchange, or it would not be the same as it is now.

Money is a sort of recognized representative of this demand. That is the reason why it is called money (νόμισμα), because it has not a natural but a conventional (νόμῳ) ex-

istence, and because it is in our power to change it, and
make it useless.

Retaliation or reciprocity will take place, when the terms
have been so equated that, as a husbandman is to a cobbler,
so is the cobbler's ware to the husbandman's. But we must
bring the terms to a figure of proportion not after the exchange has taken place — or one of the two extremes will
have both advantages, *i. e.*, *will have its superiority counted
twice over* — but when both parties still retain their own
wares; then they will be equal and capable of association,
because it is possible to establish the proper equality between them. Thus let A be a husbandman, C food, B a
cobbler, and D his wares, which are to be equated *to the food*.
But if this kind of reciprocity were impossible, there would
be no association.

The fact that it is demand which is like a principle of
unity binding society together is evident because, if there
is no mutual demand on the part of two persons, if neither
of them or one only needs the services of the other, they do
not effect an exchange, whereas, if somebody wants what
somebody else has, e. g., wine, they effect an exchange, giving the wine, e. g., in return for the right of importing corn.
Here then the wine and the corn must be equated.

Money is serviceable with a view to future exchange; it
is a sort of security which we possess that, if we do not want
a thing now, we shall be able to get it when we do want it;
for if a person brings money, it must be in his power to get
what he wants.

It is true that money is subject to the same laws as other
things; its value is not always the same; still it tends to
have a more constant value than anything else. All things,
then, must have a pecuniary value, as this will always facilitate exchange, and so will facilitate association.

Money therefore is like a measure that equates things,
by making them commensurable; for association would be
impossible without exchange, exchange without equality,
and equality without commensurability.

Although it is in reality impossible that things which are so widely different should become commensurable, they may become sufficiently so for practical purposes. There must be some single standard then, and that a standard upon which the world agrees; hence it is called money (νόμισμα), for it is this which makes all things commensurable, as money is the universal standard of measurement. Let A be a house, B ten minae, C a couch. Now A is half B, if the house is worth, or is equal to, five minae. Again, the couch C is the tenth part of B. It is clear then that the number of couches which are equal to a house is five. It is clear too that this was the method of exchange before the invention of money; for it makes no difference whether it is five couches or the value of five couches that we give in exchange for a house.

II

XENOPHON

ON THE MEANS OF IMPROVING THE REVENUES OF THE STATE OF ATHENS

NOTE

XENOPHON (c. 440–c. 355 B.C.) was a pupil of Socrates in his youth, but had no great taste for abstract speculation, being chiefly interested in the moral aspects of the philosopher's teaching. He joined the expedition of the younger Cyrus against Artaxerxes (401–400) and after the disaster at Cunaxa he was chosen leader of the disorganized Greek force. Many years later he wrote an account of this adventure in the *Anabasis*. He next entered the service of Sparta in Asia Minor, for which a decree of banishment was issued against him by his fellow Athenians. After the battle of Coroneia (394 B.C.) the Spartans furnished him a home in Scillus, where he devoted himself to literature for some twenty years. Upon the defeat of the Spartans by the Thebans, he was forced to leave Scillus, and thereafter made his home in Corinth. Besides the *Anabasis* he wrote the *Hellenica*, an historical work, the *Memorabilia*, reminiscences of Socrates, the *Cyropædia*, a sort of philosophical romance, and several minor works. The *Cyropædia* contains a remarkable analysis of the complex division of labor (Bk. VIII, 2). The *Revenues of Athens* was written about 355 B.C. It is of especial significance as a reflection of an important aspect of Greek life which had little interest for the great philosophers.

ON THE MEANS
OF IMPROVING THE REVENUES OF
THE STATE OF ATHENS [1]

CHAPTER I

ON THE SOIL OF ATTICA, AND THE POSSIBILITY
OF INCREASING ITS REVENUES

I AM always of opinion that of whatever character governors are, of a similar character also are the governments which they conduct. But as some of those who rule at Athens have been said to know what is just, no less than other men, but have declared that they are compelled, through the poverty of the common people, to act with somewhat of injustice towards the allied cities, I have in consequence set myself to consider whether the citizens may by any means be maintained from the resources of their own country, from which it is most just that they should be maintained, thinking that, if this should be the case, remedy would at once be afforded for their wants, and for the jealousy which they incur from the other Greeks.

As I revolved in my mind what I observed, it readily appeared to me that the country is well qualified by nature to afford very large revenues; and in order that it may be understood that I say this with truth, I will first of all give an account of the natural resources of Attica.

That the seasons in it are extremely mild, the products of the soil testify; for such as will not even grow in many countries bear fruit in perfection in Attica. And as the land is most productive, so likewise is the sea that surrounds the land; and whatever fruits the gods afford in their several seasons begin in this country earliest, and cease latest. Nor

---

[1] Translated by J. S. Watson. Reprinted with the permission of the publishers, G. Bell & Sons, Ltd., London.

is the land superior only in things that grow up and decay annually, but has also permanent advantages; for stone is supplied from it in abundance, from which the most magnificent temples, the most beautiful altars, and the finest statues of the gods are made, and in which many both Greeks and barbarians desire to participate. There are indeed portions of the soil which, though sown, will not produce fruit, but which, if they are penetrated by digging, will support many more people than if they produced corn, as, doubtless by divine dispensation, they contain silver beneath the surface; and though there are many states lying near, both by land and by sea, not even the smallest vein of silver is found to extend into any one of them. A person might not unreasonably suppose that the state is situate in the centre, not only of Greece, but of the whole inhabited world; for the further people are from it, the more severe cold or heat do they experience; and whatever travellers would pass from one end of Greece to the other, must all either sail by Athens, or pass it by land, as the centre of their circle. Though it is not surrounded by water, it nevertheless attracts to itself like an island, with the aid of every wind, whatever it requires, and sends away whatever it desires to export; for it has sea on each side of it. By land, too, it receives many kinds of merchandise, as it is joined to the continent. To many states, moreover, barbarians who dwell on their borders cause annoyance; but states border on the Athenians which are themselves at a distance from the barbarians.

CHAPTER II

OF THE POSSIBILITY OF ATTRACTING A GREATER NUMBER OF FOREIGNERS TO SOJOURN AT ATHENS

Of all these advantages, I think that the land is itself, as I said, the cause; and if to the blessings bestowed by nature there be joined, in the first place, an attention to the interests of strangers sojourning in it (for that source of revenue appears to me to be one of the best, since strangers, while they maintain themselves, and confer great benefits on the states in which they live, receive no pension from the public, but pay the tax imposed on aliens), such attention would seem to me likely to be of the utmost benefit; especially if we relieve them at the same time from such impositions as, while they are of no benefit to the state, appear to cast on them a mark of dishonour, and if we exempt them likewise from taking the field as heavy-armed infantry along with the citizens; for the danger which they incur is great, and it is a great trouble to them to be away from their trades and families. The state would also be much more benefited, if the citizens stood by the side of one another in the field, than if, as is the case at present, Lydians, and Syrians, and Phrygians, and other barbarians from every nation be amalgamated with them. In addition, too, to the good attendant on the exemption of strangers from joining the army, it would be an honour to the country for the Athenians to be seen to trust to themselves in the field of battle rather than to foreigners. While we give a share, moreover, to foreigners of other privileges which it is proper to share with them, we should be likely in my opinion, if we gave them admission also into the cavalry, to render them better disposed towards us, and to increase the strength and greatness of our country. Besides, as there are within the walls many pieces of ground for building, vacant of houses, I think that if the state were to allow them to become the property of those who might build upon them, and who, on applying for them, might seem to be deserving, a great number of respectable persons would by that means become desirous of a settlement at Athens. If we should institute an order of guardians of foreigners, also, as we have one of guardians of orphans, and some honour should be conferred on such of them as should bring in the greatest number of foreigners, such a plan would make the foreigners more contented under us, and, as is likely, all who have no residence in any other city would eagerly seek a settlement in Athens, and would thus increase the public revenue.

CHAPTER III

OF GRANTING PRIVILEGES TO MERCHANTS, AND THE BENEFITS TO BE EXPECTED FROM INCREASED TRAFFIC

In proof that the city is extremely pleasant and lucrative as a place of trade, I will mention the following particulars. In the first place, it has the finest and safest harbours for vessels, where navigators may moor and rest in case of a storm. In the next place, merchants, in most other cities, must barter one commodity for another; for the inhabitants use money that will not pass beyond the limits of the country; but at Athens, while there is abundance of goods, such as people require, for exportation, still, if merchants do not wish to barter, they may carry off an excellent freight by taking away our silver, for wherever they dispose of it, they will always gain more than its original value.

If we should propose rewards, however, for the judges of the tribunal of commerce, to be given to such as should decide points of controversy with the greatest justice and expedition, so that persons who wished to sail might not be detained, a still larger number of people would by that means be brought to trade with us, and with greater pleasure. It would be for our advantage and credit also, that such merchants and shipowners as are found to benefit the state by bringing to it vessels and merchandise of great account should be honoured with seats of distinction on public occasions, and sometimes invited to entertainments; for, being treated with such respect, they would hasten to return to us, as to friends, for the sake, not merely of gain, but of honour. The more people settled among us and visited us, the greater quantity of merchandise, it is evident, would be imported, exported, and sold, and the more gain would be secured, and tribute received. To effect such augmentations of the revenue, it is not necessary for us to be at any cost but that of philanthropic ordinances and careful superintendence.

For securing whatever other revenues seem likely to come in to us, I know that there will be need of a fund. Yet I am not without hope that the citizens will readily contribute for this purpose, when I reflect how much the state contributed at the period when it assisted the Arcadians under the command of Lysistratus, and how much under that of Hegesilaus. I know also that galleys have often been sent out at great expense, galleys which were built when it was uncertain whether the result of the expedition would be for better or for worse, though it was very certain that the contributors would never receive back what they had paid, or even recover any portion of it. But at present the citizens can acquire no gains so creditable as those from what they may contribute for this fund; for to him whose contribution shall be ten minae, about the fifth part will return as interest from the fleet, as he will receive three oboli a day; and to him whose contribution shall be five minae, there will be a return of more than the third. The most of the Athenians, assuredly, will receive annually more than they have contributed; for those who contribute a mina will have an income of almost two minae, and will have it in the city, being an income, too, that appears the safest and most durable of human things. I think, too, for my own part, that if the benefactors to our state were to have their names enrolled for transmission to posterity, many foreigners would give us their contributions, as well as some whole cities, through a desire for such enrolment. I should expect also that kings and other sovereign princes and satraps would feel a desire to participate in so gratifying an acknowledgment.

When a fund is established, it will be for the honour and interest of the state to build lodging-houses, in addition to those at present existing round the harbours, for the accommodation of seamen; and it would be well, also, to build others for merchants, in places convenient for buying and selling, as well as public houses of entertainment for all that come to the city. If, moreover, houses and shops were to be erected for retail dealers, at the Peiræeus and in the city, they would not only be an ornament to the city, but a great accession of income would be derived from them. It seems to me, likewise, proper to try whether it be possible for the state, as it possesses public war-galleys, to have also public vessels for conveying merchandise, and to let them out for hire, upon persons giving security for them, as is the case with other things belonging to the public; for if this should appear practicable, a large income might be derived from that source.

CHAPTER IV

OF THE EXTENT OF SILVER MINES IN ATTICA. HOW THEY MAY BE RENDERED PROFITABLE TO THE STATE. REPLIES TO OBJECTIONS THAT MAY BE MADE TO THE PLANS PROPOSED

Should our silver mines, too, be managed as they ought to be, I consider that great profits might be drawn from them, in addition to our other revenues. To those who do not know their value, I should wish to make it known; for, when you know this, you will be the better enabled to form plans for arrangements respecting them. That they were wrought in very ancient times is well known to all; for assuredly no one attempts to specify at what time they began to be formed. But though the earth containing silver has been so long dug and cast up, consider how small a portion the heaps which have been thrown out are of the hills that remain still in their natural state, and that contain silver underneath them. Nor does the space of ground that is dug for silver appear to be at all diminished, but to be perpetually extended in a wider circuit; and during the time that the greatest number of men were in the mines, no one was ever in want of occupation, but there was always more work than enough for the hands employed. At the present time, too, no one of those who have slaves in the mines is diminishing the number of them, but is indeed continually adding to it as many as he can; for when but few

are engaged in digging and searching, little treasure is
found; but when many are employed, a far greater quantity of silver ore is discovered; so that in this occupation
alone, of all those that I know, no one envies those that extend their operations. All persons that have farms would be
able to say how many yokes of oxen, and how many workmen, would be sufficient for their land; and if they send
into their fields more than are necessary, they consider it a
loss; but in the mining operations for silver, they say that
all are constantly in want of workmen. For the consequence is not the same in this case as it is when there are
numbers of workers in brass, and when, as articles made
of brass then necessarily become cheap, the workmen are
ruined, nor is it the same as when there are excessive numbers of blacksmiths; or as when there is abundance of corn
and wine, and when, as the fruits of the earth are cheap,
agriculture becomes unprofitable, so that many farmers,
quitting their occupation of tilling the ground, betake themselves to the employments of merchants, or inn-keepers, or
bankers; but, in regard to the silver mines, the more silver
ore is found, and the more silver is extracted, the greater is
the number that devote themselves to mining. Of furniture,
when people have got enough of it for their houses, they do
not much care for buying additional supplies; but nobody
has ever yet had so much silver as not to desire an increase
of it; and if people have a superabundance, they hoard it,
and are not less delighted with doing so than with putting it
to use. When communities, too, are in the most flourishing
condition, people have very great use for money; for the
men are ready to be at expense for beautiful arms, or fine
horses, or magnificent houses or furniture; and the women
are eager for expensive dresses and golden ornaments. When
communities, on the other hand, are in distress, whether
from scarcity of corn or from the effects of war, they are
still more in want of money, as the land lies uncultivated,
both for purchasing provisions and for paying auxiliary
troops.

If any one should say that gold is not less useful for such purposes than silver, I do not dispute the truth of the assertion; but I am aware at the same time that gold, if it shows itself in great quantities, becomes much less valuable, and renders silver of a higher price. These remarks I have made with a view that we should send with confidence as many workmen as possible into the silver mines, and should with confidence continue our operations in them, fully trusting that the silver ore is not going to fail, and that silver will never lose its value. The state, however, appears to me to have known this long before I knew it; for it allows any foreigner that pleases to work in the mines, on paying the same duty as the citizens.

But that I may make the subjects still more clear with reference to the maintenance of the citizens, I will state how the mines may be managed so as to be most beneficial to the country. For what I am going to say, however, I do not desire to court admiration, as if I had found out something difficult to be discovered; for part of what I shall state we all at present see before us, and the condition of things in times past, we hear, was of an exactly similar character. But we cannot but feel surprised that the state, when it sees many private individuals enriching themselves from its resources, does not imitate their proceedings; for we heard long ago, indeed, at least such of us as attended to these matters, that Nicias, the son of Niceratus, kept a thousand men employed in the silver mines, whom he let on hire to Sosias of Thrace, on condition that he should give him for each an obolus a day, free of all charges; and this number he always supplied undiminished. Hipponicus also had six hundred slaves let out at the same rate, which brought him in a clear mina a day; Philemonides had three hundred, which brought him half a mina; and others had other complements of slaves, according, I suppose, to their respective resources. But why should I dwell upon former times, when there are numbers of men in the mines let out in the same manner at present? And if what I propose be carried into effect, the only new point in it would be, that as private individuals, by the possession of slaves, have secured themselves a constant revenue, so the state should possess public slaves, to the number of three for each Athenian citizen.

Whether what I propose is practicable, let him who chooses, after considering every point of it, pronounce a judgment. As to the price for slaves, it is evident that the state can procure it better than private individuals. It is easy for the senate to issue a proclamation that he who will may bring his slaves, and then to buy all that are brought. When they are bought, why should not any person be as willing to hire slaves from the state as from a private individual, if he is to have them on the same terms? At least they hire from the state consecrated grounds, and temples, and houses, and farm the public taxes. That the slaves purchased for the public may be kept safe, the state may require sureties from those who hire them, as they require them from those who farm the taxes; and it is indeed much easier for him who farms a tax to defraud the public than for him who hires slaves. For how can any one identify the public money that is embezzled, when private money is exactly like it; but as for slaves, when they are marked with the public mark, and when a penalty is denounced against him who sells or exports them, how could any one steal them? So far, therefore, it will appear to be possible for the state to acquire and to preserve slaves.

But if any one doubts whether, after a great number of workmen have been procured, a great number of persons will also present themselves to hire them, let him be of good courage, reflecting that many of those who already possess slaves will still hire those belonging to the public (for there is plenty of work to employ them), and that many of those engaged in the works are growing old, while there are many others, both Athenians and foreigners, who would neither be able nor willing to engage in corporeal labour, but who would gladly gain a subsistence by applying their minds to the superintendence of the business. If at first, then, a thousand two hundred slaves be collected, it is probable that, with the income from that number a complement of not less than six thousand might in five or six years be obtained; and if, of this number, each brings in a clear obolus, the profit will be sixty talents a year. If of those sixty talents twenty be devoted to the purchase of more slaves, the state will be at liberty to use the other forty for whatever other purpose it may think proper; and when the number of ten thousand slaves is made up, the yearly revenue from them will be a hundred talents.

That the state will receive even a far greater profit than this, those will agree with me in thinking, who remember, if there are any that still remember, how great a height the income from the slaves reached before the occurrences at Deceleia. The fact, also, that, though innumerable workmen have been perpetually employed in the mines, their present condition is not at all different from that in which our forefathers remember them to have been, affords me additional support for this supposition. Indeed, all that is now done in the mines testifies that there can never be a greater number of slaves there than the works require; for those who are employed in digging find no limit to the depth or ramifications of their works. To cut in a new direction is assuredly not less practicable now than it was formerly; nor can any one say, from certain knowledge, whether there is more silver ore in the parts which have been opened than is to be found in those which are undisturbed. Why then, some one may ask, do not many make new cuttings now, as of old? It is because those engaged about the mines are now poorer; for it was but lately that they began to be wrought again; and great risk is incurred by a person commencing new operations; for he indeed that finds a profitable field of labour becomes rich, but he who does not find one loses all that he has expended; and into such risk the men of the present day are by no means willing to run.

I think, however, that I am able to give some advice with

regard to this difficulty also, and to show how new operations may be conducted with the greatest safety. There are
ten tribes at Athens, and if to each of these the state should
assign an equal number of slaves, and the tribes should all
make new cuttings, sharing their fortune in common, then,
if but one tribe should make any useful discovery, it would
point out something profitable to the whole; but if two, or
three, or four, or half the number should make some discovery, it is plain that the works would be more profitable
in proportion; and that they should all fail is contrary to
all the experience of past times. It is possible also for private individuals to unite and share their fortunes together,
and thus to venture with greater safety; and you need
entertain no apprehensions either that the public company
thus constituted will injure the private adventurers, or that
the private adventurers will inconvenience the public company; but as allies in the field of battle, the greater the
number in which they meet, render one another proportionately stronger, so the greater the number that are
employed in the mines, the more gain will they acquire and
bring to the state.

I have now stated how I think that public matters may
be arranged, so that sufficient maintenance may be secured
from our common resources for the whole body of the
Athenian people.

If any of us, considering that there will be need of vast
funds for all these works, think that sufficient money will
never be contributed, let them not be cast down through
that apprehension. For there is no necessity that all these
things should be done at once, or else no profit will result
from them; but whatever buildings are erected, or ships
constructed, or slaves purchased, the proceedings will
straightway be attended with profit. It is indeed more
advantageous that such things should be done gradually
than that they should all be done at once; for if we were
to build all together, we should do our work at greater cost
and with less efficiency than if we were to build by degrees;

and if we were to get a vast number of slaves at once, we should be compelled to buy them in worse condition and at a higher price. Proceeding however according to our ability, we may continue any operations that have been well planned, and if any error has been committed, we may take care not to repeat it. Besides, if everything were to be done at once, it would be necessary for us to procure means for everything at the same time; but if part be done now, and part deferred, the incoming revenue may assist in obtaining what is necessary for future proceedings.

But as to that which appears to everybody most to be apprehended, I mean that, if the state purchase an extraordinary number of slaves, the works may be overstocked, we may feel quite free from that apprehension, if we do not send into the mines every year a greater number than the operations require. Thus it appears to me that the way in which it is easiest to pursue these plans is also that in which it is best. But if, again, you think that, on account of the contributions made during the present war, you are unable to contribute anything further, you must, whatever sum of money the taxes brought in before the peace, conduct the administration with that exact sum during the next year, and whatever additional sum they may bring, through peace having taken place, through attention being paid to the sojourners and merchants, through more commodities being imported and exported in consequence of a greater number of people resorting to us, and through the sale of goods being increased at the harbour, you must take that sum and appropriate it in such a way that the revenues may be advanced to the utmost. If, however, any feel apprehensive that this course, if war occur, will prove ineffectual, let them consider that, even if war should break out, it will be far more formidable to those who attack us than to our state. For what acquisition would be more useful for war than a great number of people, since they would be able to man many of the public vessels, while many of them also, serving for the public on land, would offer a powerful resistance to the enemy, provided that we do but treat them well?

I consider, too, that even if war takes place, it is possible to prevent our mines from being abandoned; for there is, we know, a fortress near the mines at Anaphlystus, on the sea towards the south, and another at Thoricus, on the sea towards the north; and these two are distant from each other about sixty furlongs. If, then, a third fort should be built between these on the summit of Besa, the workmen might then retire into some one of all these fortresses, and, if they should see an enemy approaching, it would be but a short distance for each to retreat to a place of safety. Should even an overpowering number of enemies come, they would, doubtless, if they found corn, or wine, or cattle, without the works, carry them off; but if they even occupied the mining ground, of what more would they possess themselves than a heap of stones? But how, indeed, could our enemies ever make an inroad on our mines? for the city of Megara, which is nearest to them, is distant much more than five hundred stadia; and Thebes, which is the nearest city after Megara, is distant much more than six hundred. If they should advance upon the mines, then, from any part in that direction, they will be under the necessity of passing by the city of Athens; and if they come in small numbers, it is probable that they will be cut off by the cavalry and the guards of the frontier; while it is difficult to imagine that they will march out with a large force, leaving their own country unguarded; for the city of Athens would be much nearer to their cities, than they themselves would be when they are at the mines. But, even if they should come in great force, how could they stay, when they would have no provisions? since, should they go out to get provisions in small parties, there would be danger both to those who went out for provisions, and to those who remained behind to fight; and, if their whole force went out foraging on every occasion, they would be besieged rather than besiegers.

Not only the profit from the slaves, then, would increase the resources of the city, but, as a vast number of people would collect about the mines, there would also arise a great income from the market held there, from the rent of the public buildings around the mines, from the furnaces, and from all other sources of that kind. Our city, too, if it be thus supported, will become extremely populous, and land about the mines will grow as valuable to those who possess it there as to those who have it around Athens. Should all indeed be done that I have proposed, I maintain that the state will not only be better supplied with money, but will be more quiet and orderly, and better prepared for war. For those who are appointed to exercise the youth would discharge their duties in the gymnasia with greater care, as they would then receive more pay than those now receive who act as gymnasiarchs for the torch-race; and those who are sent to be stationed in garrisons, as well as those who are to serve as peltasts, and to keep guard round the country, would perform all their occupations more efficiently, if pay were given them for each of their duties.

CHAPTER V

NECESSITY OF PEACE FOR THE MAINTENANCE AND IMPROVEMENT OF THE REVENUE

But if it appears evident, that, if the full revenues from the state are to be collected, there must be peace, is it not proper for us also to appoint guardians of peace? for such an office, if established, would render the city more agreeable for all men to visit, and more frequented. Should any persons imagine, however, that if our state continues to maintain peace, it will be less powerful, and esteemed, and celebrated through Greece, such persons, in my opinion, entertain an unreasonable apprehension; for those states, assuredly, are most prosperous, which have remained at peace for the longest period; and of all states Athens is the best adapted

by nature for flourishing during peace. Who, indeed, if the
city were in the enjoyment of peace, would not be eager to
resort to it, and shipowners and merchants most of all?
Would not those who have plenty of corn, and ordinary
wine, and wine of the sweetest kind, and olive oil, and
cattle, flock to us, as well as those who can make profit by
their ingenuity and by money-lending? Where would artif-
icers, too, and sophists, and philosophers, and poets, and
such as study their works, and such as desire to witness
sacrifices, or religious ceremonies worthy of being seen and
heard, and such as desire to make a quick sale or purchase
of many commodities, obtain their objects better than at
Athens? If no one can answer in the negative to these questions, and yet some, who desire to recover the supreme
dominion for our state, think that that end would be effected
better by war than by peace, let them contemplate, first of
all, the Persian invasion, and consider whether it was by
force of arms or by good offices to the Greeks that we attained the head of the naval confederacy, and the management of the treasury of Greece. Besides, when our state,
from being thought to exercise its power too tyrannically,
was deprived of its supremacy, were we not then also, after
we abstained from encroachment, again made rulers of the
fleet by the unanimous consent of the islanders? Did not
the Thebans, in consideration of the benefits which they
had received, allow the Athenians to lead them? Even the
Lacedaemonians, not from being forced, but from having
been assisted by us, allowed the Athenians to settle matters
as they pleased respecting the supreme command. And at
the present time, through the disturbances prevailing in
Greece, it seems to me that an opportunity has offered itself
to our city to attach the Greeks to it again without difficulty, without danger, and without expense; for we may
endeavour to reconcile the states that are at war with one
another, and we may try also to unite such as are divided
into factions. If you should make it evident, too, not by
forming warlike confederacies, but by sending embassies

throughout Greece, that you are anxious for the temple at Delphi to be free as it was formerly, I think it would not be at all surprising if you should find all the Greeks ready to agree, and to form confederacies and alliances with you, against those who sought to gain the mastery over the Delphic temple when the Phocians relinquished it. If you indicate, moreover, that you are desirous that peace should prevail over the whole land and sea, I consider that all the Greeks, next to the security of their own countries, would pray for the preservation of Athens.

But if any one still thinks that war is more conducive to the wealth of our city than peace, I know not by what means this point can be better decided than by considering what effect events that occurred in former times produced on our city. For he will find that in days of old vast sums of money were brought into the city during peace, and that the whole of it was expended during war; and he will learn, if he gives his attention to the subject, that, in the present day, many branches of the revenue are deficient in consequence of the war, and that the money from those which have been productive has been spent on many urgent requisitions of every kind; but that now, when peace is established at sea, the revenues are increasing, and that the citizens are at liberty to make whatever use of them they please.

If any one should ask me this question, "Do you mean that, even if any power should unjustly attack our state, we must maintain peace with that power?" I should not say that I had any such intention; but I may safely assert, that we shall retaliate on any aggressors with far greater facility, if we can show that none of our people does wrong to any one; for then our enemies will not have a single supporter.

CHAPTER VI

ADVANTAGES THAT WILL ARISE FROM THE PLANS PROPOSED.
DIVINE AID AND PROTECTION TO BE SOUGHT

IF, then, of all that has been said, nothing appears impossible or even difficult, and if, in case that what I propose be effected, we shall secure increased attachment from the Greeks in general, dwell in greater security, and be distinguished with greater honour, — if the common people will have plenty of provisions, and the rich be eased of the expenses for war, — if, as abundance increases, we shall celebrate our festivals with greater magnificence than at present, shall repair our temples, rebuild our walls and docks, and restore their civil rights to the priests, the senate, the magistrates, and the cavalry, is it not proper that we should proceed to execute these plans as soon as possible, that, even in our days, we may see our country flourishing in security? Should we resolve on pursuing these measures, I should recommend that we should send to Dodona and Delphi to inquire of the gods whether it will be better and more advantageous for the state, for the present time and for posterity, thus to regulate itself. If the gods should give their assent to the proceedings, I should say that we ought then to ask which of the gods we should propitiate in order to execute our designs in the best and most efficient manner; and whichever of the deities they name in their reply, it will be proper to seek favourable omens from them by sacrifices, and then to commence our operations; for if our undertakings are begun with the support of the gods, it is likely that the results from them will lead continually to that which is still better and more advantageous for the state.

III
ST. THOMAS AQUINAS

SUMMA THEOLOGICA

NOTE

ST. THOMAS AQUINAS (1225–1274), greatest of the Schoolmen, was the son of Landulph, count of Aquino. Despite the opposition of his family, he entered the Dominican order at an early age. His superiors, recognizing his great talents, sent him to study with Albertus Magnus, at first in Cologne, later in Paris, where he obtained his doctorate about 1257. His fame as a teacher was already great, and the remainder of his life was devoted to labors in this field at various seats of learning. He was extraordinarily industrious and wrote no less than sixty works, some of them of great length. The most important of these is his famous *Summa Theologica*, a complete exposition of theology and summary of Christian philosophy. This served for centuries as a point of departure for all discussions in its field. It is divided into three parts, but the same plan of exposition is followed throughout. Part I considers the nature of God; Part II (from which our extract is taken), the nature and consequences of human actions; Part III, Christ and His service to the world. His other works include commentaries on Aristotle's *Ethics* and *Politics*, part of the widely-read treatise on politics, *De Regimine Principum*, and many tracts on theological questions. Like Aristotle, he never discussed economic subjects abstractly, but always in connection with larger problems of ethics or politics.

SUMMA THEOLOGICA

QUESTION LXXVII

ON FRAUD COMMITTED IN BUYING AND SELLING

(Divided into four articles)

WE next have to consider the sins which have to do with voluntary exchanges; first, fraud committed in buying and selling; second, usury taken on loans. For in the case of other forms of voluntary exchange, no kind of sin is noted which is to be distinguished from rapine or theft.

Under the first head there are four points to be considered: 1. sales unjust with respect to price, that is, whether it is lawful to sell a thing for more than it is worth; 2. sales unjust with respect to the thing sold; 3. whether a seller is bound to point out a defect in the thing sold; 4. whether it is lawful to sell a thing in trade for more than was paid for it.

FIRST ARTICLE

*Whether a man may lawfully sell a thing for more
than it is worth*

The first article is analyzed as follows:

1. It seems that a man may lawfully sell a thing for more than it is worth. For in the exchanges of human life, justice is determined by the civil law. But according to this it is lawful for the buyer and seller to deceive each other (Cod., lib. IV, tit. 44, *de rescindenda Venditione*), and this takes place when the seller sells a thing for more than it is worth, or the buyer pays less than it is worth. Therefore, it is lawful for a man to sell a thing for more than it is worth.

2. Furthermore, that which is common to all men seems to be natural and not sinful. But as Augustine relates (13

de Trin., cap. 3) the saying of a certain actor was accepted by all: *you wish to buy cheap, and sell dear;* which agrees with the saying in Proverbs xx, 14: *It is naught, it is naught, saith every buyer; and when he is gone away, then he will boast.* Therefore it is lawful to sell a thing for more and to buy it for less than it is worth.

3. Furthermore, it does not seem to be unlawful to do by agreement what the claims of honor require. But according to the Philosopher (*Ethics*, VIII, 13), in friendships based on utility recompense ought to be according to the advantage accruing to the beneficiary; and this sometimes exceeds the value of the thing given, as happens when a man needs something very much, either to escape danger or to obtain some advantage. Therefore in contracts of buying and selling it is lawful to sell a thing for more than it is worth.

But opposed to this is the saying in Matthew vii, 12: *All things whatsoever you would that men should do to you, do you also to them.* But no man wishes to have a thing sold to him for more than it is worth. Therefore no man should sell a thing to another for more than it is worth.

I answer that it is wholly sinful to practise fraud for the express purpose of selling a thing for more than its just price, inasmuch as a man deceives his neighbor to his loss. Hence Cicero says (*de Offic.*, III): *All deception should therefore be eliminated from contracts: the seller should not procure some one to bid up nor the buyer some one to bid down the price.*

If there is no fraud, we may speak of buying and selling in two ways: first, considering them in themselves, and in this respect buying and selling seem to have been instituted for the common advantage of both parties, since one needs something that belongs to the other, and conversely, as explained by the Philosopher (*Polit.*, I, 6). Now what has been instituted for the common advantage ought not to be more burdensome to one than to the other; hence a contract between them ought to be based on the equality of

things. The value of a thing which is put to human use is
measured by the price given; and for this purpose money
was invented, as is explained in *Ethics*, V, 5. Hence,
whether the price exceeds the value of a thing or conversely,
the equality required by justice is lacking. Consequently,
to sell dearer or to buy cheaper than a thing is worth is in
itself unjust and unlawful.

We can speak of buying and selling in another sense,
namely, the case where it accidentally turns out to the advantage of one and to the injury of the other; for example,
when a man has great need of something, and another is
injured if he is deprived of it; in such a case the just price
will be one which not only takes into account the thing sold,
but also the loss incurred by the seller in parting with it.
And thus a thing may lawfully be sold for more than it is
worth in itself, though not more than it is worth to its
possessor. If, however, a man is greatly aided by something
he has obtained from another, and the seller does not suffer
any loss from doing without it, he ought not to charge more
for it, since the advantage which accrues to the other is not
due to the seller but to the condition of the buyer. Now no
one has a right to sell to another what does not belong to
him; though he may charge him for the loss he suffers.
He, however, who derives great advantage from something
received from another, may of his own accord pay the seller
something in addition. This is a matter of honor.

In reply to the first argument above, it is to be said that,
as explained earlier (I–II, quaest. 96, art. 2), human law is
given to the people, among whom many are deficient in
virtue, not to the virtuous alone. Hence human law could
not prohibit whatever is contrary to virtue; it suffices for it
to prohibit the things which destroy the intercourse of men,
treating other things as lawful, not because it approves
them, but because it does not punish them. Hence it treats
as lawful, imposing no penalty, the case where a seller without deception obtains a higher price or a buyer pays a lower
price; unless the discrepancy is too great, since in that case

even human law compels restitution to be made; for example, if a man were deceived as to the just price by more than half. But divine law leaves nothing unpunished which is contrary to virtue. Hence, according to divine law, it is considered unlawful if the equality required by justice is not observed in buying and selling; and he who has more is bound to recompense the one who suffers loss, if the loss is considerable. I say this, because the just price of things is not absolutely definite, but depends rather upon a kind of estimate; so that a slight increase or decrease does not seem to destroy the equality required by justice.

In reply to the second argument, it is to be said that, as Augustine remarks in the same passage: *that actor, either from looking into himself or from experience with others, believed that the desire to buy cheap and sell dear was common to all men. But since this is indeed wicked, each man can attain such justice as to resist and overcome this desire.* And he cites the example of a man who paid the just price for a book to one who, through ignorance, asked too little for it. Hence it is evident that this common desire is not natural but due to wickedness, and hence is common to many who travel the broad road of sin.

In reply to the third argument, it is to be said that in commercial (*commutativa*) justice the chief consideration is the equality of things; but in friendships based on utility the equality of advantage is considered; hence recompense ought to be according to the advantage derived; but in buying, according to equality of things.

ARTICLE II

Whether a sale is rendered unlawful by a defect in the thing sold

The second point is analyzed as follows:

1. It seems that a sale is not rendered unjust and unlawful by a defect in the thing sold. For other considerations should be given less weight in a thing than its essential sub-

stance. But a sale does not seem to be rendered unlawful by a defect in the essential substance; for example, if a man should sell as the real metal alchemic silver or gold, which is suitable for all human uses for which gold and silver are necessary, such as vessels and the like: then still less will a sale be unlawful because of a defect in some other respect.

2. Furthermore, a defect in a thing with respect to its quantity seems to be chiefly opposed to justice, which is based upon equality. Quantity, however, is determined by measuring; the measures of things which are put to human use are not definite, but in some places more and some places less, as explained by the Philosopher (*Ethics*, V, 7). Therefore, just as defects in the things sold cannot be avoided, so it seems that a sale is not rendered unlawful for this reason.

3. Furthermore, it is a defect in the thing sold if any proper quality is lacking in it. But to determine the quality of a thing great skill is needed, which most buyers lack. Hence a sale is not rendered unlawful by a defect.

But opposed to this is the dictum of Ambrose (*de Offic.*, III, 11): *It is a manifest rule of justice that it is not fitting for a good man to deviate from the truth, or to inflict unjust injury on anyone, or to practise any fraud.*

I answer that with respect to a thing sold three kinds of defects may be considered. The first has to do with the substance of the thing; and if a seller knows of such a defect in a thing he sells, he commits fraud: so that the sale is rendered unlawful. Hence it is written against certain people (Isaias i, 22): *Thy silver is turned into dross, thy wine is mingled with water;* for what is adulterated is defective as to its substance. The second kind of defect is as to quantity, which is recognized by means of a measure; and so if a man knowingly uses a short measure in selling, he commits fraud, and the sale is unlawful. Hence it is written in Deuteronomy xxv, 13: *Thou shalt not have divers weights in thy bag, a greater and a less; there shall not be in thy house a greater bushel and a less;* and further on: *For the Lord*

abhorreth him that doth these things, and hateth all injustice.
The third kind of defect is with respect to quality, such as
selling a broken-down animal as sound: if a man does this
knowingly, he commits fraud in the sale, and hence the sale
is unlawful. And in all such cases a man is not only guilty of
sin in making an unjust sale, but he is also bound to make
restitution. If, however, without his knowledge, any of the
aforesaid defects happens to exist in a thing sold, the seller
is not guilty of sin, on account of doing injustice in a material sense; nor is his action unjust, as is evident from what
had been said above (quaest. 59, art. 2). He is, however,
bound to make the loss good to the buyer, when it is brought
to his notice. And what has been said concerning the seller
is also applicable to the buyer. For it sometimes happens
that a seller thinks his article is less valuable in substance,
as if a man should sell gold in place of brass; in this case the
buyer buys unjustly, if he knows it, and is bound to make
restitution. Similar reasoning applies to defects in quality
and quantity.

In reply to the first argument, then, it is to be said that
gold and silver are valuable, not only on account of the
utility of vessels or similar things made of them, but also on
account of the dignity and purity of their substance. Hence,
if gold and silver made by alchemists do not possess the true
substance of gold and silver, the sale is fraudulent and unjust, especially since there are some properties of gold and
silver, in their natural action, which are not found in gold
made by alchemy; such as its property of making glad, and
its medicinal value in certain diseases; true gold can also be
utilized more frequently, and retains its purity longer than
artificial gold. If true gold were made by alchemy, it would
not be unlawful to sell it for true, for nothing prevents art
from using natural causes to produce natural and true
effects, as Augustine says (*de Trin.*, III, 8) concerning those
things which are done by the art of evil spirits.

In reply to the second argument, it is to be said that the
measures of saleable things are necessarily different in dif-

ferent places, on account of differences in the plenty and
scarcity of things; since where a thing is more plentiful,
measures are generally larger. In each place, however, it is
the function of the rulers of the state to determine what are
the just measures of saleable things, taking into account the
conditions of places and things. Hence it is not lawful to
ignore the measures established by public authority or by
custom.

In reply to the third argument, it is to be said that, as
Augustine says (*de Civit. Dei*, XI, 16) the price of saleable
things does not depend upon their rank in nature, since
sometimes a horse is sold for more than a slave; but depends
upon their usefulness to man. Hence a seller or buyer does
not have to know the hidden qualities of a thing sold, but
only those which render it fit for human use; such as the
fact that a horse is strong, runs well, and so on. These qualities, however, the seller and buyer can easily recognize.

ARTICLE III

*Whether a seller is bound to declare a defect in a
thing sold*

The third point is analyzed as follows:

1. It seems that a seller is not bound to declare a defect
in a thing sold. For since the seller does not force the buyer
to buy, he seems to submit the thing he sells to the buyer's
judgment. But judgment and knowledge belong to the same
man. Hence it does not seem that the seller should be held
responsible if the buyer is deceived in his judgment, through
buying hastily and without careful investigation into the
condition of the thing.

2. Furthermore, it seems foolish for a man to do anything
which would hinder his action. But if a man points out defects in an article offered for sale, he hinders the sale; hence
Cicero makes a man say (*de Offic.*, III): *What is so absurd as
that a public crier should announce by order of the owner that*

he has an unwholesome house for sale? Therefore the seller is not bound to declare defects in a thing sold.

3. Furthermore, it is more necessary for a man to know the way of virtue than to know the defects of things sold. But a man is not bound to give advice to all, and to tell them the truth concerning things which pertain to virtue, although he should tell no one a falsehood. Much less, therefore, is a seller bound to declare the defects in a thing sold, giving advice, as it were, to the buyer.

4. Furthermore, if a man is bound to declare a defect in a thing sold, this is only in order that the price may be lowered. But sometimes the price may be lowered even apart from any defect in the thing sold, for some other reason; for example, if a seller, bringing wheat to a place where grain is dear, knows that many are following with more wheat, knowledge of which on the part of the buyers would cause them to pay less. This, however, the seller does not have to tell, apparently. Hence, for analogous reasons, he does not have to declare defects in a thing sold.

Opposed to this is the statement of Ambrose (*de Offic.*, III, 10): *In contracts defects in the things sold must be revealed; and unless the seller has made them known, though the goods have passed into the possession of the buyer, the contract is void on the ground of fraud.*

I answer that to expose a man to danger or loss is always unlawful; though it is not necessary that a man should always give another any help or advice likely to be of service to him, this being necessary only in certain cases, such as when a person is in his care, or cannot be helped by anyone else. But a seller who offers a thing for sale exposes the buyer to loss or danger by the very act of offering him a defective article, if he may incur loss or danger through the defect in it — loss, if the thing offered for sale is worth less because of such a defect, and he does not reduce the price on account of it; danger, if the use of the thing is hindered or rendered harmful by such a defect, as in the case of a man who sells a lame horse as a fast one, a ramshackle house as sound, decayed or poisonous food as good. Hence if such defects are concealed, and the seller does not point them out, the sale will be unlawful and fraudulent, and he is bound to make good the loss.

But if the defect is obvious, as in the case of a horse with only one eye, or when the use of the thing, though not suitable for the seller, may be satisfactory for others, and if he makes a proper deduction from the price, because of this defect, he is not bound to point out the defect in the thing, because the buyer might wish to deduct more from the price on account of this defect than ought to be deducted. Hence the seller may lawfully provide against his own loss by keeping silent about the defect in the thing.

In reply to the first argument, it is to be said that one can not form an opinion except on the basis of evidence. For every man judges according to what he knows, as is stated in *Ethics*, I, 3. Hence if the defects in a thing offered for sale are concealed, the buyer is not enabled to form a satisfactory opinion, unless they are pointed out by the seller. It would be different, however, if the defects were obvious.

In reply to the second argument, it is to be said that a man does not have to announce a defect in a thing by means of a public crier, because if he did so, buyers would be deterred from buying, not knowing the other qualities of the thing, which make it good and useful. But the defect is to be pointed out individually to anyone considering the purchase, who can then weigh all the qualities together, good as well as bad. For there is no reason why a thing which is defective in some respect may not be useful in many others.

In reply to the third argument, it is to be said that, although a man is not strictly bound to tell everyone the truth about things pertaining to virtue, still he is bound to tell the truth about them in a case where another would be exposed to danger by his action, to the detriment of virtue, and so it is in this case.

In reply to the fourth argument, it is to be said that a defect in a thing makes its present value less than it seems;

but in this case the thing is expected to fall in value in the future through the arrival of merchants, which is not expected by the buyers; hence a seller who sells at the prevailing price does not seem to act contrary to justice, in not telling what is going to happen. If, however, he did tell, or lowered his price, he would act more virtuously; though he does not seem to be bound by the requirements of justice to do this.

Whether in trading it is lawful to sell a thing for more than was paid for it

The fourth point is analyzed as follows:

1. It seems that in trading it is not lawful to sell a thing for more than was paid for it. For Chrysostom says on Matthew xxi (hom. 38. in Op. imperf.): *Whoever buys a thing in order to make a profit in selling it, whole and unchanged, is the trader who is cast out of God's temple;* and Cassiodorus writes to the same effect in commenting on the passage *Because I have not known learning* (*trading,* according to another version) in Psalm lxx. *What else is trading,* he says, *but buying cheap and wishing to sell dear at retail?* and he adds: *Such traders the Lord cast out of the temple.* But nobody is cast out of the temple except on account of sin. Therefore such trading is sinful.

2. Furthermore, it is contrary to justice for a man to sell a thing for more than it is worth or to buy for less, as is shown in the first article of this question. But he who in trading sells a thing for more than he paid for it must have paid less than it was worth or be selling for more. Therefore this cannot be done without sin.

3. Furthermore, Jerome says (epist. ii ad Nepotian.): *Shun, as you would a pestilence, a trader cleric, who out of poverty has become rich, and out of obscurity famous.* Now trading seems to be forbidden to clerics for no reason except its sinfulness. Hence to buy a thing cheap and sell it dear in trade is a sin.

Opposed to this is Augustine's commentary on the passage *Because I have not known learning*, in Psalm lxx: *The avaricious trader blasphemes over his loss, lies and perjures himself about the prices of his wares. But these are vices of the man, not of the craft, which can be carried on without such vices.* Therefore, trading is not in itself unlawful.

I answer that it is the function of traders to devote themselves to exchanging goods. But, as the Philosopher says (*Polit.*, I, 5, 6), there are two kinds of exchange. One may be called natural and necessary, by means of which one thing is exchanged for another, or things for money to meet the needs of life, and this kind of trading is not the function of traders, but rather of household managers or of statesmen, who have to provide a family or a state with the necessaries of life. The other kind of exchange is that of money for money or of things for money, not to meet the needs of life, but to acquire gain; and this kind of trading seems to be the function of traders, according to the Philosopher (*Polit.*, I, 6). Now the first kind of exchange is praiseworthy, because it serves natural needs, but the second is justly condemned, because, in itself, it serves the desire for gain, which knows no limit but extends to infinity. Hence trading in itself is regarded as somewhat dishonorable, since it does not logically involve an honorable or necessary end. Gain, however, which is the end of trading, though it does not logically involve anything honorable or necessary, does not logically involve anything sinful or contrary to virtue; hence there is no reason why gain may not be directed to some necessary or even honorable end; and so trading will be rendered lawful; as when a man uses moderate gains acquired in trade for the support of his household, or even to help the needy; or even when a man devotes himself to trade for the public welfare, lest there be a lack of the things necessary for the life of the country; and seeks gain, not as an end, but as a reward for his efforts.

In reply to the first argument, then, it is to be said that the words of Chrysostom are to be understood as applying to trade insofar as gain is its ultimate end; and this seems to be the case chiefly when a man sells a thing at a higher price without making any change in it: for if he charges a higher price for a thing that has been improved, he seems to receive a reward for his efforts; though the gain itself may also be sought, not as an ultimate end, but for some other necessary or honorable end, as explained above.

In reply to the second argument, it is to be said that not everyone who sells for more than he paid is a trader, but only the one who buys for the express purpose of selling dearer. Now if he buys a thing, not for the purpose of selling it, but with the intention of keeping it, and later wishes to sell it, for some reason, it is not trading, though he sells at a higher price. For this can be done lawfully, either because he has improved the thing in some way, or because the price has changed with a change of place or time, or because of the risk he takes in transporting the thing from one place to another, or even in having it transported for him. According to this reasoning, neither the purchase nor the sale is unjust.

In reply to the third argument, it is to be said that clerics should abstain not only from what is evil in itself but also from what has the appearance of evil. This is the case in trading, both because it aims at earthly gain, which clerics should disdain, and also because of the frequent sins of traders, since *the trader finds it hard to avoid sins of the lips*, as it is written in Ecclesiasticus xxvi, 28. There is also the further reason that trading involves the mind too much in secular interests, and consequently distracts it from spiritual ones: hence the Apostle says (2 Timoth. ii, 4): *No man being a soldier to God entangleth himself with secular businesses*. Clerics may, however, practise the first kind of exchange, which is directed to meeting the needs of life, either in buying or selling.

QUESTION LXXVIII

OF THE SIN OF USURY, WHICH IS COMMITTED IN LOANS

(Divided into four articles)

WE next have to discuss the sin of usury, which is committed in loans; and under this head there are four points to be considered: 1. whether it is sinful to receive money as a price for money lent, that is, to receive usury; 2. whether it is lawful in the same case to receive any advantage, as a sort of compensation for the loan; 3. whether a man is bound to restore what he has made as a just profit on usurious gains; 4. whether it is lawful to borrow money upon usury.

FIRST ARTICLE

Whether it is sinful to receive usury for money lent

The first point is analyzed as follows:

1. It seems that it is not sinful to receive usury on money loans. For no one sins in following the example of Christ. But the Lord says of himself (Luke xix, 23): *At my coming I might have exacted it with usury*, that is, the money lent. Hence it is not sinful to receive usury for a loan of money.

2. Furthermore, as it is written in Psalm xviii, 8, *The law of the Lord is unspotted*, that is, because it prohibits sin. But in the divine law some usury is allowed, according to the passage of Deuteronomy (xxiii, 19): *Thou shalt not lend money to thy brother upon usury, nor corn, nor any other thing, but to the stranger;* and what is more, it is promised as a reward for keeping the law, according to Deuteronomy (xxviii, 12): *Thou shalt lend to many nations, and shalt not borrow of any one.* Hence to receive usury is not sinful.

3. Furthermore, in human affairs justice is determined according to the civil laws. But according to these it is allowed to receive usury. Hence it seems to be lawful.

4. Furthermore, to neglect counsels does not bind to sin. But, among other counsels, is found (Luke vi): *Lend,*

hoping for nothing thereby. Hence it is not sinful to receive usury.

5. Furthermore, to receive a price for what one is not bound to do does not seem to be, in itself, sinful. But in no case is a man who has money bound to lend it to his neighbor. Hence it is lawful for him to receive a price for a loan in some cases.

6. Furthermore, silver made into money does not differ essentially from silver made into vessels. But it is lawful to receive a price for vessels of silver that are lent. Hence it is also lawful to receive a price for the loan of silver in the form of coins. Hence usury is not, in itself, sinful.

7. Furthermore, any man may lawfully receive a thing which the owner gives him voluntarily. But he who receives a loan pays usury voluntarily. Hence he who lends may lawfully receive it.

But opposed to this is the saying of Exodus xxii, 25: *If thou lend money to any of my people that is poor, that dwelleth with thee, thou shalt not be hard upon them as an extortioner, nor oppress them with usuries.*

I answer that to receive usury for money lent is, in itself, unjust, since it is a sale of what does not exist; whereby inequality obviously results, which is contrary to justice.

In proof of this, it should be noted that there are some things the use of which is the consumption of the things themselves; as we consume wine by using it to drink, and consume wheat by using it for food. Hence, in the case of such things, the use should not be reckoned apart from the thing itself; but when the use has been granted to a man, the thing is granted by this very fact; and therefore, in such cases, the act of lending involves a transfer of ownership (*dominium*). Therefore, if a man wished to sell wine and the use of the wine separately, he would be selling the same thing twice, or selling what does not exist; hence he would obviously be guilty of a sin of injustice. For analogous reasons, a man commits injustice who lends wine or wheat, expecting to receive two compensations, one as the restitution of an equivalent thing, the other as a price for the use, which is called *usury*.

There are some things, however, the use of which is not the consumption of the thing itself; thus the use of a house is living in it, not destroying it. Hence, in such cases, both may be granted separately, as in the case of a man who transfers the ownership of a house to another, reserving the use of it for himself for a time; or, conversely, when a man grants someone the use of a house, while retaining the ownership. Therefore a man may lawfully receive a price for the use of a house, and in addition expect to receive back the house lent, as happens in leasing and letting a house.

Now money, according to the Philosopher (*Ethics*, V, 5 and *Polit.*, I, 5, 6) was devised primarily for the purpose of effecting exchanges; and so the proper and principal use of money is the consumption or alienation (*distractio*) of it, whereby it is expended in making purchases. Therefore, in itself, it is unlawful to receive a price for the use of money lent, which is called *usury*; and just as a man is bound to restore other things unjustly acquired, so he is bound to restore money received through usury.

In reply to the first argument above, it is to be said that usury is there used in a figurative sense, to indicate the increase of spiritual goods which God requires of us, wishing us always to increase in the goods received from Him; which is for our advantage, not His.

In reply to the second argument, it is to be said that the Jews were forbidden to receive usury from their brothers, that is, from Jews; by which we are given to understand that to receive usury from any man is strictly evil: for we ought to regard every man as a neighbor and brother, especially in the state of the Gospel, to which all are called. Hence it is written in so many words (Psalm xiv, 5): *He that hath not put out his money to usury;* and Ezechiel xvii, 8: *He who hath not taken usury.* The permission to receive usury from strangers was not accorded them as something lawful, but as something allowed with a view to avoiding a greater evil, that is, lest through avarice, to which they were addicted (Isaias lvi), they should take usury from the Jews who worshipped God. In the promise of it as a reward: *Thou shalt lend to many nations*, etc., the word (*feneraberis*) is to be taken in the broad sense of lending (*mutuum*), as in Ecclesiasticus xxix: *Many have not lent (fenerati), not out of wickedness*, that is, they have not lent in the broader sense (*mutuaverunt*). Therefore the Jews are promised an abundance of riches as a reward, whereby they may be able to lend to others.

In reply to the third argument, it is to be said that human laws leave some sins unpunished, on account of the conditions among imperfect men, who would be deprived of many advantages, if all sins were strictly forbidden and penalties provided. Hence human law had allowed usury, not in the sense of considering it to be according to justice, but in order not to prevent the advantage of many. Hence in the civil law itself (Constit., lib. II, tit. 4, *de Usufructu*) it is written that *things which are consumed in use do not receive a usufruct, either according to natural reason or civil law, and that the senate did not create a usufruct in their case (for it could not), but a quasi usufruct*, that is, allowing usury. And the Philosopher, led by natural reason, says (*Polit.*, I, 7) *that the acquisition of money by means of usury is especially contrary to nature*.

In reply to the fourth argument, it is to be said that a man is not always bound to lend; hence, to this extent, it is placed among the counsels. But that a man should not seek gain from lending is a matter of precept. It may, however, be called a counsel in comparison with the sayings of the Pharisees, who considered some usury lawful; just as loving our enemies is a counsel. Or he speaks in this passage, not about the hope of usurious gain, but about the hope that is placed in man; for we ought not to lend or do any other good deed on account of hope in man, but on account of hope in God.

In reply to the fifth argument, it is to be said that he who is not bound to lend may receive compensation for what he has done: but he ought not to exact more. He is recompensed, however, according to the equality required by justice, if as much is returned to him as he lent. Hence if he exacts more for the use of a thing which has no use except the consumption of the substance, he exacts a price for what does not exist; and so it is an unjust exaction.

In reply to the sixth argument, it is to be said that the principal use of silver vessels is not the consumption of them; hence the use of them can be sold, though the ownership of the thing be retained. The principal use of coined silver, however, is the alienation (*distractio*) of the money in making purchases; hence it is not lawful to sell the use of it, while desiring the restitution of what was lent. It is to be noted, however, that a secondary use of silver vessels may be exchange; and it is not lawful to sell this use of them. And, similarly, there may be a secondary use of coined silver, as in the case of lending coined money for the purpose of display or for deposit as a pledge; and a man may lawfully sell this use of money.

In reply to the seventh argument, it is to be said that he who pays usury does not really do it voluntarily, but under some compulsion, for he needs to obtain the loan, and the one who has the money will not lend it without usury.

ARTICLE II

Whether it is lawful to ask any other consideration for money lent

The second point is analyzed as follows:

1. It seems that a man may ask some other consideration for money lent. For every man may lawfully provide against his own loss. But sometimes a man suffers loss through lending money. Hence it is lawful for him to ask or exact something over and above the money lent, to make up for his loss.

2. Furthermore, every man is bound by a kind of requirement of honor to make some recompense to one who has done him a favor; as is stated in *Ethics*, V, 5. But he who lends money to a man in need, does him a favor, for which some expression of gratitude is due. Hence he who receives is bound by natural duty to make some recompense. But it does not seem to be unlawful for a man to bind himself to something to which he is bound by natural law. Hence it does not seem to be unlawful for a man, in lending money to another, to contract for some compensation.

3. Furthermore, just as there are gifts *by the hand*, so also there are gifts *by the tongue* and *by service*, as a gloss says on Isaias xxxiii, 15: *Blessed is he that shaketh his hands from all bribes*. But it is lawful to receive service or even praise from one to whom money has been lent. Hence for analogous reasons it is lawful to receive some other gift.

4. Furthermore, there seems to be the same relation between gift and gift as between loan and loan. But it is lawful to receive money for other money given. Hence it is lawful to receive compensation in the form of another loan for money lent.

5. Furthermore, a man who transfers the ownership of money to another in a loan alienates it more than a man who entrusts it to a merchant or craftsman. But it is lawful to receive gain for money entrusted to a merchant or craftsman. Hence it is also lawful to receive gain from money lent.

6. Furthermore, a man may receive a pledge for money lent, the use of which may be sold for some price; as when the pledge is a field or a house which is inhabited. Hence it is lawful to make some gain from money lent.

7. Furthermore, it sometimes happens that a man sells his goods dearer in a sort of loan, or buys the property of another cheaper, or even increases the price in proportion to the delay in payment, or lowers it in proportion to the promptness; in all of which cases some compensation seems to be given as if for a loan of money. This, however, does

not seem to be obviously unlawful. Hence it seems to be lawful to ask or exact some consideration for money lent.

Opposed to this is the mention (Ezechiel xviii, 17) among other things required in a just man: *If he hath not taken usury and increase;* as also verse 8: *If he hath not taken any increase.*

I answer that, according to the Philosopher (*Ethics*, IV, 1), everything is considered money of which the price can be measured by money. Hence, just as a man who, by a tacit or explicit agreement, receives money for the loan of money or anything else which is consumed by use, sins against justice, as explained in the preceding article, so also anyone who, by tacit or explicit agreement, receives anything else, the price of which can be measured by money, is likewise guilty of sin. If, however, he receives something of this kind, not asking it and not according to any tacit or explicit obligation, but as a free gift, he does not sin; because even before he lent the money, he might lawfully receive a free gift, and he is not put at a disadvantage by the act of lending. Compensation in the form of things which are not measured by money may, however, be exacted lawfully, such as good will and love for the lender, or something similar.

In reply to the first argument, it is to be said that a lender may without sin contract with the borrower for compensation to cover the loss arising from the fact that he gives up something which belongs to him; for this is not selling the use of money, but avoiding loss; and it may be that the borrower avoids greater loss than the lender incurs; so that the borrower makes good the other's loss with advantage to himself. Compensation for loss, however, cannot be stipulated on the ground that the lender makes no profit on his money, because he should not sell what he does not yet possess, and which he may be prevented in various ways from getting.

In reply to the second argument, it is to be said that compensation for a favor may be made in two ways; first, as a requirement of justice, to which a man may be bound by definite agreement; and this obligation depends upon the amount of benefit received. Hence a man who receives a loan of money, or of something similar, the use of which is its consumption, is not bound to pay back more than he received in the loan: so that it is contrary to justice, if he is bound to return more. Secondly, a man is bound to make compensation for a favor as a requirement of friendship; in which more consideration is given to the spirit in which the benefit was conferred than to the extent of it; and to such a debt no civil obligation attaches, whereby a certain element of compulsion is introduced, making the compensation no longer spontaneous.

In reply to the third argument, it is to be said that if a man, by a sort of obligation tacitly or explicitly agreed to, expects or exacts compensation in the form of *service* or of *words*, it is just as if he exacted a gift *from the hand*; because both can be valued in money, as we see in the case of those who offer for hire the work they do with their hands or tongues. If, however, a gift *of service* or *of language* is not given as an obligation, but out of good will, which is not subject to valuation in money, it is lawful to receive, and exact, and expect this.

In reply to the fourth argument, it is to be said that money cannot be sold for more money than the amount lent, which is to be repaid. Nor is anything to be exacted or expected except a feeling of good will, which is not subject to valuation in money; from which a spontaneous loan may arise. The obligation to make a loan later is inconsistent with this, however, because such an obligation can also be valued in money. Hence, it is lawful for a lender to receive another loan in return, at the same time, but it is not lawful to bind the borrower to make a loan later.

In reply to the fifth argument, it is to be said that a lender of money transfers the ownership of the money to the borrower; so that the borrower holds it at his own risk, and is bound to restore it intact: hence the lender should not exact more. But he who entrusts his money to a merchant or craftsman, by means of some kind of partnership, does not transfer the ownership of his money to the latter, but it remains his; so that the merchant trades with it or the craftsman uses it at the owner's risk; hence he may lawfully claim a part of the gain arising therefrom, as being from his own property.

In reply to the sixth argument, it is to be said that if a man, in return for money lent to him, pledges something, the use of which can be valued at a price, the lender ought to count the use of this thing as part of the repayment of the loan; otherwise, if he wishes to have the use of that thing granted him without charge, it is just as if he received money for a loan, which is usury; unless the thing happened to be such as are usually lent without charge among friends, as in the case of a book.

In reply to the seventh argument, it is to be said that if a man wishes to sell his goods for more than their just price, expecting the buyer to pay later, it is plainly a case of usury, because such waiting for payment has the character of a loan. Hence whatever is exacted for such waiting, in excess of the just price, is a kind of price for a loan, which comes under the head of usury. And likewise, if a buyer wishes to buy for less than the just price, on the ground that he pays the money before the thing can be delivered to him, it is a sin of usury, because that paying of money in advance has the character of a loan, the price of which is the amount deducted from the just price of the thing bought. If, however, a man wishes to deduct from the just price, in order to obtain the money sooner, he is not guilty of a sin of usury.

ARTICLE III
Whether a man is bound to restore anything he may
have made out of usurious gains

The third point is analyzed as follows:

1. It seems that a man is bound to restore anything he may have made out of usurious gains. For the Apostle says

(Romans xi, 16): *If the root be holy, so are the branches.* Hence by the same reasoning *if the root be tainted, so are the branches.* But the root was usurious. Hence whatever was acquired thereby is usurious. Hence he is bound to make restitution of it.

2. Furthermore, as stated in the Decretal *Cum tu, sicut asseris (extrav. de Usuris): property acquired by means of usury should be sold, and the price thereof restored to those from whom it was extorted.* Hence by the same reasoning anything else acquired from usurious gains should be restored.

3. Furthermore, what a man buys with usurious gains belongs to him by reason of the money which he paid for it. Hence he has no greater right to the thing acquired than to the money he paid. But he was bound to restore usurious gains. Hence he is also bound to restore what he acquired therewith.

Opposed to this is the principle that a man may lawfully keep what he has legitimately acquired. But what is acquired with usurious gains is sometimes legitimately acquired: hence it may lawfully be retained.

I answer that, as stated above in the first article of this question, there are some things of which the use is the consumption of the things themselves, and which have no usufruct, according to the civil law (Instit. II, tit. 4, *de Usufructu*). Hence, if such things were extorted by usury (for example, money, wheat, wine, or something similar), a man is not bound to make restitution beyond what he has received: because what is acquired by this means is not the fruit of such a thing but of human industry; unless perchance the other man suffer a loss through the withholding of such a good, losing a part of his property; for then he is bound to make compensation for the injury.

There are some things, however, of which the use is not their consumption; and such things have a usufruct; such as a house or a field or something of the kind. Hence, if a man has extorted the house or the field of another by usury, he is bound to restore not only the house or field but also the fruits obtained therefrom, because they are the fruits of things of which another is the owner; and hence they belong to him.

In reply to the first argument, it is to be said that the root not only has the character of material, as in the case of usurious gains, but also has in some degree the character of an active cause, since it furnishes nourishment; hence it is not the same thing.

In reply to the second argument, it is to be said that property acquired by means of usury does not belong to the same persons as the usury, but to those who bought it; those from whom the usury was taken have some claims on it, however, as on the other property of the usurer. Hence it is not prescribed that such property be assigned to those from whom the usury was taken, because it may be worth more than the usury paid; but it is prescribed that the property be sold, and the price restored, that is, up to the amount of the usury received.

In reply to the third argument, it is to be said that what is acquired with usurious gains belongs to the purchaser, not on account of the usurious gains he paid for them, as instrumental cause, but on account of his industry, as principal cause; hence he has more right to a thing acquired with usurious gains than to the usurious gains themselves.

ARTICLE IV

Whether it is lawful to borrow money upon usury

The fourth point is analyzed as follows:

1. It seems that it is not lawful to borrow money upon usury. For the Apostle says (Romans i, 32) that *they are worthy of death, not only they that do these sins, but also they that consent to them that do them.* But he who borrows money upon usury consents to the usurer in his sin, and gives him an occasion for sin. Hence he also sins.

2. Furthermore, for no temporal advantage should one give another any occasion for sin; for this is in the nature of active scandal, which is always sinful, as stated above (quaest. 45, art. 2). But he who seeks a loan from a usurer directly gives him an occasion for sin. Hence he is not excused by reason of any temporal advantage.

3. Furthermore, it seems to be no less necessary to deposit one's money sometimes with a usurer than to borrow from him. But depositing one's money with a usurer seems to be entirely unlawful, just as it would be unlawful to put a sword in the keeping of a madman, a maiden in the keeping of a libertine, or food in the keeping of a glutton. Hence it is not lawful to borrow from a usurer.

Opposed to this is the argument that a man who suffers an injury does not sin, according to the Philosopher (*Ethics*, V, 11); hence justice is not a mean between two vices, as stated in the same place (cap. 5). But the usurer sins, in doing injustice to the one who borrows upon usury. Hence the borrower upon usury does not sin.

I answer that it is in no way lawful to induce a man to commit sin; but it is lawful to use the sin of another for a good end; because even God uses all sins for some good end; for He draws some good out of every evil, as is stated in the *Enchiridion* (August. xi). Hence when Publicola asked whether it was lawful to use the oath of a man swearing by false gods, in which he plainly sins, by paying them divine homage, Augustine answered (Epist. xlvii) that *he who uses the oath of one who swears by false gods, not for evil but for good, does not become a party to his sin in swearing by evil spirits, but to his good faith whereby he kept his word. If, however, he induced him to swear by false gods, he would sin.* So, in the present question, it is also to be said that it is in no way lawful to induce a man to lend upon usury; one may, however, borrow upon usury from a man who is ready to do it and practises usury, provided it be for some good purpose, such as helping oneself or somebody else out of difficulty; just as it is also lawful for one who falls among robbers to point out what goods he has, in order to save his life, though the robbers commit sin in plundering him, like the ten men who said to Ishmael (Jeremiah xli, 8): *Kill us not, for we have stores in the field.*

In reply to the first argument, it is to be said that he who borrows money upon usury does not consent to the sin of the usurer, but uses it; nor does the taking of usury please him, but the loan, which is good.

In reply to the second argument, it is to be said that he who borrows money upon usury does not give the usurer occasion for taking usury, but for making a loan. The usurer, himself, however, takes the occasion for sin from the malice of his heart. Hence, it is a passive scandal on his part, not an active one on the part of the borrower. Nor should the other, on account of such passive scandal, refrain from seeking a loan, if he is in need; because such passive scandal does not arise from infirmity or ignorance, but from malice.

In reply to the third argument, it is to be said that if a man deposited his money with a usurer who had no other with which to practise usury, or with the intention of making greater gains by way of usury, he would provide the material for sin; and so he himself would share the blame; but if a man deposits his money for safe-keeping with a usurer who has other money with which to practise usury, he does not commit a sin, but uses a sinful man for a good end.

IV

NICOLE ORESME

TRAICTIE DE LA PREMIERE INVENTION DES MONNOIES

NOTE

Nicole Oresme (c. 1320–1382) was one of the most distinguished French churchmen of the fourteenth century. He was born in or near Caen, but went early to Paris for study, and was presently (1356) made grand master of the College of Navarre. Six years later he was made dean of Rouen, and in 1377 bishop of Lisieux, where he died. He was a man of wide interests and wrote ably on several theological subjects and on mathematics, as well as translating several works of Aristotle from the Latin version into French. The date of composition of his *Traictie* is unknown, but it is believed to have been not far from 1360. Though its originality has quite properly been questioned, this work is nevertheless of great significance; first, because it does summarize the best Scholastic opinion fairly well, and second, because it shows unmistakable beginnings of the secular, detached point of view which was later to transform economic discussion. Oresme, himself, translated the original Latin into French at the request of King Charles V. Several manuscripts and printed editions of it are known, and it appears to have been quite widely read.

ON THE FIRST INVENTION OF MONEY

Here beginneth the Treatise on the first origin, the nature, and the law of moneys; and firstly, why money was first devised.

QUANDO *dividebat Altissimus gentes, quando separabat filios Adam, constituit terminos populorum juxta numerum filiorum, etc.* When the most high and sovereign God almighty divided the nations and separated the sons of Adam, he set boundaries for the peoples, according to the number of the children of Israel; thence in the course of time men multiplied over the earth, and their possessions were divided and shared among them, as was expedient. Thus it came about that one man had more of one thing in his possession than his needs required, while another had little or none of the same thing, but on the contrary had a plenty of something else, of which the first was in need. As if, for example, a man had a surplus of sheep and other cattle but needed grain and bread, while the laborer, on the other hand, had bread enough but lacked cattle. Similarly one region abounded in a thing of which another was greatly in need. For this reason, therefore, men began to traffic and exchange their riches with one another, without money, one giving a sheep for some grain, another his labor for bread or wool, and similarly for everything else. And this practice was long the custom in several cities and countries, as Justinus, the historian, and other ancient authors recount. But since many difficulties and disputes arose among them under this method of exchanging things, clever men devised an easier way — the making of money, an instrument for measuring and exchanging one with another those natural riches by means of which men most easily supply their necessities; for all money is called artificial wealth, as indeed it is, since a man might have an abundance of it and yet die of hunger, as the philosopher Aristotle illustrates by the example of a covetous King, called Midas by Ovid in his *Metamorphoses*, who prayed the Gods that whatever he touched might become gold. This foolish prayer the Gods granted him, and so he died of hunger amid his gold, as the poets tell us; for money does not readily meet the needs of human life, but is an artificial instrument devised to facilitate the exchange of natural riches. Thus it can easily be seen without further proof that money is of great use to the commonwealth, and indeed very necessary, as Aristotle agrees in the fifth book of his *Ethics*, though the poet (Ovid) declares:

> Effodiuntur opes irritamenta malorum.
> Jamque nocens ferrum ferroque nocentius aurum, etc.

Which is to say that riches, i. e. gold and silver, which are dug from the bowels of the earth, are the mockeries and deceits of wicked men, for many evils are caused by them, including numberless murders, as men have seen in days gone by and see to-day. This results from the perverse greed of wicked men, and not from money itself; for it is very helpful and necessary to human life, and the use of it is a very good thing. On this point Cassiodorus remarks that, although this money may, from common use, seem a base thing, it is to be noted that the use of it was adopted by the ancients for very good reasons. And in another passage he says that the invention of money was necessary, especially to contribute to the public welfare.

The second chapter: Of what material money should be made.

And since money, therefore, is an instrument for the mutual exchange of natural Riches, as explained in the preceding chapter, it was expedient that such an instrument should be convenient to handle, easy to carry, and such that a small portion of it might buy and exchange natural Riches in greater quantity, as well as several other conditions which will be noted hereafter. It is desirable, therefore, that Money be made of precious material which is not

plentiful, such as gold; but a material of which the country
has an adequate supply. And when gold does not suffice,
Money is made of silver also. Where these two metals do
not suffice, and adequate supplies cannot be found, then
Money should be made of alloy or simply of base metal, like
the bronze or copper money of ancient times, as Ovid nar-
rates in the first book of his *De Fastis*, where he says,—

> Æra dabant olim, melius nunc omen in auro est,
> Victaque concessit prisca moneta novae.

Which is to say that the ancients in early times made their
money of copper, but now the moderns make it more satisfactorily, of gold. And indeed the ancient world has left
examples of good money to the new. Our Lord, moreover,
promised through Isaias, the prophet, a similar change, saying: *For copper will I bring gold, and for iron will I give
silver.* The two metals are therefore well adapted and suitable for money. And, as Cassiodorus says, the first to discover these two metals are said to have been Cutus, who
discovered gold, and Indus, who discovered silver, both
Kings of Scythia; and to their great honor they gave them
over to the use of men, for which they were reputed divine
by the peoples of those days. And therefore we should not
allow so much of these metals to be used for other purposes
that not enough will be left for use as money. Realizing
this, Theodoric, a former king of Italy, being informed of
the gold and silver which, according to ancient pagan custom, was placed in the tombs of the dead, ordered this treasure to be removed and made into money, for the good of the
commonwealth, saying it was a sort of crime to leave lying
idle, in the tombs of the dead, a thing by which the lives of
men might be sustained and aided. Moreover, it is not
politically expedient that such a material, i. e. gold and
silver, should be too plentiful; for this was the reason why
copper Money was driven out of use, as Ovid says. Perhaps
it is for this reason, too, that the human race has not been
provided with abundant supplies of gold and silver, which

are very suitable for making money, and that men are unable to make them easily by alchemy, as some endeavor to do. To such I say: thus nature justly resists the man who vainly strives to outdo her in her own works.

The third chapter is on the diversity of materials used for money and on alloying.

Money, as was pointed out in the first Chapter, is an instrument for trading. Now since trading is a privilege and necessity for the whole community and each of its members — sometimes on a grand scale and very important, sometimes moderate, and most frequently quite small — it was convenient and necessary to have money of gold, which is precious and easily carried or moved, and hence more adapted to large transactions; and likewise money of silver, which is less precious, and suitable for paying balances in money-changing, and for buying inexpensive merchandise. And since sometimes there is not enough silver in a region, in proportion to its natural riches, with the result that the small quantity of silver which would justly be given for a pound of bread, or something of that kind, would be too small to be easily handled, therefore it was mixed with a less valuable material, thus giving rise to *black money*, which is convenient for small purchases. Hence in a region where silver is not plentiful, mixed Money may very properly be made. There are therefore three sorts of materials suitable for use as money: the first is gold, the second silver, and the third *black mixed*. But it is to be noted as a general rule that money should never be alloyed, except in the case of the less valuable metal of which small Money is ordinarily made; if a country, for example, was using money of gold and silver, the gold Money should never be alloyed, so long as the gold was of such quality that it could be coined without admixture. The reason for this is that all such mixtures naturally arouse suspicion, and in them neither the quality nor the quantity of the gold can be easily recognized. Therefore no alloy should be used in gold money, except in case of great necessity, as already explained; and when alloy is to be added, it should be in the money least subject to suspicion and deception, i. e. in the least precious metal, silver. Moreover, no such mixing should take place except for the common advantage, for the sake of which money was first devised, and which is its natural purpose, as is clear from the preceding chapters. But the common advantage plainly does not require the use of alloy in gold money, when there is enough silver money; such a policy never seems to be adopted in good faith, and it has never been followed in well-governed communities.

The fourth chapter treats of the form and stamp of Money.

When men first began to trade and buy things by means of money, there was as yet no stamp or image upon it, but men simply gave a piece of copper or silver for food or drink, measuring the piece by weight. And since it was a bother to have to make use of scales so often, and money could not be satisfactorily equated with commodities by weight in this way; and since, moreover, the seller in many cases could not determine the quality of the metal in mixed Money; therefore the wise men of that time prudently arranged that the pieces of money should be made of certain quality and definite weight, that they should be marked with a stamp familiar to all, indicating the quality of the material and its weight, so that by eliminating suspicion the value of money might be made easy to determine without difficulty or doubt. That the stamp on coins was adopted as a guaranty of quality and weight is clearly shown by the ancient names of coins known to us by their stamp, such as the pound, the sou, the penny, the obol, and the like, which are names of weights suitable for money, as Cassiodorus says Similarly *shekel* is properly the name of a coin and also the name of a weight, as appears in Genesis. Other names of coins are proper names, accidental or derived from the place, the image, the maker, or something of the kind. The pieces of

money which are called *deniers* [1] should be of a size and
stamp adapted to handling and counting, and of divisible
material which can take and keep an impression. Hence
not all precious things are suitable for coining into money,
for precious stones, pepper, glassware, and such things are
not naturally fit for this, but only gold, silver, and copper,
as explained above.

The fifth chapter: Who has the right to coin money?

It was further wisely ordained in ancient times, to put an
end to deception, that not everyone should have the right to
coin money, or to stamp the figure or image on his own gold
and silver, but that the stamping of the letters and char-
acters upon money should be done by one or more public
officials appointed by the community; and since the prince
of a country enjoys the greatest prestige and authority, it
is fitting that he, rather than anyone else, should have
money coined and marked with an honest stamp for the
whole community. This stamp, made by the prince and at
his command, should be of fine workmanship and very
difficult to imitate. It should also be forbidden under pain
of death for any of his vassals or even neighboring princes to
coin money stamped like his or of less value, making it impossible for the common people to distinguish between this
unauthorized money and that of the prince. Such action
would cause much harm, and no vassal should have the
privilege of doing anything of the kind; for it would lead to
much fraud, and on the part of a foreign prince would be a
just cause for war.

The sixth chapter: Who is and should be the owner of this money?

Although, as a matter of public policy, the coining and
stamping of money is left to the prince, as we have said, it
does not follow that the Lord and prince is and ought to be
proprietor and lord of the money in circulation in his coun-

---

[1] A term loosely applied to various coins of small denomination. — ED.

try; for money is a legal instrument for exchanging natural Riches among men, as is shown in the first chapter. Money, therefore, really belongs to those who own such natural Riches; for if a man gives his bread or the labor of his body for money, it certainly belongs to him alone, just as did his bread or his labor, which he had full power to dispose of as he wished, unless he was a serf. God, in the beginning of his beautiful world, did not give free control of things only to the princes, i. e. our first parents, but also to all their descendants, as is written in the book of Genesis. For this reason, therefore, money does not belong to the sovereign alone. But someone may seek to attack this conclusion with the argument that Our Lord Jesus Christ, when he was shown a penny, asked whose image and superscription it was, and being told that it was Caesar's, replied: Render therefore to Caesar the things that are Caesar's, and to God the things that are God's; as if he meant to imply: The money is Caesar's since his image is stamped upon it. But if we examine the text of the Gospel, it is clear that we should not say the penny belonged to Caesar because it bore his image, but because it was tribute belonging to Caesar, and for no other reason. For, as the Apostle says, let tribute be given to whom tribute is due; rent to whom rent is due. Jesus indicates, by this saying, to whom tribute is due, viz. the one who protects the commonwealth, and who for the defense of the Realm and the general welfare has the right to coin money. For the reasons set forth above, therefore, money belongs to the community and its individual members, as Aristotle maintains in the seventh book of his *Politics* and Cicero towards the end of his *Rhetoric*. To render to Caesar what belongs to him means simply to render him obedience, as St. Peter says in his second Epistle; but for some time now this obedience has been refused him to such a degree that everyone, ignoring the King's regulations, presumes to sell or pay his gold or silver money as he wishes, rather than according to the price set upon it by the King and the Estates of his Realm. As a result, it has come about that nowadays nobody, whatever his class, can obtain a gold coin except at the rate set by the giver, who sells it as if it were natural Riches, which is directly contrary to the original purpose for which money was devised, as explained above. The toleration of this practice causes the gold of one country to be withdrawn and transported to another where it passes at a higher price. Thus, no standard being maintained, the Kingdom becomes so impoverished that in the course of time the King and the community may suffer grave inconvenience. And what is still more harmful is the way people disregard the clipping of the King's moneys, and pass them at the same rate as good ones of full weight. This cannot last long, because of the confusion which may result.

The seventh chapter: At whose expense money should be coined.

Just as money belongs to the community, as we have said, so it should be coined at the expense of the community. This may be done satisfactorily by deducting the expense from the money itself; the money material, such as gold, being received and purchased for coinage at a lower price than it makes when coined, a definite price fixed by the Lords and experienced officers. For example if LXII sous can be made from one mark of silver, and the necessary labor costs two sous for each mark, then a mark of uncoined silver will be worth only LX sous, the difference being the expense of coining. The amount thus deducted should be ample for the expenses of coinage at all times. If the money can be coined for less, the balance may properly be at the disposal of the Prince or of the master of the mint, as a sort of perquisite; but this should be moderate and need not be much, even if the money could bear it well enough, as will be explained later. For if this deduction were excessive, it would be harmful to the whole community, as anyone of clear understanding can easily see.

The eighth chapter: On alterations in general.

Above all, it is to be noted that no change should ever be made, without clear necessity, in the fundamental laws, statutes, customs and regulations affecting the community. Thus, according to the philosopher Aristotle in the second book of his *Politics*, legislation of long standing should never be repealed in favor of new, even if better, unless the improvement is obviously great; for such changes weaken the authority and sanctity of the laws, especially if they occur frequently.   Such changes give rise to scandal and complaint among the people and danger of disobedience, particularly if they are changes for the worse, for then they become intolerable and unjust.   Now it is certain that the rate and price of money should be regarded as a law or ordinance not to be changed under any circumstances. Evidence of this is to be seen in the fact that all salaries and annual revenues are fixed in terms of money, i. e. a certain number of pounds, sous, and deniers, from which it is plain that no change should ever be made, unless necessity or the obvious advantage of the whole community requires it.   On this point Aristotle remarks in the fifth book of his *Ethics*, speaking of money: *Certainly the thing which should be most stable in character is money.*   Now, speaking generally, Money may be altered in several ways: in form and stamp, in the proportion between the metals, in price and name, in size and weight, and finally in the quality of the material. These five methods may be employed separately or in combination.   It will be well to consider them briefly, and to inquire whether any of them can be just, under what conditions, by what authority, in what way, and for what reason.

·   ·   ·   ·   ·   ·   ·   ·   ·   ·   ·

The tenth chapter: On altering the proportion of Money.

A proportion is a comparison or relation between one thing and another, such as the proportion between gold Money and silver Money, which should always bear a definite relation in value and weight to each other. For inasmuch as gold is naturally more noble, more precious, and better than silver, as well as more difficult to obtain, it is certainly very reasonable that a given weight of gold should be worth a good deal more than the same weight of silver, in some definite ratio, such as twenty to one; thus one pound of gold would be worth as much as twenty pounds of silver, one mark of gold as much as twenty marks of silver, and so on. Similarly there might be some other ratio, such as twenty-five to three or the like; but this should follow the natural ratio or proportion between the values of gold and silver; and when thus established it should not be arbitrarily ignored, or changed except for good reasons arising from changes in the material itself, which are rare. Thus if gold became less plentiful than before the establishment of the currency, it ought to be worth more as compared with silver, and its price ought to be changed; but if the change were slight or nil, the Prince would have no right to make such alteration. For if he changed the ratio arbitrarily, he could unjustly draw to himself the money and property of his subjects; as if, for example, he rated gold at a low price and bought it up in exchange for silver, and then, having raised the price of gold, sold it again or coined it into money at the new rate, which would be the same as setting a price on all the grain in his Realm, buying it up, and later reselling it at a higher price. Surely anyone can easily see that this exaction would be unjust and truly tyrannical, worse than what King Pharaoh did in Egypt. Of this Cassiodorus writes: We read that Joseph gave permission to buy grain to meet the terrible famine, but set such a price on it that the starving people sold themselves into subjection to him, to obtain sustenance. What a miserable thing it was to live, when bitter relief seemed to take away one's liberty, when the rescued lamented no less than the captive. I believe that the holy man was compelled to do this in order to satisfy his avaricious lord and rescue the suffering people. These are his

words. Although this seems unjust and evil, this monopoly
of money is still more truly tyrannical, inasmuch as it is not
voluntary and not necessary for the community, but indeed
harmful.   If anyone objects that it is not the same case
as grain, since some things are the special concern of the
sovereign, upon which he places whatever price he chooses,
as some say of salt in France, and especially money, etc.,
I answer that *this monopoly or tax on salt or anything else
necessary to the community is unjust and wicked*. And if any
princes have established laws giving themselves such privileges, let them know they are the ones of whom Our Saviour
says, in the words of the prophet Isaias: *Woe unto them that
make unrighteous decrees and impose such injustice upon the
people*. Again, it is clear enough from the first and sixth
chapters that money is something that belongs to the community.   Therefore, in order that the sovereign may not
maliciously pretend one of the causes for altering the proportion of money set forth in this chapter, the community
alone has the right to decide whether this can and should be
done, and when, and how, and to what extent; nor has the
prince the right to usurp this function in any way.

·   ·   ·   ·   ·   ·   ·   ·   ·   ·   ·

The twelfth chapter: On altering the weight of money.

Changing the weight of money, and at the same time
changing its price in proportion and its stamp, is simply
making another kind of money; as if one should make two
obols out of a denier, or the like, without loss or gain. This
may sometimes be justly done on account of some real
change in the money material, which seldom happens, as
explained in the tenth chapter. Here, however, I wish to
speak of another kind of alteration — where the name and
price are not changed.   In my opinion, such a change is
utterly wrong, especially for the prince, who cannot under
any circumstances practise it without injustice and grave
dishonor.   For, in the first place, the image and inscription
of the Prince are placed on coins to show the correctness of

the weight and the quality of the material, as set forth in the fourth chapter. If, therefore, the weight and quality were not truly indicated, there would evidently be base falsity and fraudulent deception. Measures for wheat, wine, and other less important things are often marked with the public stamp of the King, and if anyone is found guilty of practising fraud upon them, he is considered an infamous falsifier. In the same way the inscription placed upon a coin indicates the correctness of its weight and quality. Who, then, would trust a prince who should diminish the weight or fineness of money bearing his own stamp? On this point Cassiodorus says: What is so wicked as to allow sin in the very standard of weight, that what is properly devoted to justice should be known to be corrupted by fraud? In this way, indeed, the prince could acquire the money of others, nor could he be led by any other motive to make such a change; he would receive money of correct weight and from it coin and issue money of less weight. Such a course would not differ from what Our Lord forbids in many passages of Holy Scripture. In the words of the Sage: *One weight and another weight, one measure and another measure, both are abominations before God;* and in Deuteronomy it is written that Our Lord abominates him who has done such things. And so Riches acquired in this way are soon consumed and lost, to the injury of their possessor; for as Cicero says: Riches acquired in evil will be lost in evil.

The thirteenth chapter: On altering the material of money.

The material of money, as explained above, is either simple or mixed. If it is simple, coinage may be stopped from lack of material; for example, if little or no gold could be found, it would be fitting to cease coining; and if later sufficient supplies became available again, then the coining of money should be resumed, as at various times in the past. On the other hand, coinage of a material may be stopped because of the excessive supplies available. For this reason copper money went out of use at one time, as pointed out above in the third chapter. Such reasons, however, arise very seldom, and under no other circumstances is the pure or simple material of money to be abandoned or adopted anew. If there is any alloying of the materials, it should be only in the least precious metal coinable by itself, as conceded in the said third chapter, and in black money, in order that the pure and good may be distinguished from the adulterated. This mixture, moreover, should be according to a certain proportion, such as ten marks of silver to one of gold, as may be expedient and ordered by officials experienced in these matters. This proportion may be changed on account of some real variation in the nature of the materials or their relationship, and this in two ways: either from lack of a material, as when there is no silver or much less than formerly, in which case more alloy should be mixed with the silver; or from a greater abundance of silver, in which case more of it should be placed in the mixture. But these cases occur infrequently, as pointed out above; and if such a situation should happen to arise, the change of this proportion or mixture should be made by the community, for the greater security of the money, and to avoid the malice and deception which might be practised, as explained in the tenth chapter in discussing the alteration of the proportion in money. In no other case, then, should the mixture or proportion of money be changed, and, what is more, this is not lawful for any prince, for the reasons advanced in the preceding chapter, which are directly applicable here; for the stamp on money is a sign of the honesty of its material and of its alloy, if any, and therefore to change this is to falsify the money. For these reasons the name of God is inscribed on some coins, or the name of a Saint, or the Sign of the Cross, a practice devised and established long ago to testify to the honesty of the money in quality and weight. If a prince, therefore, changes the weight or fineness of money bearing such a sign, he seems to lie tacitly, to commit perjury, and to bear false witness, besides breaking God's commandment: *Thou shalt not take the name of thy God in vain.* For according to the opinion of Hugues, money is derived from *moneo*, since it warns us against fraud or deception in its metal or weight. Again, the prince might by such improper alteration draw to himself unjustly a good part of the property of his people, as explained in connection with altering the weight of money in the preceding chapter; and many other bad results would follow. Moreover, this deception would surely be worse than altering the weight, for it is more subtle and less perceptible, and hence may harm the community more. Therefore, when such alloyed or black money is coined, the community should keep the standard of proportion and alloy in some public place or places to avoid risk, lest the prince (which God forbid) or others falsify the money secretly; just as the community keeps the standards of various other measures in its control.

. . . .

The fifteenth chapter: Gain made by the prince through altering money is unjust.

It is my opinion that the principal and final reason why the prince desires the power of altering money is simply his desire to acquire gain in that way; otherwise there would be no point in making so many kinds of changes. Therefore I wish 'to demonstrate more clearly that such gain is unjust and evil. In the first place, every alteration of money, except the infrequent cases explained above, involves so much deception and falsity that the prince should not have the right to make them, as is proved above; hence he usurps an unjust privilege unjustly, and it is impossible to make just gains in that way. Moreover, insofar as the prince makes a profit there, the community necessarily suffers harm from it. As Aristotle says, whatever the prince does to the detriment of the community is unjust and tyrannical, not befitting a king. If he should say, as Tyrants falsely do, that he is using this gain for the advantage of the public, his mere word is not to be relied on; for by the same reasoning he might take away my cloak or other possession, and say that he needed it for the general welfare; and according to the words of the Apostle, it is never right to do evil in order that good may come of it. For this reason, therefore, nothing should be unjustly taken from anyone under pretense of spending it in works of charity. Moreover, if the prince has the right to make a profit by a simple alteration of money, he may, for the same reason, make a greater alteration and derive greater gain and repeat this several times, then make a compound alteration and increase his gain still more, as explained above. And it is probable that the prince or his successors would follow this course, either on their own initiative or as a result of advice, such action being lawful, for human nature is prone to increase its Riches, when it can do so easily; and thus in time the prince might draw to himself practically all the property and Riches of all his subjects, and so reduce them to servitude. This would be direct tyranny and the act of a genuine tyrant, not of a prince, as is made plain by the philosophers and by all ancient histories.

.   .   .   .

The seventeenth chapter: Gain made by altering
money is worse than usury.

There are three ways, in my opinion, in which one may make profit from money, aside from its natural use. The first of these is the art of exchange, the custody of or trafficking in money; the second is usury, and the third is the altering of money. The first is base, the second is bad, and the third is even worse. Aristotle mentioned the first two but not the third, for in his time such wickedness had not yet been devised. That the first is base and dishonorable Aristotle proves by the reasoning set forth above, saying that this amounts to making money produce offspring, and even calling it *abolostaticon*, or a kind of toll. Hence the apostle St. Matthew, who had been a money-changer, did not return to his former trade, after the resurrection of

Jesus Christ, as did St. Peter, who had been a fisherman. In explaining this St. Gregory says that it is one thing to get your living as a fisherman and another to increase your wealth by the gain from tolls. And he points out, furthermore, that there are some occupations which cannot be carried on without some sin; for there are menial tasks which soil the body, such as cleaning sewers or chimneys, and others which stain the soul, like those now in question. As for usury, it is certain that it is bad, detestable, and unjust, as we learn from Holy Scripture. It remains now to show that making a profit from the alteration of money is even worse than usury: the usurer gives his money to one who receives it voluntarily and who can use it to meet his urgent needs, and what the latter returns over and above what he received is a matter of definite contract satisfactory to both; but the prince, by unnecessary altering of money, takes the property of his subjects against their will; for he forbids the circulation of the former money, which is worth more and which everyone would rather have, and substitutes a poorer money without any possibility that profit or advantage will thereby accrue to his subjects. And if it happens that he makes the money better than before, this is in order to debase it later, and thus return less than the equivalent of the good he had received. In any case he keeps a part for himself. This making of profit by the prince through the altering of money, beyond the natural and customary amount, is the same as usury, and indeed even worse, since it is less voluntary and contrary to the wishes of his subjects, besides being of no advantage to them and unnecessary. Since the gain made by a usurer is not so excessive or so generally harmful as this alteration, which is imposed upon the whole community, I say it is not only like usury, but so tyrannical and fraudulent that I am uncertain whether it should be called violent theft or fraudulent exaction.

.   .   .   .

*The nineteenth chapter: On some disadvantages to
the prince which result from altering money.*

Many great disadvantages arise in divers ways from the
alteration of money; some of them chiefly affecting the
prince, some all the people of his Realm, and some the
greater part of the community, as we have seen within a
short time in France and its dependencies. Some of these
have been referred to already, but it will be well to enu-
merate them again. In the first place, it is too disgraceful in a
prince to commit a fraud by falsifying his money, calling
gold what is not gold, and a pound what is not a pound.
Moreover it is the sovereign's function to condemn and
punish counterfeiters and those who practise any fraud
upon money. How ashamed he should be, therefore, to be
found guilty of a crime which he should punish in another
by a disgraceful death! Furthermore, it is scandalous and
disgraceful for a prince to allow the money of his Realm to
have no fixed value, but to fluctuate from day to day at the
will of the possessor, while sometimes a gold or silver piece
is worth more in one place than another at the same time,
as nowadays. As a result of these alterations, people are
often unable to tell how much a coin of gold or silver is
worth, so that they have to bargain as much about their
Money as about their wares, which is contrary to its nature;
and that which ought to be very certain is quite uncertain
and confused, to the dishonor of the prince, who ought to
take care to punish those guilty of such alterations. It is
likewise disgraceful and everywhere foreign to the nobility
of a prince to prohibit the circulation of good money in his
country, and, for the sake of gain, to order and even compel
his subjects to use his own which is poorer, as if to say that
the good is bad and his bad is good. For Our Lord declares,
in the words of the prophet: *Woe unto you who call good evil
and evil good.* Again, it is very dishonorable for a Prince not
to respect his predecessors, for everyone is bound by the
divine commandment to honor his parents; and he seems to

detract from the honor of his ancestors, when he forbids the circulation of their money, replaces their image by his own, and coins debased money instead of their gold. Of this we seem to have a figure in the Book of Kings, where we read that King Rehoboam removed the gold shields which his father Solomon had made, and erected brass ones in their stead. For this crime and others Rehoboam lost the rule over ten of the tribes of Israel; for he burdened his subjects excessively and tyrannically from the beginning of his Reign. In view of these examples, the prince or King ought to have a horror of such tyranny as altering his money, which is so dangerous and harmful to all his posterity, as will be demonstrated later.

The twentieth chapter: On the disadvantages to the whole community.

Of the many disadvantages arising from the alteration of money which affect the whole community, one was referred to in the fifteenth chapter, namely, that princes could thereby acquire practically all the wealth of the community and thus impoverish their subjects. And just as certain maladies are more dangerous than others because less perceptible, so this evil of alteration is the more dangerous and harmful as it is less noticed; for the evil that results from it is not as promptly felt or perceived by the people as by other bodies, and yet no evil of this kind can be greater. Moreover, the amount of gold and silver in a Realm decreases as a result of such alterations and debasements, and despite all precautions they are carried out to places where they are rated higher; for men prefer to take their money to markets where they know it is worth more. Hence the supply of the money material decreases in countries where debasement is practised. And sometimes people in foreign countries counterfeit the debased money and take it into the country where it is current, obtaining by this fraud the gain which the prince expected. Furthermore, the money materials are partly consumed by the meltings and remelt-

ings involved in these alterations. Hence the money materials are diminished in three ways by these debasements
and alterations. Thus the country's stock cannot last long,
unless it has abundant resources in mines or otherwise, and
the prince will finally lack material for an ample supply of
good money. Again, as a result of alterations and debasements, merchants cease coming from foreign countries with
their good merchandise and natural riches to countries
where they know such bad money is current; for what most
encourages a merchant to bring his natural riches and good
money into a country is the fact that good and stable money
is used there. Moreover, in the country itself where such alterations take place, traffic in merchandise is so disturbed
that merchants and artisans do not know how to deal with
each other. While such alterations last, the revenues of the
prince and the nobility, as well as all annual pensions, salaries, and dues, cannot be justly fixed or paid, as has been
and is now the case; and, what is worse, money cannot be
safely loaned to anyone. Thus is the world troubled by such
alterations, and even divine service and works of charity for
the poor among God's children are checked; and yet an
adequate supply of money material, of merchandise, and all
the things just mentioned are necessary or highly useful to
humanity, and the lack of them a great harm to the whole
community.

*The twenty-first chapter: On the disadvantages to a part of the
community arising from these alterations.*

Some people in the community are engaged in honorable
tasks, useful to the whole commonwealth, such as acquiring
natural Riches, offering prayers and supplications, administering Justice, or doing anything else for the common
necessity or advantage. Such are Ecclesiastics and Religious, Judges, Soldiers, merchants, laborers on the land,
artisans, and so on. But the other part of the community is
free to increase its wealth by base means; such are money-
changers, money-merchants, melters and the like, whose

trades are dishonorable, as shown in the eighteenth chapter. These men, for whom the community has practically no need, and certain others, such as receivers and handlers of large sums, obtain a great part of the gain resulting from the alteration of money, and through chance or fraud grow rich contrary to God and justice, for they are unworthy of having such great wealth. In this way others, who make up the best part of the community, are impoverished. Thus the prince brings loss upon the most numerous and best of his subjects, while the gain does not accrue to him, but mostly to those whose business is base and tainted with fraud and deception, as we have said. Moreover, when the Prince does not give public notice of the time and nature of the alteration he proposes to make in his money, some, by schemes or through friends, discover it secretly, and then buy up merchandise with the poor money to sell it later for good money, thus becoming rich suddenly, and profiting more than the natural course of trade would justify. St. Augustine marvels much at this, and indeed it does seem to be a kind of monopoly prejudicial to the whole community. Furthermore, in case of such alterations, rents and other incomes fixed in money units by count have to be raised or lowered in proportion, as explained in the chapter on altering the name of money. Again, the Prince by such manipulation of the coinage gives wicked men occasion to make false money, either because it is less against their conscience to do this when their prince seems to be doing it too, or because they think their fraud will not be detected so quickly. Thus in time of such alterations more evils can be perpetrated than would be possible if there were always good money in circulation; and innumerable perplexities, errors, and difficulties arise in connection with accounts and receipts, leading to disputes and litigation over debts, irregularities and abuses innumerable, besides many greater evils, which I cannot develop further. And it is no wonder; for, as Aristotle says, one trouble always brings many others in its train, as we know all too well.

The twenty-second chapter: Whether the community may
alter money.

Since money belongs to the community, as demonstrated
in the sixth chapter, it would seem that the community may
control it as it wills, and therefore may make as much profit
from alteration as it likes, and treat money as its own property. And if the community has great need of a large sum of
money for a war or for the ransom of its prince from cap-
tivity, or for some other emergency, then it might raise it
by altering the money, and this would not be contrary to
nature or usurious, since it would not be the act of the prince
alone, but of the community to whom the money belongs.
Hence many of the reasons advanced above against alteration would not apply in this case. Not only may the community do this for the reasons just stated, but in my opinion
it ought to do it, provided the levy is necessary; for in this
arrangement about all the conditions desirable for such a
levy seem to be combined; it brings in a large revenue in a
short time, it is very easy to collect and assess without the
services of many officials, and it involves little expense or
opportunity for fraud by the collectors. Indeed no other
more equitable or proportional plan can be imagined; for he
who has more pays more, and being relatively less felt, it is
more tolerable without danger of rebellion and complaint by
the people. It is also very general, for neither cleric nor
noble can escape it by privilege or otherwise, as frequently
happens in the case of other levies, causing various jeal-
ousies, dissensions, lawsuits, scandals, and other undesirable
results which do not arise from the alteration of money.
Therefore, in the circumstances mentioned above, alteration
may be ordered by the community. In my opinion, however, saving better judgment, it should be resorted to only
when the money is to be transported into distant parts, and
spent among people with whom we have no communication,
and when the sum required is so large that the community's
supply of money metal would be diminished thereby for a

considerable time. In this case the levy may be made by altering money in material or fineness; for if it were managed otherwise, a similar alteration would have to take place later for the reason and in the manner explained in the twelfth chapter. And if the sum required were not so great, or if the conditions were such that the community would not suffer a prolonged scarcity of the money material, then, apart from the undesirable effects pointed out in the present chapter, several dangers would result from making the levy by an alteration, which would be worse than those already mentioned. The chief danger would be that the Prince would eventually desire to have this privilege accorded to him. Then all the inconveniences described above would appear again. Nor is the first argument valid here — that the money belongs to the community; for nobody can justly abuse his property or make illicit use of it, as would the community in altering its money. And if the community should in any way make such an alteration, the money ought to be restored to its proper basis as soon as possible, and the making of gain in that way should cease.

V

CAROLUS MOLINAEUS

TRACTATUS CONTRACTUUM ET USURARUM REDITUUMQUE PECUNIA CONSTITUTORUM

NOTE

CAROLUS MOLINAEUS (1500–1566) was the Latinized name of Charles Dumoulin, one of the greatest jurists of the sixteenth century. After studying law at Orleans and Poitiers, and lecturing for a time in the former place, he went to Paris to appear as advocate before the Châtelet and the Parlement. Not being very successful as a pleader, he turned to work as a consultant. In 1539 he began the publication of his *Commentarium in Consuetudines Parisienses*, which won him great distinction. His *Tractatus Contractuum et Usurarum* (1546) aroused a storm of protest, which became so intense after the appearance of his *Comment. ad edict. Henr. II contra parvas datas et abusus curiae Romanae* (1552), an attack on ecclesiastical abuses, that he was forced to take refuge in flight. The rest of his life was stormy. He lectured at various German universities, served some of the German princes, and took an active part in the religious controversies of the day. His extraordinary self-esteem probably contributed to his troubles, but he also seems to have been the victim of envy and malice. He died in Paris, two years after the publication of his *Conseil sur le fait du concile de Trente*, which had made him enemies in both religious camps.

A TREATISE
ON CONTRACTS AND USURY

I

HERE it is to be noted[1] that Scholastic theologians, as well as canonists & jurists, considering the letter rather than the spirit or intent & purpose of the divine law, have believed there was something peculiarly & inherently vicious about usury or usurious gains, more than in unjust, deceitful sales, or other similar kinds of fraud. And this, not because one's neighbor is more harmed thereby; but because in a loan something more than the principal is received; as if usury *per se* were more detestable & more wicked, or *per se* more unlawful. Thus some hold (Bernardi., *de Contract.*) that, although usury may sometimes not be contrary to charity, as if it were harmful, still there is always something rather dishonorable about it; or again (Petr. Anchar.), that the prohibition of usury is so strict according to divine law that it cannot be modified by legislation, even in cases where it is a question of public utility & the common good, & the civil amity which nature has established among men. Hence they have fallen into the infinite evasions & numerous errors & fallacies with which their very confused books are filled; all because they have not considered the purpose of the divine law, which is charity, as Christ himself testifies (Matth. 7): *All things, therefore, whatsoever you would that men should do to you, do you also to them. For this is the law & the prophets.* That is to say, this is its purpose. And St. Paul (I Timothy): *The end of the law is charity.* Also Romans 13 & Galatians 5: *He who loveth his neighbor hath fulfilled the law.* Therefore,

---

[1] This passage is preceded by a summary of the chief scriptural texts cited by opponents of usury. — ED.

usury is not forbidden & unlawful according to divine law, except insofar as it is contrary to charity. Since, however, usury is taken in many ways, that form alone is prohibited & condemned which offends against charity & love of one's neighbor. This is the interpretation of the passages cited & all similar passages of Scripture.

Suppose a merchant of means borrows money in order to make a profit from legitimate business, & promises to pay usury monthly or annually, instead of a portion of the expected profit: Should you say that the creditor, if unable to prove his claim to that much *interest*,[1] or perhaps any *interest* at all, cannot lawfully contract for or receive such usury without injury to the debtor? Whatever all this crowd may have written, I see no harm in this, nothing contrary to divine or natural law; since nothing is done in it contrary to charity, but rather from mutual charity. It is plain that one grants the favor of a loan from his property; the other remunerates his benefactor with a part of the gain derived therefrom, without suffering any loss. Therefore the creditor lawfully receives more than his principal; & by the same reasoning, he may from the beginning covenant to this effect, within legitimate limits, however, & provided that the one who covenants does not plan any fraud against his neighbor, or demand usury unfairly. Indeed he should not receive it at all, if the debtor would suffer a loss by giving it; but he should take & exact only as much as he, in good faith & fair judgment, would wish to have taken or exacted from him, if he were in the same circumstances, or caught in a similar emergency. I know what these sophists prattle in reply (such as Conrad, *de Contract.*, quaest. 22): that the debtor, forsooth, cannot give a part of his gain without suffering loss to that extent, even if he keeps the greater part of it; since all the gain belongs to him, inasmuch as it

---

[1] *Tanti sua intersit.* The word *interesse* has no exact English equivalent. It is used by Molinaeus to refer to loss sustained or gain prevented through delay in repaying the principal. *Interusurii* has a similar meaning. See below, pp. 114–118.

is not derived from the property of the creditor, but from property or money which is now wholly the property of the debtor alone. But the answer is easy: that this subtlety is not based upon any divine or natural precepts, but upon human & positive interpretations; nay, not upon any human light or law, but upon the confused dreamings of certain ill-informed men. Therefore it cannot prevail against us. Moreover, I prove that it is pure sophistry, by the argument that the creditor, by making the loan, furnishes the immediate & efficacious cause, or, as the popular saying is, the *sine qua non* of this gain; hence he seems to give the gain itself. Therefore, he can covenant for a part of the gain, at least if there is any, according to divine & natural law, even according to civil regulations. And since the debtor makes a greater profit out of the loan, even with this burden, than if he had not had the loan, it is plain that the loan with this burden is an advantage to the debtor & not a disadvantage. Finally, since by hypothesis the debtor has the wherewithal to return the principal with usury, conveniently & retaining the better part of the gain, it follows that usury of this kind does not injure or defraud one's neighbor, but rather works to his not inconsiderable advantage. So far is it, then, from being in any way contrary to charity or love of one's neighbor: therefore it is not contrary to divine or natural laws; & hence it is lawful in conscience, which strictly follows correct reasoning — a kind of divine thing — & clings to pure truth, limiting the scope of artificial law, as Baldus says, most philosophic of professors of law. Again, he says, *Conscience does not bind those whom nature does not oblige.* What they have written & taught hitherto, therefore, is not true but erroneous & superstitious: that usury or any other return whatever received by a creditor for the lending of money is condemned by divine law; for usury is not condemned unless it defrauds or oppresses one's neighbor.

The general negative (Luke 6): *hoping for nothing thereby*, is not opposed to this conclusion: for in this passage

Christ is speaking, not of usury, but of the repayment of the principal or the return of the favor. This is evident, because He is speaking there against men who lend only to those who are expected to return equal amounts, as Heathens & sinners do. But He teaches & requires fuller justice from His people; namely, to lend to those in need, with the feeling that, even if they are not likely to return anything, you rejoice in assisting a neighbor. So far is the benefit from perishing, He teaches, that God will repay it the more abundantly as it was less repaid & expected by men. As Christ, therefore, does not wish us to lend only when there is certain hope of repayment, but to consider how we can aid the needy, rather than how we can be sure of our money, so if your brother is not so much in need as to prevent his returning the principal with interest to his benefactor with profit to himself, He does not prohibit it, as He does not prohibit demanding back the principal, even in the public courts. But He desires that charity toward one's poor neighbor be always & everywhere considered. And He teaches often with what kindness we should deal with the poor who cannot pay at all or conveniently. Therefore, it is not the receiving of any usury whatever that conflicts with brotherly love, but receiving it to the injury of one's brother. If, therefore, your brother acquires gain by means of your money, & gives you a part of the gain, you are not sharing in a divine blessing that belongs to another; nor is the offense of usury to be estimated from the amount which you receive, but from the harm done to your neighbor, the debtor; so long as the limits fixed by laws or public ordinances are not exceeded. This opinion appears to be accepted by Innocent & Aretino. And this is what I have written elsewhere, myself, concerning the true & simple law of contracts, rejecting the nice distinctions made by others, briefly indeed (as suited that discussion), but in equally effective language

.   .   .   .

II

It is agreed by all learned & good authors, & the derivation of the word indicates, that usury is not taken for the thing but for the use of the thing. Now this (to demand payment for the use of a thing or principal) the scholastic theologians declare to be inherently evil & unjust, in the case of a loan, and contrary to natural law, basing this conclusion upon several reasons, but chiefly these three. The first is Thomas Aquinas's argument that the usurer sells that which does not exist or sells the same thing twice, or receives double compensation for the same thing. This he proves as follows. In loans the use of the thing is the consumption of it, & therefore it cannot be separated or computed apart from the thing itself: consequently he who receives anything over & above the sum lent, either receives it for the use of the thing & for nothing, or for what does not exist; or he receives it for the principal, & thus sells twice or receives double compensation for the same thing. The second reason is Scotus's point that I ought not to sell you what is not mine but yours: but in a loan there is a transfer of ownership, as shown by the derivation of the word (*mutuum*) from *meum* & *tuum*. Hence for the use of money which is already yours, I cannot demand any payment from you. The third reason is also from Scotus: that money lent is not of itself reproductive, even if we grant that it remains the property of the lender. Therefore, since the principal remains intact, it is not lawful to demand anything more than the principal: because that would be to receive gain, not from money (which is barren), but from the industry of another. These are the three principal reasons of the Theologians. For all their other reasons are derived from these, however much the verbal forms may seem to be multiplied & diversified. For example, the three arguments advanced by Petrus de Palude. First, that in commutative justice one man should not receive more from another than he gave him in value: but this is the same as the first argument above from Thomas. Second, that in a loan I transfer ownership, & therefore I ought not to sell you what is yours, namely, the use of your money: but this is the same as the second argument above from Scotus. Third, following Durand, that it is not lawful to sell one thing as two, & to receive two for one: but this is no different from the first argument above from Thomas, except for the shell & the sound of the words. Similarly, the twenty-five arguments recently collected by Conrad in his treatise on contracts may for the most part be reduced to the three given above. The others, indeed, are irrelevant to a natural process of reasoning. He even, with ridiculous pedantry, gives the same argument with slight verbal changes seven times: namely, his first, fifth, sixth, ninth, tenth, & eleventh. Let him who has leisure look them up; I do not care to pursue them in further detail, lest I fall myself into the pedantry I have criticized, & delay our argument. So much for the arguments of the sophists. I pass over their opinion that usury is wholly prohibited by divine law, according to the passages cited above, which they apply to loans in the strict sense only, & according to the custom of the people, who do not realize there is usury in anything but formal or suspected loans, not observing that the Holy Scriptures mean by the word usury any superabundance & excess in dealing with one's neighbor, as Jerome declares in commenting on Ezechiel, & likewise the ancient canons (14, q.3; 14, q.4). I also pass over many absurd suggestions, which men unmindful of the limits of speech & unacquainted with civil laws & business have foolishly made in this connection.

Another & fourth argument, which is more plausible than the foregoing, is advanced by John Teutonicus, an old canonist, who says that when the money is at the risk of the borrower from the beginning, it is improper to put any further burden on him & to look for additional gain. Other more reasonable arguments are advanced by philosophers & men of experience, which may be reduced to two, namely (continuing the previous series, for the sake of more

convenient numbering) fifth, with reference to the interest
of the state: lest men abandon agriculture, commerce, &
other useful & necessary arts, or attend to them less carefully, enticed by the richer & easier gains from usury; or
lest a few usurers absorb the property of all other men.
Innocent treats this explicitly, & is of the opinion of Aristotle. For the business of usury is not like trade in commodities, by means of which a state is preserved: since in the
latter trade an equivalent is always given & received; while
in usury, though the use of the money gives the user a
greater advantage for a time than does the use of merchandise for the same period, still it is not perpetual, & yet the
interest continues until the principal is returned intact.
Thus, in the course of time, if usury multiplied & continued,
the result would be that the property of all would be transferred to the usurers. Sixth, with reference to the origin and
development of the practice & the order & end of nature:
that money was not devised as an end but as a means of acquisition, & so it should not be a merchandise, but a price;
therefore usury is especially contrary to nature, which is the
original & explicit opinion of Aristotle. I add a seventh:
that the more usury takes advantage of the poverty or need
of men, so much the more should it be excluded. And the
more frequent & common is the necessity of borrowing
money, so much the less should it be permitted to seek gain
therefrom, & to render such necessary transactions difficult.

Analyzing the arguments outlined above, the first three
can be refuted in almost the same way, inasmuch as they all
err on one point especially. For they do not distinguish between the use, or the benefit accruing from the use, of the
principal for a time, and the principal itself. But not only
civil laws but also experience & common sense demonstrate
that the use or fruition of money has a utility suitable &
valuable for the uses of men, over & above the amount or
restitution of the principal itself. And so there is no force in
the first argument that the lender sells what does not exist
or the same thing twice; for it is plainly false, provided that

what he takes in addition to the principal for the use thereof does not exceed the just *interest:* for this is not selling the principal, inasmuch as payment is not received for the principal; nor is it selling nothing, but a true & real benefit, due, moreover, to him to whom the principal is due, & which meanwhile, in addition to the principal itself, & pending its repayment, is out of the possession of the creditor & in the hands of the debtor. Thus it is childish to say that the use of money cannot be considered apart from the principal, on the ground that the use of money is the consumption of it; for the use & fruition of money consists not only in the first momentary spending or disposal of it, but also in the ensuing use of the merchandise or things purchased with it, or replaced by it, or preserved in one's patrimony, which otherwise would have had to be disposed of, had not assistance been received from the money of another, or would have to be sold, if the money had to be returned at once. . . . Indeed, the dictum of Thomas & all the Scholastics is refuted by himself, & he is not consistent; for he admits, & they all agree, that one may lawfully sell the use of money lent, say, for the purpose of display, the ownership being retained: therefore, if the ownership of the same money is transferred, so that the recipient can have the use of it more freely & more profitably, until he has to return an equal sum, then there will be much stronger grounds for selling the use & benefit of money in this case than in the former, in proportion as a greater & richer benefit is transferred in this case than in the former. Nor is it a valid objection to say that in the former case the money is at the risk of its owner, the creditor, but in the latter case is at the risk of the debtor: first, because it is lawful in the first case to covenant that the money be at the risk of the borrower or hirer (& the contract will be valid), along with a contract to pay for the use; & second, because the lender or lessor can obtain security against the risk by pledges or otherwise. It is true that, insofar as the risk falls upon the user, the payment for the use, or usury, should be that much smaller, just as it may reasonably be greater, when the risk falls upon the creditor, as in the case of bottomry loans. And thus the transfer of ownership does not, of itself, prevent the use from being sold in addition to the principal. And thus the first argument is completely overthrown, along with all those depending upon it.

The second argument, about what is not mine but thine, is easy to answer: if, however, you owe me a debt unconditionally, I can sell it to you; in fact, even if it is only a conditional debt, I can sell it to you. But the use of money which you owe me unconditionally is likewise owed to me unconditionally; therefore I can sell it to you. Likewise the claim itself, or the benefit of it, can be sold to the debtor himself, or to anyone else.

The answer to the third argument is evident from the foregoing, & everyday commercial practice shows that the utility of the use of a considerable sum of money is not slight, & in law it is often called the product. Nor does it avail to say that money by itself does not fructify: for even fields do not fructify by themselves, without expense, labor, & the industry of men; money, likewise, even when it has to be returned after a time, yields meanwhile a considerable product through the industry of man. Indeed, without gain-seeking activity, the mere delay itself yields a not inconsiderable profit, since the debtor can meanwhile procure enough from the product of his estates or otherwise to pay back the principal without any grievous & irreparable breaking-up of his patrimony. And sometimes it deprives the creditor of as much as it brings to the debtor.

The three principal arguments being refuted, all the other subtleties of the sophists, which depend on them, fall too. To the fourth I reply, in the first place, that it merely leads to the conclusion that not all the product should go to the creditor who does not share the risk, nor as much as if he retained or shared in the risk, for which even the civil law provides. And so it is not inappropriate that some part of the profit be given to the creditor: since in giving an appreciable use of money, he does give something, though he does not bear the risk. In the second place, I answer that to escape risk is of the very nature of the material involved, which is loaned on condition, not that the identical bodies, but the same amount in kind, is owed. Moreover, it does not ordinarily happen that money perishes & becomes useless to the debtor, but on the contrary, it is utilized for the advantage of the debtors in the majority of cases. Hence usury should not be universally prohibited, on account of what happens only rarely & unexpectedly; for laws ought to be adapted to what happens frequently, not to what happens rarely. And yet it is sometimes true that, when it is established that the debtor has lost all the money as a result of an accident, it is not proper for the creditor to demand usury, or even the principal in some cases.

The fifth argument proves nothing except that usury should not be excessive: for the disadvantages of discouraging the desirable arts & of disturbing the condition of the state cannot result from small & moderate usury.

Similarly the sixth & seventh arguments prove nothing except that usury is hated & should be restricted, especially the more extreme & immoderate; but they do not make out a case for the complete exclusion of even moderate & reasonable usury. Therefore, all just hating, condemning & punishing of usury should be understood as applying to excessive & unreasonable, not to moderate & acceptable usury.

. . . .

The scholastic doctors, not only theologians but canonists & jurists (to judge from their writings), generally have the idea that a loan may involve usury or increase in two ways. First, on account of the mere service of lending. Only in this case do they consider that usury is present, & this they think is what is meant in all the civil laws on usury which they condemn. Second, on account of delay in repayment, or, apart from technical delay, as a compensation for real or probable *interest* due to being deprived of the money loaned.

This they do not consider usury or what is meant by laws limiting usury. But they are wholly mistaken, as a result both of ignorance of the law & lack of practical experience. For who ever contracted for usury for the mere service of lending, & not as a compensation for loss to be incurred or gain to be prevented, or in order to participate in the gains which the debtor expected to make? Do you think so many jurisconsults & revisers of the civil law have labored with the sole purpose of setting a limit in those cases of usury where the service rendered in lending was specified, & not rather in those cases where the contract is for compensation for the *interest* due the creditor, or which will be due until the principal is returned. This, indeed, is the plain answer, both of common sense & of practical experience, as well as the whole series of laws on this point. The first form, therefore, is to be rejected as a purely fantastic conception, or a foolish dream. It follows, therefore, according to the opinion of all theologians & jurists, that the usury laws of our civil law are not usury laws; since they have to do with compensation, not for service, but for *interest*. Hence, since the limit is not a limitation of usury but of *interest*, it will be lawful even in conscience, according to their interpretation. And in general it follows that the jurisconsults & Justinian never approved real & pure usury, but moderate & reasonable compensation for ordinary *interest*, necessary in commerce and civil life. For it is demonstrated that all usury laws aimed simply at this, not at the compensating or selling of the mere service of lending, & never even thought of compensating the service itself. . . . If you should say that only Philip Melancthon has, in a recent work, defined usury as being only gain derived from the service of lending, & that others have defined it in various other ways, the answer is easy: that although the older theologians & jurists did not use those particular words (service of lending), because of their less refined vocabulary, still that is just what they thought, as their writings show. Melancthon, however, in his elegant & graceful language, has neither added nor subtracted anything whatever; but has simply expressed their meaning more elegantly & skillfully. I submit that the meaning of all is that, unless there is genuine & just *interest*, there is no other reason for receiving more than the principal, except on account of the service of lending; & so it is, and is assumed to be, usury, except insofar as real & just *interest* is proved. But I say, first, that the civil law is not impugned by this, but justified; since it never considered the mere service of the loan or the delay, but only reasonable compensation for real *interest* in general. Hence, although some, who are not really entitled to *interest*, may abuse it, this is not a defect of the law but of man. Second, I say that practical experience teaches & has always taught that only rarely is there no *interest;* but that it is frequent & customary for creditors to have a claim to *interest* on account of appreciable delay or the amount involved. Therefore, if the compensation of this *interest* is allowed in conscience, according to all, then the civil laws must be exonerated from all offense & impiety, for they tend only to restrict as far as possible, not to extend, the *interest* that is commonly & generally involved; especially since they ought to be adapted to those conditions which happen frequently & commonly, not to those of rare occurrence.

.   .   .   .

To return to the subject, just as the invention of money was necessary for the sake of exchange & the needs of men, so for a similar, though not so great, necessity, usury was invented & tolerated; for it is clear that people in business often need to use other people's money, nor is it expedient in all cases to arrange a partnership, a single man's industry being involved; & none are found who will lend for nothing. Indeed, a free loan is not due to those who are in business for profit, as it is to people in temporary need. Or people not in business often (though not so frequently) happen, for very just, unexpected, & urgent reasons, to have serious need of the temporary use of the money of others, & they are not among those to whom a loan should be made for nothing, or if they are, other people do not know it; or perhaps it is not expedient that it should be known they are in need, or if it is known, there does not happen to be anyone who can and will lend for nothing. Now you see that, just as exchange would be very cumbersome & even harmful, if we were deprived of the use of money, so if we were deprived of all use of usury, the business of lending money, which is especially necessary for a state, would be very cumbersome & harmful. For the result will necessarily be, either that the needy will be forced to grievous, base, & irreparable selling of portions of their property, or there will be public & general sanction of creditors covenanting for all alleged *interest*, even of gain prevented (*lucrum cessans*), however much it may be; as happened & was *de facto* allowed, after that stupid & no less pernicious than superstitious opinion gained acceptance, that usury in itself is thoroughly evil, & that the principles of the civil law concerning usury are impious & unjust.

Therefore, the necessity of allowing some usury is similar to the necessity of using money, but not so great. For the use of money is necessary in almost all exchanges, but the use of usury is necessary only to procure the use of other people's money, & only for those who need it, & as long as they do. The use of money, being of general & greater necessity, is more just & commendable, as it is always useful & necessary to all; it cannot prove deceptive or harmful to anyone, since it always procures equal & greater advantage in itself. If this sometimes does not take place, it is not due to money itself, or to the use thereof *per se*, but to some other cause. Usury, on the other hand, being less useful & necessary, is less just & commendable; since it is often deceptive & harmful to one of the parties — the debtor — & involves an especial falling away from the nature of all contracts. Hence it is odious.

Two conclusions follow, namely, the first & third below, which, though most paradoxical to the sophists, are very true & thoroughly established. First, that it is necessary

& useful to retain & tolerate some usury. Second, that it ought to be moderated & restrained as far as possible, by whatever title or name it is called or represented. Third, that under these conditions, it is lawful, not only according to human law but also according to all law, divine & natural. Fourth, that it is not lawful to exceed in any way the determined moderation, either directly or indirectly, by any pretext or trick, either in the competitive market or in conscience, or by pretext of any *interest*, either gain prevented, even where it is established, or loss incurred or anticipated, except in cases where special (*casuale*) interest may be due & demanded, to prevent fraud.

III

The refutation being complete, it remains to discuss briefly the question of proper limitations.   First it should be noted that there are two kinds of usury in the broad sense; the first, commercial (*negociativus*), always contractual & the most strict; the second, punitive or compensatory, punishing delay or compensating for postponement & *interest*. The first is rated variously in the civil law; but the second is always put at six per cent a year, except in the case of a bona fide merchant, to whom eight per cent a year may be due by explicit agreement, or by implicit agreement in the case of a banker. This rate was never in itself unjust; but, though maximum & adequate in its day, in the course of time, on account of the abuse of men, it was found too lax & vague in certain cases. And in general, with respect to commercial loans, the form of the civil law appeared too inconvenient & harmful to debtors; wherefore it was deservedly abandoned & another safer & more convenient form devised, namely, the sale of the principal, the debtor retaining full liberty of redemption. And this new form, being milder & more agreeable, is less in the nature of usury, on account of the sale of the principal, than the form of the civil law.   In a broad sense, however, it is a true kind of usury. Similarly, the rating of the civil law in the case of

incidental usury, compensating for mere delay or postponement, was found too vague & harsh. And so it also
deservedly disappeared; not immediately, however, as the
inexperienced think, concluding that every form of usury
on account of delay or postponement was abolished; but
(abandoning the too vague & harsh form of the civil law)
it was merely left to the decision of a good & prudent judge,
according to all the circumstances of the whole subject in
each case. Hence, although it is not possible to define it
absolutely, we can set up a probable definite limit, which it
is not proper to exceed.

Nothing, however, is more moderate & more in accord
with natural reason in this matter than to restrict it to the
gain or income derived from investing a principal in the
purchase of estates, according to common & just estimate.
In this, since there are many degrees, we must note three
points. First, that it should not be restricted to the minimum yield of estates; for in this case it would be profitable
to be a delayer, & delay would not be punished but fostered:
the delayer, indeed, by making the maximum gain, & paying his creditor the minimum, would grow rich at the latter's
expense. It should, therefore, not be restricted to that
minimum, except where usury ought to be fixed without
reference to delay & blame, not as a punishment but simply
in lieu of the advantage of having the products. . . .
Second, it should be noted that it is not even expedient to
set the limit at the average yield of investments in estates;
for the delay would not be considered punished, nor would
sufficient provision be made for indemnifying the one who
suffered the delay; unless equity made it advisable, as in the
case of one who is sued for the non-delivery of a promised
gift, for which he ought not to be held to a penalty, &
therefore not the highest or regular usury, which is a kind
of penalty. . . . Third, that nevertheless it is expedient
to establish a definite, regular limit, not to prescribe the
amount of the usury, even generally, (for the very great &
uncertain variety of business transactions would find this

inconvenient), but to fix a limit which it is not lawful to exceed; & this not absolutely, but allowing for exceptions, where special reasons require more than ordinary usury. From the foregoing it appears most fitting & natural that this limit should ordinarily be the maximum yield from estates: in this way simple delay is regularly penalized sufficiently, & ordinary *interest* is compensated liberally enough.

VI

LA RESPONSE

DE

JEAN BODIN

AUX PARADOXES DE MALESTROIT TOUCHANT L'ENCHERISSEMENT DE TOUTES CHOSES & LE MOYEN D'Y REMEDIER

NOTE

JEAN BODIN (1530–1596) is chiefly noted for his work in political theory, in which he was one of the most important figures after Aristotle. He was born at Angers and studied law at the university there. After spending twelve years in Toulouse as a lecturer on law, he went to Paris; and not being very successful at the bar, he presently entered government service. In 1576 he was a member of the States General at Blois, and worked ardently for toleration and peace. Having incurred the king's displeasure by opposing his financial schemes, he retired to Laon, where he held a minor post for many years, though under much suspicion from the League. He was a man of vast erudition, and very liberal views on many questions. His chief works are: *Les Six Livres de la République* (1576) and *Methodus ad Facilem Historiarum Cognitionem* (1566). The sixth book of the *Republic* contains an important discussion of public finance. His *Réponse* to Malestroit, though not the first to mention the influence of the new American mines, is the most interesting discussion evoked by the price revolution of the sixteenth century. The substance of this tract was incorporated into the *Republic*, and thus became widely known.

JEAN BODIN'S REPLY
TO THE PARADOXES OF MALESTROIT
CONCERNING THE DEARNESS OF ALL
THINGS AND THE REMEDY THEREFOR

I WILL begin by giving a summary of Malestroit's arguments. People cannot complain, he says, that a thing is now dearer than it was three hundred years ago: unless one now has to pay more gold or silver for it than was paid then. Now the fact is that we do not pay more gold or silver now for things than we did then. Therefore nothing has grown dearer in France during this period. This is his conclusion, which necessarily follows, if we grant his minor premise. In proof of the latter, he points out that in the time of King Philip of Valois a yard of velvet cost only four *escus* as good as our *escus de soleil*, or of even better weight & value, & each *escu* was worth only twenty *solds* in silver: while now, when the *escu* is worth fifty *solds*, velvet costs ten *livres* a yard, which are worth no more than the four *escus*. Therefore the said yard of velvet is no dearer now than it was then. He reasons similarly about all Latin merchandise, even our wines & wheat, but nevertheless he has no proofs.

As for velvet, the seigneur de Malestroit is mistaken in saying that the yard cost only four *escus* in the time of Philip the Fair: for it would first be necessary to make sure there was velvet in France at that time: for those who have tried to show this by what Justinian says about Holoberis & Holoburis have not been accepted. Moreover, the ordinance of Philip the Fair to this effect, issued in the year 1294 & registered with the chamber of accounts, & not printed, which the seigneur de Malestroit, master of the accounts, could see in the volume entitled *Ordinationes sancti Ludovici, pro tranquillo statu regni* (fol. 44) describes elaborately & in more than fifty articles the style of dress which each one should

wear, from Princes to the humblest servants; & yet there is
no mention, directly or indirectly, of silk, or satin, or velvet,
or damask, or half-silk, or brocade, or any stuff resembling
it, though the ordinance allows certain persons to wear gold
chains & girdles, without any prohibition of wearing silk,
either for men or women, Princes or merchants, masters or
servants; which it would not have overlooked, inasmuch as
the first article begins with this prohibition: No *bourgeoise*
shall have a chain; secondly, no *bourgeois* or *bourgeoise* shall
wear gold or precious stones, or a gold girdle, or a crown of
gold or silver, or trimmings of squirrel or ermine, which is
not forbidden for nobles.

It is therefore a mistake to cite the example of velvet
which was not used in France at that time, or perhaps anywhere in the world: for many spices were brought from India, from which silk came, from Araby the blessed, which is
much farther away than Brusa, where velvet was invented.
And even if I should concede him the example of velvet, it is
not reasonable to draw conclusions as to the price of everything else from velvet, which must have been the most expensive merchandise from the Levant at that time, when
there were almost no cities except Damascus in Syria, and
Brusa in Anatolia, called Prusa by the ancients, where velvets & damasks were made. Gradually Greece & Italy came
to use them, & it is not a hundred years back that silk mills,
which we took from the Genoese, were unknown in France.
Now that Tours, Lyons, Avignon, Toulouse & other cities of
this Kingdom are full of such merchandise, though everyone
wears it, which was not the case then, at least to such an extent, a yard of the best velvet ought not to cost more than an
escu of the standard of that period, as I shall demonstrate
later. But it is enough for the present to have shown that
velvet must not be taken as typical of other Latin merchandise, & still less of things in general.

As for wine & wheat, it is quite certain that they cost
twenty times as much as they did a hundred years ago;
which I can say I saw in the Registers of Toulouse, where a

bushel of wheat, equal to about half as much as ours, was worth only five *solds*, while now it costs sixty *solds* most commonly, which is twenty times as much as it was then. And without seeking further than this city, we find in the registers of the Châtelet that a quarter of wheat in rentals [*de rente*], Paris measure, cost only a hundred & twenty *livres* in the year fifteen hundred & twenty-four, although two years earlier wheat had been frozen, upon which estimate the judgments of the Châtelet were based; in the year fifteen hundred & thirty the price rose to a hundred & forty-four *livres*, & by a decree of the court handed down in the year 1531, a certain contract made at a lower price was annulled. Now, when the ordinary price has risen by more than a third, contracts made at the price of the decrees of the year fifteen hundred & thirty-one would be declared usurious, if the debtor did not have the option of paying silver instead of grain at the rate of the twelfth penny. I do not speak of the year fifteen hundred & sixty-five, when the quarter of ordinary wheat cost two hundred & sixty *livres* in straight sales [*en pur achet*] in the month of May; but I am speaking of average conditions during forty years only, where we see that wheat in rentals, which cost fifty *escus de soleil*, not to quote in *livres*, now costs twice as much, so that the best wheat in straight sales costs ordinarily a hundred & twenty *livres*, which is as much as it cost in rentals forty years ago. Thus Malestroit should not have taken produce as an example.

But to verify my statements more fully, let us turn from produce & consider the price of lands, which can neither increase nor decrease, or be altered in their natural excellence, provided they are not mocked, as the saying is, but cultivated as has been the practice since Ceres, a lady of Sicily, taught it. For it is not probable that land loses its vigor as it grows old, as many think (though God, with just vengeance, has sent sterility for some years past). Moreover, since God placed France between Spain, Italy, England, & Germany, He provided also that she should be the foster-mother, bear-

ing in her bosom the horn of plenty, which has never been
empty & never will be; which the peoples of Asia & Africa
have known well & confessed, as may be seen from all their
writings, & likewise in the speech of King Agrippa, when he
wished to bring the rebellious & mutinous Jews under obedience to the Romans. "Consider Gaul," said he, "which
has three hundred fifteen peoples surrounded by the Alps,
the Rhine, the Ocean, & the Pyrenees, which supplies almost all the earth with inexhaustible sources of all goods;
yet these war-like peoples succumbed to the power of this
Empire, after having fought bravely for eighty years, more
astonished at the good fortune & grandeur of the Romans
than overcome by weariness, inasmuch as they are gar-
risoned by only twelve hundred soldiers, which is hardly as
many men as they have good cities." Thus we see that
France was no more sterile then than it has been since: let
us also show that it is no less fertile today. Cicero, speaking
of the fertility of Sicily, which the Romans called their granary, says that the best land yielded only twelve for one,
favored though it was by the gods: We have today in our
valley of the Loire, in Brie, in Xaintonge, in Alimange d'Auvergne, in Languedoc, & even in the isle of France, better
lands, in the opinion of all peasants. And yet in fifty years
we have seen the price of land increase, not to double but to
triple: so that an acre of the best arable land in the open
country, which used to cost in former times only ten or
twelve *escus*, vineyards thirty, today sells for twice, even
thrice as many *escus*, weighing but a tenth less than they did
three hundred years ago. Which Malestroit will concede, if
he will take the trouble to glance through our registers even
the least bit. And without going into contracts made by individuals, which may be seen everywhere, I call you to witness, Sir, who have handled all the records of the chamber &
all the contracts of the treasury of France, whether the Bar-
onies, Counties, Duchies, which have been alienated or re-
united to the crown, are not worth as much rental as they
once sold for outright.

.   .   .   .

I find that the high prices we see today are due to some four or five causes. The principal & almost the only one (which no one has referred to until now) is the abundance of gold & silver, which is today much greater in this Kingdom than it was four hundred years ago, to go no further back. Moreover, the registers of the court & of the chamber do not go back more than four hundred years; the remainder has to be obtained from old histories with little assurance of accuracy. The second reason for the high prices arises in part from monopolies. The third is scarcity, caused partly by export & partly by waste. The fourth is the pleasure of Kings & great lords, who raise the price of the things they like. The fifth has to do with the price of money, debased from its former standard. I will treat all these points briefly.

The principal reason which raises the price of everything, wherever one may be, is the abundance of that which governs the appraisal & price of things. Plutarch & Pliny testify that, after the conquest of the Kingdom of Macedonia, under the King of Persia, the Captain Paulus Æmilius brought so much gold & silver to Rome that the people were freed from paying taxes, & the price of lands in the Romagna rose by two thirds in a moment. And Suetonius says that the Emperor Augustus brought so much wealth from Egypt that usury fell, & the price of lands was a good deal higher than formerly. Now it was not the scarcity of lands, which can neither increase nor diminish, or monopoly, which cannot exist in such a case: but it was the abundance of gold & silver, which causes the depreciation [*mespris*] of these & the dearness of the things priced [*prisees*]; as happened at the coming of the Queen of Candace, whom holy Scripture calls the Queen of Sheba, into the city of Jerusalem, whither she brought so many precious stones that people trampled them under foot. And when the Spaniard made himself master of the new world, hatchets & knives were sold for much more than pearls & precious stones; for there were only knives of wood & stone, & many pearls. It is therefore abundance which causes depreciation. Wherein the Emperor Tiberius was much mistaken, when he had a man beheaded who had made glass soft & pliable, fearing, as Pliny says, that if the news got out, gold would lose its vogue; for the abundance of glass, which is made of almost all stones & of several plants, would have caused its depreciation anyway. Thus it is with everything.

It is therefore necessary to demonstrate that there was not as much gold & silver in this Kingdom three hundred years ago, the time of which Malestroit speaks, as there is now: which is evident at a glance. For if there is money in a country, it cannot be so well hidden that Princes will not find it, when they are in straits. Now the fact is that King John was unable to obtain a loan of sixty thousand *francs* (let us call them *escus*) in his extreme need; & during the eight years he was held prisoner by the English, after the battle of Poitiers, neither his children, nor his friends, nor his people, nor he himself, who came in person, could find his ransom, & he was compelled to go back to England, to wait till money was made for him. . . . Moreover, we read in our old histories that, because of a lack of silver, money was made of leather with a silver nail in it, which shows well the extreme need of gold & silver at that time in France.

Now if we come down to our own times, we shall find that in six months the King obtained in Paris, without going outside, more than three million four hundred thousand *livres*, besides the household charges, which were also obtained in Paris, as well as the subsidies & domainal revenues.

.   .   .   .

But, someone will say, where did so much gold & silver come from since that time? I find that the merchant & the artisan, who cause the gold & silver to come, were inactive at that time; for the Frenchman, having one of the most fertile countries in the world, devoted himself to tilling the soil & feeding his cattle, which is the greatest industry [*mesnagerie*] in France, neglecting the trade with the Levant, because of fear of the Barbary pirates, who hold the coast of Africa, & of the Arabs, whom our fathers called Saracens, who controlled the whole Mediterranean sea, treating the Christians they captured like galley slaves. And as for the trade with the West, it was entirely unknown before Spain had sailed the Indian sea. There was also the fact that the English, who held the ports of Guyenne & of Normandy, had closed the routes to Spain & the Isles to us. On the other hand, the quarrels of the houses of Anjou & of Arragon cut us off from the ports of Italy. But a hundred fifty years ago our fathers drove out the English; & the Portugese, sailing the high seas by the compass, made himself master of the Gulf of Persia, & to some extent of the red sea, & by this means filled his vessels with the wealth of the Indies & of fruitful Arabia, outwitting the Venetians & Genoese, who obtained the merchandise from Egypt & from Syria, whither it was brought by the caravans of the Arabs & Persians, to sell it to us in small lots & for its weight in gold. At the same time the Castilian, having gained control of the new lands full of gold & silver, filled Spain with them, & prompted our Citizens to make the trip around Africa with a marvelous profit. It is incredible, and yet true, that there have come from Peru since the year 1533, when it was conquered by the Spaniards, more than a hundred millions of gold, & twice as much silver. The ransom of King Atubalira brought 1,326,000 *pesans* of gold. At that time in Peru cloth hose cost three hundred ducats; a cloak, a thousand ducats; a good horse, four or five thousand; a bottle of wine, 200 ducats: as the history of the Indies testifies. And yet Augustin de Zarate, master of accounts of his Catholic Majesty, found that the officers of his Catholic Majesty in Peru showed a balance in their accounts rendered of eighteen hundred thousand *pezans* of gold, & six hundred thousand *livres* of silver; not counting the incredible profit which the King of Portugal makes by trade in the Moluccas, where cloves, cinnamon, & other precious drugs grow, which he obtained from the Emperor Charles V as a pledge for 350,000 ducats, when he went through Boulogne, to be crowned Emperor; which the Italians wished to redeem & pay the sum in cash, but the

Emperor would not consent, on account of the alliance of the two houses.

Now the fact is that the Spaniard, who gets his subsistence only from France, being compelled by unavoidable necessity to come here for wheat, cloths, stuffs, dye-stuffs, paper, books, even joinery & all handicraft products, goes to the ends of the earth to seek gold & silver & spices to pay us with.

On the other hand, the English, the Scotch, & all the people of Norway, Sweden, Denmark, & the Baltic coast, who have an infinity of mines, dig the metals out of the center of the earth to buy our wines, our saffron, our prunes, our dye, & especially our salt, which is a manna that God gives us as a special favor, with little labor: for the heat being lacking for people North of the forty-seventh degree, salt cannot be made there, & below the forty-second degree, the excessive heat renders the salt more corrosive; especially the salt of the mines in Spain, Naples, & Poland, which often injures persons & things, so that the salt-works of Franche Comté & the rock salt in Spain & Hungary are nowhere nearly equal to ours in quality. This often causes the English, the Flemings, & the Scotch, who carry on a large trade in salt fish, to load their vessels with sand, in default of other merchandise, in order to come & buy our salt with good hard cash. The other cause of the great amount of wealth that has come to us in the last hundred & twenty or thirty years is the huge population which has grown up in this Kingdom, since the civil wars between the houses of Orleans & Bourgogne were ended: which allowed us to experience the sweetness of peace, & enjoy the fruit thereof for a long time, down to the Religious troubles; for the foreign war which we have had since then was only a purging of bad humors necessary for the whole body of the Republic. Formerly the open country was deserted & the cities nearly so, as a result of the ravages of the civil wars, during which the English had sacked cities, burned villages, murdered, pillaged, killed a good part of the people of France, & gnawed the remainder to the

bones: which led to the breakdown of agriculture, trade &
all mechanical arts. But in the last hundred years we have
cleared a vast territory of forests & moors, built several villages, peopled the cities, so that the greatest wealth of Spain,
which otherwise is a wilderness, comes from the French set-
tlers who go into Spain in a steady stream & principally
from Auvergne & from Limousin: to such an extent that in
Navarre & Arragon almost all the vine-dressers, laborers,
carpenters, masons, joiners, stone-cutters, turners, wheel-
wrights, waggoners, carters, rope-makers, quarry-men, sad-
dlers, harness-makers are French. For the Spaniard is aston-
ishingly indolent, except in arms & trade, & therefore likes
the active & willing Frenchman; as he made plain in the case
of the prior of Capouë's enterprise in Valencia, where there
were ten thousand French servants & artisans, who were
threatened with trouble for having had a part in the con-
spiracy against Maximilian, then lieutenant general in Spain:
but it turned out that the masters & inhabitants of Valencia
warned them all. There are also many in Italy.

Another cause of the riches of France is the trade with the
Levant, which was opened to us as a result of the friendship
between the house of France & the house of the Ottomans
in the time of King Francis the first; so that French merchants since that time have done business in Alexandria, in
Cairo, in Beirut, in Tripoli, as well as the Venetians & Genoese; & have as good standing at Fez & at Morocco as the
Spaniard, which was discovered when the Jews, driven out
of Spain by Ferdinand, withdrew into the country of Languedoc, & accustomed the French to trading in Barbary.

Another cause of the abundance of gold & silver has been
the bank of Lyons, which was opened, to tell the truth, by
King Francis the first, who began to borrow money at the
twelfth penny, & his successor at the tenth, then the sixth,
& up to the fifth in emergencies. Suddenly the Florentines,
Luccans, Genoese, Swiss, Germans, attracted by the high
profit, brought a vast amount of gold & silver into France;
& many settled here, partly because of the mildness of the

climate, & partly because of the natural goodness of the
people & the fertility of the country. By the same means, the
annuities charged upon the city of Paris, which amount to
three million three hundred fifty thousand *livres* every year,
have enticed the foreigner, who brought his money hither to
make a profit, & eventually settled here: which has greatly
enriched this city. It is true that the mechanical arts & merchandise would flourish much more, in my opinion, without
being diminished by the traffic in money which is carried on,
& the city would be much richer, if people did as they do in
Genoa, where the house of Saint George takes the money of
all who wish to bring any, at the twentieth penny, & lends
it to merchants to trade with, at the twelfth or fifteenth
penny; which is one of the causes of the grandeur & wealth
of that city, & which seems to me very expedient for the
public & for the individual.

.   .   .   .

These, Sir, are the means which have brought us gold &
silver in abundance in the last two hundred years. There is
much more in Spain & Italy than in France, owing to the
fact that in Italy even the nobility engage in trade, & the
people of Spain have no other occupation; & so everything
is dearer in Spain & in Italy than in France, & dearer in
Spain than in Italy. This is true even of servants & artisans,
which attracts our Auvergnats & Limousins into Spain, as
I learned from them myself, because they earn three times as
much as they do in France; for the rich, proud, & indolent
Spaniard sells his labor very dear, as Clenard testifies, who
writes in his letters, in the chapter on expenses, in a separate entry: for being shaved in Portugal, fifteen ducats per
year. It is therefore the abundance of gold & silver which
causes, in part, the high prices of things.

I will pass over the second reason for high prices, because
it is not so important in the present case, namely, monopolies of Merchants, artisans, & day laborers: when they get
together to fix the price of merchandise or to raise the price
of their day's work & of their products. Since such assem-

blies usually conceal themselves under the cloak of religion, the Chancellor Poyet wisely advised that the confraternities should be abolished & restricted, which was later confirmed at the request of the Estates at Orleans, so that there is no lack of good laws.

The third cause of high prices is scarcity, which arises in two ways. One is the excessive export from the Kingdom, or the hindrances to bringing in the things that are needed; the other is the wasting of them. As for export, it is certain that we have wines & wheat at lower prices during the war with the Spaniard & Fleming than afterwards, when export is allowed; for the farmers in part are compelled to raise money, the merchant does not dare to load his vessels, the lords cannot long keep what is perishable, & consequently the people must live cheaply. For our fathers taught us an old proverb, that France was never famished, that is to say, that she is richly supplied with the wherewithal to feed her people, whatever bad year may come, provided foreigners do not empty our barns. Now it is certain that wheat is no sooner ripe than the Spaniard takes it away, especially since Spain, except for Arragon & Granada, is very barren, & the people are naturally indolent, as I have said. Hence in Portugal grain merchants have every possible privilege; & among other things it is forbidden to take prisoner anyone bringing wheat to sell, otherwise the people would overwhelm the officer, provided the one bringing wheat cried out, "Traho dridigo," that is to say, "I am bringing wheat." And although it is forbidden to take gold & silver out of Spain under heavy penalties, it is allowed in the case of wheat alone. Hence the Spaniard takes out a large amount of wheat. On the other hand the country of Languedoc & of Provence supplies almost all of Tuscany & Barbary. This causes abundance of money & dearness of wheat; for we import practically no merchandise from Spain, except oils & spices; the best drugs, moreover, coming to us from Barbary & the Levant. From Italy we have all the alums & some serges & silks: although the lowlands of Languedoc &

Provence have more oil than we need. And as for serges &
silk, just as good are made in this Kingdom as in Florence
& in Genoa, in the opinion of experts, & merchants know
well how to make a profit on them, selling them at their pleasure. As for the alums, if we wished to open the veins in the
Pyrenees, it is certain that we would find sources not only of
alum but also of gold & silver, seeing that several Germans
report well of it; & master Dominic Bertin showed me in
these regions, & has demonstrated to King Henry the existence of all metals, with an infinity of copperas, alums, &
pyrites. Among other things it was found that there is more
alum than is needed for all France, although more than a
million of it comes from Italy every year, as has been ascer-
tained. It is to him that we owe the beautiful marbles, —
black, white, mottled, jaspered, serpentine, — which he
sent from the Pyrenees as far as Paris; & he assures me that,
if he had any influence, we would have no more to do with
the alums of Italy. In this way Italy would be left with only
trinkets, artificial gems, & perfumery to draw away the
money of this Kingdom. This is the means they have found,
having nothing else to barter for our merchandise, to sell us
vapors; which are so dear that a certain Italian perfumer
sold a lord of this Realm, as you know, four hundred *escus*
worth of gloves, & that was a supply for only one year. If I
could have my wish, I should like to have Princes esteem
them as little as did the Emperor Vespasian; I am sure the
perfumes of Gascony would do away with the dearness of
those from Italy.

As for the fourth cause of high prices, it arises from the
pleasure of Princes, who make the price of things; for it is a
general rule in matters of state & of the Republic, which
Plato was the first to perceive, that Kings not only make
laws for their subjects, but they also change the customs &
fashions of living at their pleasure, whether in vice, or virtue,
or indifferent matters. I will cite only the example of King
Francis the first, who had his hair clipped to cure a wound
on his head: suddenly the courtiers & then all the people

had theirs clipped, so that nowadays people make fun of
long hair, which used to be a mark of beauty & freedom.
(Moreover, their blond hair was considered the beauty of
the people of the North by the ancients.) Hence our first
Kings forbade their subjects, with the exception of native
Frenchmen, to wear long hair, as a sign of servitude: a custom which lasted till Peter Lombard, Bishop of Paris, had
the restriction removed, under the authority which Bishops
at that time had over Kings. Which suffices, in passing,
to show that the people always conform to the will of the
Prince, & consequently esteem & enhance everything that
the great lords like, even though the things be unworthy of
it; as the Emperor Nero made yellow amber extraordinarily
dear, as history tells us, because it was the same color as his
sweetheart's hair.

.   .   .   .

The other cause of high prices is the wasting of things
which ought to be economized. Silk ought to be very cheap,
since so much of it is made in this Kingdom, besides what
comes from Italy. Dearness results from waste: for people
are not satisfied to dress rascals & lackeys in it, but they also
cut it up in such ways that it cannot last or serve more than
one master; for which the Turks, as I have heard, reproach
us rightly, calling us foolish & mad to spoil, as if in despite
of God, the goods which He has given us. They have far
more of it than we, but it is death to cut any of it. We use as
much more for drapery, & especially for hose, where three
times as much is used as is necessary, with so many slashes
& cuttings, that poor people cannot use them, after monsieur is tired of them; & what is more, three pairs are worn
instead of one, & to give grace to hose, a yard more of stuff
is needed to make a jacket than formerly. Fine edicts have
been issued, but they do no good: for since what is forbidden
is worn at court, it will be worn everywhere, the officials
being intimidated by some & corrupted by others.

.   .   .   .

We have considered the reasons for the higher prices of things; it remains to show that Malestroit was also mistaken with respect to the standard of the moneys coined in this Kingdom in the last three hundred years. For he says that Saint Louis had the first *solds* coined worth twelve *deniers*, & that there were only sixty-four of them to the mark. He also says that in the time of Philip of Valois the "fleur-de-lis" *escu* of gold, of better weight & alloy than ours, was worth only twenty *solds*. Then later King John had fine gold "foot & horse" *francs* coined, which were worth only twenty *solds*. Moreover, that the silver *sold* of that time was worth five of ours. He does not say of what standard, of what weight & alloy the moneys were.

As for this last point, he contradicts himself: for he agrees that the old *escu*, which weighs three *deniers trebuchans*, is worth only sixty of our *solds*, coined according to the ordinance of King Francis I, so that the old *sold* of fine silver would be worth only three of them; & yet the "foot & horse" *francs* weigh less than the old *escus* by four grains, & are not of better alloy, on the average. There is also a quarter of a carat remedy, according to the ordinance of the year fifteen hundred sixty-one, the old *escu* being at sixty *solds*, & the "foot & horse" *franc* at fifty *solds*. Thus he is mistaken by about half as to the proportion between the old *solds* and ours; for if it was as he says, that the old *sold* of fine silver was worth five of ours, the old *escu* would be worth a hundred *solds;* the "foot & horse" *franc*, four *livres* ten *solds*.

In the second place monsieur de Malestroit is mistaken in leaving out a hundred twenty-three years between Saint Louis & Philip of Valois, during which time Philip the Fair, grandson of Saint Louis, in the year thirteen hundred, so debased the silver money that a *sold* of the old money was worth three of the new, as we find in our registers, & even in our Annals, & in the history of Antonine, to which monsieur de Livre, a man of great learning, called my attention. And although, to appease the mutiny of the people, the money was restored to the old value, the fact is that ten years afterwards it was so much debased that the *sold* contained only three *deniers* & a half of silver, two & a half quarters being of copper; which is the poorest money seen in our time, for in the year fifteen hundred fifty-one the *solds* coined according to the ordinance of King Henry II contain three *deniers* & a half of silver. We must conclude, therefore, since the *sold* was of the same standard, of the same weight, of the same alloy, & since there was as much alloy three hundred years ago as now, that the demonstration of Malestroit & his examples cannot be accepted; for although King Charles the Fair restored the old standard of the *solds* to twelve *deniers* in the year thirteen hundred twenty-two, nevertheless, six months later he debased it by all of a half.

. . . .

So much for higher prices in general, without considering the particular developments which make things rise above their ordinary price, such as provisions in time of famine, arms in time of war, wood in winter, water in the deserts of Lybia, where there is a tomb in the plain of Azoa, bearing witness in graven letters that a merchant bought a cup of water from a carter for ten thousand ducats, & yet the buyer & the seller died of thirst, as Leo of Africa writes; or handicraft products & hardware in places where there is none made, which are usually cheaper in cities full of artisans, as at Limoges, Milan, Nuremberg, Genoa, Paris, Rouen, Damascus, Venice. Or, on account of the abundance of people & money in one place as compared with another, as in Stamboul, Rome, Paris, Lyons, Venice, Florence, Antwerp, Seville, London, where the courts of Kings or great lords or merchants attract people & money, provisions are dearer; as was usually the case in Rome, where there was abundance of gold & silver & of people, who came thither from every quarter of the earth, & famine was frequent; so that Augustus was compelled to drive the mob of slaves & gladiators & all foreigners out of the city, except teachers of youth & physicians, together with twenty-eight colonies

which he sent from Rome to various parts of Italy. Sometimes, too, the change comes as a result of a new edict, as
happened at Rome, where houses suddenly rose in price by
a half, as a result of the edict of Trajan ordering all who
wished to have estates & offices of honor to employ a third of
their property in the purchase of properties in Rome or in
the vicinity. All these individual things are unimportant in
the present case, which is general.

Now that we know that prices are higher & the causes of
the higher prices, which are the two principal points we had
to prove against Malestroit, it remains to remedy the situation with as little harm as possible; which Malestroit has
not considered at all, since he believed it certain that prices
had not risen.

In the first place, the abundance of gold & silver which is
the wealth of a country, should in part excuse the dearness:
for if there was such a scarcity of it as in times gone by, it is
very certain that all things would be as much less esteemed
& purchased as gold & silver were more valued.

As for monopolies & waste that occur, I have indicated my
views above. But in vain do we make fine ordinances concerning monopolies or extravagance in living & dressing, if
people will not enforce them; yet they will never be en-
forced, if the King in his goodness does not have them observed by his courtiers, for the remainder of the people
model their actions after the example of the courtiers in matters of display & extravagance; & there was never a Republic in which health or disease did not flow from the head to
all the members.

As for the export of merchandise from this Kingdom,
there are several important personages who try & have
tried, by speaking & writing, to stop it altogether if possible:
believing that we can live happily & cheaply without sending out anything or receiving anything from abroad; but
they are mistaken, in my opinion, for we have business with
foreigners & could not get along without them. I admit that
we send them wheat, wine, salt, saffron, dye, prunes, paper,

cloth & coarse stuffs, & obtain from them in exchange, first, all the metals except iron — gold, silver, tin, copper, lead, steel, quicksilver, alum, sulphur, vitriol, copperas, cinnabar, oils, wax, honey, pitch, Brazil wood, ebony, fustet, guaiacum, ivory, morocco, fine cloths, cochineal, scarlet, crimson, drugs of all kinds, spices, sugars, horses, salt salmon, sardines, mackerel, salt cod, & an infinity of good books & excellent handicraft products.

And even if we could get along without such merchandise, which is not at all possible, when we had something to sell, we should still have to trade, sell, buy, exchange, lend, even give away, a part of our goods to foreigners, and even to our neighbors, if only to communicate & keep up friendship between them & us.

I say further, that, being endowed by God with all that can be given to men, in arms & in laws without fear or hope of others, we owe them this charity, as a natural obligation, to share with them the favors which God has bestowed on us, to teach them & mould them in all honor & virtue. Wherein the Romans showed themselves unworthy of ruling, when the grandeur of their power reached to Heaven, & they had extended their Empire from the setting of the Sun to the rising of the Sun. Several peoples then sent embassies to them offering to submit to their rule, & to obey them voluntarily, but the Romans, seeing that there was nothing to be gained, refused these offers, as Appian writes, which is one of the basest actions & vilest insults to God there ever was; as if the majesty of ruling & administering justice, even over poor and ignorant peoples, were not the greatest gift of God, & the greatest honor a man can receive in this world. It was very far from sharing their goods & wealth with them, as they ought to have done.

But, some one will say, Plato & Lycurgus forbade trade with foreigners, fearing that their subjects would be corrupted. It is true: but one dreamed what he could never carry out, though he tried; the other carried out what man never dared to hope; & yet both would have done better, if I am not much mistaken, to allow trade as Moses wisely did, who showed clearly that he was a greater leader than these two. For the light of virtue is so clear, that it not only drives away the shadows of wickedness, but also shines the more for being passed on to others. Yet we cannot excel so much in our virtues that foreigners will be unable to repay us in kind.

Again people say we ought not to give our goods for nothing to foreigners & even to our enemies, besides treating them well: & yet, if we did so, when we have enough ourselves, we would gain their friendship better than by making war on them; as God, against whom we have blasphemed & made war unceasingly, shows us by example, with unstinted prodigality. But since this can not enter the heads of those who consider nothing but gain, though it be sordid & dishonorable, God with admirable foresight has arranged things well: for he has so divided his favors that there is no country in the world so fruitful that it does not lack many things. Which God seems to have done to keep all the subjects of his republic in friendship, or at least to prevent them from making war on each other for very long, being always dependent one upon another.

. . . .

There remains but one argument, to which I must reply briefly. When export takes place, people say, everything becomes dearer in a country. I deny this point, for what enters in place of the things exported makes what was scarce cheap. Moreover, one would think, from what they say, that the merchant gives his goods for nothing; or that the riches of the Indies & of Araby the blessed grow in our country. I will except only wheat, of which export ought to be regulated more wisely than is now the case; for we witness intolerable high prices & famines through our failure to provide for this. Thus France, which ought to be the granary of all the West, receives ships full of poor, black wheat, generally brought from the Baltic coast, which is a great disgrace to us. The way to regulate this is to have in each city a public

granary, as they had formerly in well regulated cities, & in
this Kingdom, before the quarrels between the houses of Orleans & Bourgogne; & every year the old wheat should be
replaced. In this way we would never see such high prices
as we do; for, besides making provision for bad years, we
would also check monopolies by merchants, who store up all
the wheat & often buy it in the sheaf, in order to fix its price
at their pleasure.

VII

ANTONIO SERRA

BREVE TRATTATO DELLE CAUSE CHE POSSONO
FAR ABBONDARE LI REGNI D'ORO E D'ARGENTO
DOVE NON SONO MINIERE

NOTE

ANTONIO SERRA was a native of Cosenza, and on the title-page
of his treatise he called himself "Doctor," but no details of his
life are known, except that he was in prison at Naples, apparently on a charge of coining, when he wrote and published
his work (1613). The immediate occasion of his discussion was
Marc' Antonio de Santis' *Discorso intorno alli effetti, che fa il
cambio in Regno*, which argued that the scarcity of money was
due to high exchange, and advocated public regulation to keep
it down; but this led him to discuss the larger question of
national wealth, and to formulate what is probably the first
systematic statement of the Mercantilist philosophy. The
book had no influence and attracted little attention among his
contemporaries, who were chiefly interested in the question
immediately at issue — the regulation of exchange.

A BRIEF TREATISE
ON THE CAUSES WHICH CAN MAKE GOLD AND SILVER PLENTIFUL IN KINGDOMS WHERE THERE ARE NO MINES

I

Of the causes which can bring abundance of gold and silver

HOW important it is, both for peoples and for princes, that a kingdom should abound in gold and silver, and what great advantages this conveys, and how potent a means it is of preventing many crimes (though some capriciously pretend the contrary), I do not propose to discuss in this place; nor how great harm is caused by the lack thereof; for it is my opinion that this is understood by everyone, if not distinctly, at least vaguely. Taking it, therefore, as a proved proposition, and assuming that those who hold the contrary opinion ought to be sent to Anticyra,[1] I shall discuss the causes which can produce this result. These fall into two classes, the natural and the collateral (*accidentali*). The natural class comprises only one sort, namely, when there are mines of gold and silver in a country; and where this cause exists, the prince needs to make different regulations for his kingdom than he would if there were no mines. This cause I do not intend to discuss, since it is not found in our Kingdom or even in all Italy; where no mines of these metals are worked except in Saravez, by the grand duke of Tuscany. Therefore, I shall consider the collateral causes, these being the ones that are chiefly applicable in our Kingdom and all of Italy; so that, by comparing similar things with respect to the same factors, the truth may be seen more clearly.

---

[1] A place famous among the ancients as a resort for hypochondriacs. — ED.

II

Of the collateral causes and particular factors

The collateral causes subdivide into what will be called particular factors and common factors (*accidenti*). Particular
factors are those which occur and can occur in only one
kingdom and no others; common factors, those which occur
and may occur in all kingdoms alike. The particular factors
which can make a kingdom abound in gold and silver are
chiefly two. First, a surplus of products grown in a kingdom
in excess of its own needs and convenience; since, if these
goods are transported into countries where they are lacking,
or if people come from these countries or other places to buy
them, gold or silver necessarily has to be brought in. This
factor will be called particular, because not every kingdom
has or can have it; and it is more conspicuous in our Kingdom than in any other part of Italy, as is well known. The
other particular factor is the situation of a country with respect to other kingdoms and other parts of the world. Being
a potent occasion, and almost a cause, of extensive trading
in a kingdom, both for its own account and for the account
of other parts of the world, and therefore also bringing an
abundance of gold and silver, it should be counted among
the particular factors; and I shall speak of it when I come to
discuss the common factor of commerce. In this the city of
Venice holds the first place, not only in Italy but in Europe
and Asia; while our Kingdom, on the other hand, is more
deprived of this factor than any other country, as will be
fully explained in the above-mentioned discussion of the
factor of commerce.

III

Of the common factors

The common factors are divided into four chief classes:
quantity of industry, quality of the population, extensive
trading operations, and regulations of the sovereign. They
will be called common factors, because they may occur in

any kingdom; and the combination of them in any place, though it raises nothing in excess of its own needs, but must procure everything from abroad, and though it has no mines of gold or silver, will surely make it abound in these metals.

The quantity of industry will make a kingdom or city abound in money, when many and varied trades, necessary or convenient or pleasant for human use, are carried on there, in quantities in excess of the needs of the country. This factor ought not only to be placed at the head of the common ones, but in many respects should be rated higher than the particular factor of surplus produce. First, because of its greater certainty, since the artisan is more certain of making a profit by working at his trade than the peasant or other persons by cultivating or preparing their products; this profit being dependent, not upon man's work alone, but upon the nature of the weather, according to the varying needs of the land, which at some times needs rain, at others sun, as well as other conditions. If these are lacking, or if unseasonable weather comes, the labor is of no avail; and instead of a profit, there is sometimes a loss: but in the trades, the application of labor is always sure to bring gain.

Second, in the trades there can be extension, and thus the profit can be increased; which is not possible in the case of produce, this not being subject to increase. Nobody, for example, having a territory upon which only a hundred *tomola* of wheat can be sown, will be able to have a hundred and fifty sown; but among the trades, it is just the other way, since they may be multiplied not only two-fold but two hundred-fold, and with proportionately less expense.

Third, the trades have a surer market than produce does, and consequently the profit is surer. That their market is surer should be clear from this reason alone: that produce is hard to keep for any length of time without spoiling; hence its export from one country to another distant one is exposed to risk on this score; and in case such goods can not be sold for the time being, and if it is desired to keep them for the future, the same danger threatens. But in the case of the trades, it is quite the opposite, their products being easily preserved, not only for a short but also for a long time; and for the same reason, they may be exported with every facility to any distant country. And the art of navigation being nowadays so improved that in this alone the moderns have surpassed the ancients, having developed trade not only between the east and the west and between the south and the north, but even between one hemisphere and the other, so that commodities are readily transported from one place to another, who will not admit that the market for the trades is surer than that for produce, and the profit consequently more certain?

Fourth and last, in most cases more profit is made from industry than from produce, as is seen in the manufacture of wool, especially fine cloths, in the manufacture of linen, of silks, arms, pictures, sculptures, printing, and in all branches of the drug industry, with an infinite number of others which it would be superfluous to mention. For all of which reasons this factor ought to be placed ahead of the factor of surplus produce; for when it is found in perfection in a city or kingdom, it will be one of the most potent of the causes bringing in an abundance of gold and silver — much more than surplus produce. In Italy the city of Venice will hold the first place, possessing this factor in perfection; whereby so much produce is obtained through manufactures, and money is brought in, as is well known. The city of Naples, on the contrary, will be rated as the one in which this factor is found in no perfection. For not only are all or the greater part of the trades lacking there, but such as do exist, except the silk manufactures, are not sufficiently extensive to provide any exports, as is necessary in order to produce the effect in question; or even adequate for its own needs and for the Kingdom of which it is the head, so that it may not have to pay for the manufactures from abroad; as will be shown when we come to make a comparison between it and the city of Venice with respect to plentifulness of money.

IV

Of the common factor of the quality of the population

In the second place should come the factor of the quality of the population; and this factor may be said to exist in a kingdom or city, when the inhabitants thereof are by nature industrious, or diligent and ingenious in building up trade not only in their own country but outside, and on the watch for opportunities to apply their industry. By this means their city will surely abound in gold and silver, since they will get money not only from the industry which can be carried on in their own country, but also from that which can be carried on in other countries; and this factor holds first place in making a city or kingdom abound in money in particular, more than in general. In this respect Genoa will be the first city of Italy, this factor existing in perfection there, and bringing in more money than in any other city of Italy in particular; and after this Florence, and next Venice, which, though it has more commerce than all the cities of Italy together, will nevertheless hold third place with respect to this factor. On the other hand, the city of Naples will be the one, together with its Kingdom, where this factor is not found, but quite the contrary; since the inhabitants of the country are so unenterprising that they do not traffic outside their own country, either in the other provinces of Europe, such as Spain, France, Germany and others, or even in Italy itself; nor do they carry on the industries of their own country, the inhabitants of other places coming in for this purpose, principally from their own province, such as Genoese, Florentines, Venetians and others. And for all their seeing these people carrying on industries in their country and enriching themselves thereby, they have not the energy to imitate them and to follow their example by working in their own houses; quite the opposite of the Genoese, who, not content with the industries which they can carry on in their own province (I mean Italy), since in their own country there are few, spare no labor or danger, traveling through every province, not only of Europe but of the other parts of the world, and even in the new Indies, when they can obtain permission from his Catholic Majesty. From the effect it is clear how important is this factor of the quality of the population: these people, though their country is very barren, having such an abundance of money, and the citizens of this Kingdom, though their country is so rich, being so poor.

V

Of the common factor of a great trade

In the third place will come the factor of a great trade, of which the most potent occasion, and almost the cause, is generally the particular factor of situation, as was pointed out in the chapter on the particular factors. This factor will make a country abound in money, when it has an extensive trade in the produce of other places rather than its own; since the trade in any place arising from the export of its own surplus produce can not be great, and the money which comes in this way should be attributed to the particular factor of surplus goods as cause, and not to commerce; and that which has to do with goods which are imported from abroad, because of need thereof, will impoverish it, not make it abound in money. Hence we may conclude that great commerce will have the effect referred to, insofar as it shall be concerned with the goods of other countries for other countries, that is, with trading; not with domestic commodities, in which case it produces the contrary effect. And of this traffic (as I have said), situation is the most potent occasion and cause. That where there is great commerce there must necessarily be much money, requires no proof, since commerce cannot be carried on without it, and that is its purpose.

And as was said in an earlier chapter, the city of Venice holds the first place with respect to situation, not only in Italy itself, but in all Europe; as is shown by the fact that all the commodities which come from Asia into Europe pass through Venice, and from there are distributed into other parts; while the commodities which go from Europe into Asia are likewise shipped from there. Thus a great commerce develops from the shipping of so many commodities into so many places. In this she is aided, first of all, by the convenience of her position for traffic from Asia to Europe and from Europe to Asia, and with respect to Italy itself; since the greater part of its rivers flow into her sea, which facilitates the transportation of commodities into various places, and since, moreover, she is situated almost in the flank of Italy, not far from the head or from the foot, which is a convenience for such transportation. She is also aided by her extensive manufactures; which factor brings a great many people there, not only by reason of the trades themselves, in which case the effect would be attributed to them, but also as a result of the conjuncture of these two factors; for one furnishes strength to the other, the great concourse due to commerce and to the situation being increased by the manufactures, and the manufactures being increased by the great concourse due to commerce, while commerce is made greater by this same assembling of people.

On the other hand, the city and the Kingdom of Naples have no commerce pertaining to foreign countries, but only their own trade, as is shown by the fact that, except for the produce grown there, few or no commodities are exported. The cause of this is the very bad position of the Kingdom for this purpose; for Italy extends from the land like an arm from the body, being for this reason called a peninsula, while the Kingdom is situated in the hand and outermost part of this arm, so that it is not to the advantage of anyone to bring commodities there to distribute them to other places. Indeed, the situation of the Kingdom in this respect is so bad, that nobody ever has to go through there to go to other countries, whatever part of the world he comes from or desires to go to; unless it be for pleasure and to lengthen the trip, or on account of his own business. Hence it is not only not convenient for merchants to bring goods there to distribute them into other places, but is inconvenient and expensive. And with the combination in the Kingdom of this factor of situation and that of a population without enterprise, together with scarcity of manufactures, the factor of commerce is bound to be lacking, except for domestic needs; and this, besides being necessarily small, cannot cause an abundance of money, but scarcity, except through the export of surplus commodities, as has been said.

VI

Of the common factor of the regulations of the sovereign

The last class is the regulations of the sovereign, who, observing the situation in his State, and the various factors which are found there, together with conditions in the neighboring and distant States with which his kingdom has or may have commerce, and considering the causes or occasions which can make his domain abound in money, and those which can impede this, adopts various regulations according to the different effects which he wishes to produce, removing the impediments which might prevent the effect desired. But, as was said in the introduction, it is not so easy to know how to arrange this factor well. The sovereign needs to consider carefully not one thing alone but many, to have regard for the inconveniences and other effects which may be caused by the regulations, and not to make any mistake as to the principal means to be employed; for sometimes the difficulty of a problem causes one to mistake one alternative for the other; principally in cases where the effect depends not upon some necessary cause, but only upon a contingent one, which is the will of man. To provide for this it is necessary to attend to more than one cause, since the same cause generally produces different effects with respect to different subjects (as the sun hardens clay and softens wax, and a light whistle rouses dogs and quiets horses); the observance of the regulations depending upon the will of men, as has been said. And although he could use force upon his own subjects, he needs to consider how they may impede him in various indirect ways, of which there are many; while as for men who are not his subjects, the regulations should be made attractive to them, and changed if necessary, so that they may come readily, as well as an infinite number of other considerations; and this being understood, he should consider how to employ them in his State: the difficulty of which has been pointed out. To this excellence very few have attained, among whom, in my judgment, should be numbered and ranked high, among both the ancients and the moderns, Pope Sixtus the Fifth; who in knowledge of the resources of his States, of their causes, and of the remedies necessary for their defects, in being quicker to act than to speak, and in whatever else was necessary for the perfect ordering of the political State, should without doubt be placed ahead of any that have ever lived. Not only is there this difficulty, but after the regulations are decided upon, the prince must not yield to personal feelings which might impede sound reasoning, or at any rate might cause little attention to be paid to it, making him consider his own desire, rather than the public good. When this factor is found in perfection in any kingdom, there is no doubt that it will be the most potent of all in making it abound in gold and silver, since it may be called the efficient cause, more important than all other factors; for it can produce these, as well as an infinite number of other occasions, keep them in good condition, remove impediments, and in other ways bring about the same result, not only in countries where there is a good situation with respect to these factors, or they have been produced, but also in countries where there is no such situation and none of these factors. . . .

VII

Whether the low or high rate of exchange in Naples on other cities of Italy is or can be the cause of the plenty or scarcity of money in that kingdom

In all his *Discourse* Mark Antony de Santis [1] undertakes to prove no more than that the high rate of exchange in Naples on the other cities of Italy is the sole cause of the scarcity of money in the Kingdom. This he bases on the argument that the high rate of exchange does not permit remittance to be made in cash for the commodities exported from the Kingdom, rather than by exchange; while remittance for commodities imported is made in cash instead of exchange, because of the profit to be made in each case. A low rate of exchange, on the other hand, should cause money to be plentiful, the opposite effect being produced for analogous reasons. And for greater proof of this he points to the fact that fifteen, twenty, thirty years ago, when exchange was low, the Kingdom had plenty of money, domestic and foreign; while for about fifteen years back, when exchange has been high, the Kingdom has become poor, for the reason assigned. This is the first and principal conclusion of his *Discourse*, the root and foundation, as it were, of his thought; the destruction of which will necessarily cause everything to fall to the ground which depends upon it. It is necessary, therefore, to consider carefully what truth this conclusion contains, and the reasons and proofs which are given for it. For without doubt, if this conclusion were true, both by reason of the gain, which moves all men, and in the light of experience (for he asserts that his reasons are sensible, and that he has never been able to find any contradiction, however much he has tried), he would not have been mistaken as to the remedy, and the regulation he proposed would have been expedient and would have produced the desired effect. But since this

---

[1] The reference is to de Santis' *Discorso intorno alli effetti, che fa il cambio in Regno*, the work which led Serra to write his treatise. — ED.

conclusion is not sound, even though the arguments and the facts be as stated, still less if these are false, then it follows that the remedy was not good, and that the regulation neither would nor could produce the effect. To make this truth clear I shall discuss both the arguments and the facts adduced: that is, whether they would prove the said conclusion, if true, and then whether they are true; for if the falsity of one of these be enough to prove the conclusion unsound, then all the more if both are found so.

And beginning with the first point, namely, whether they prove the conclusion, if true, I shall develop the argument according to his reasoning, in order that it may be known and better understood; it being a property of the truth to reveal itself through discussion. The same may be said of error, which ordinarily occurs when there is no discussion, and the intellect is satisfied with first appearances. The argument then is as follows: the high rate of exchange makes it profitable for anyone who wishes to bring funds into the kingdom to use exchange rather than cash; and since the purpose of everyone in such matters is profit, therefore everyone who has to bring funds into the Kingdom will do so by exchange and not in cash; therefore the conclusion is true, that the high rate of exchange, which yields a profit, causes funds to be brought into the Kingdom by exchange rather than in cash; and hence it necessarily follows that the high rate of exchange is the cause of the scarcity of money in the Kingdom.

This argument appears to contain a clear and simple truth, obvious at first glance, as he says; but in order to avoid error it is necessary to discuss the parts and the conclusion of the argument with care. And beginning with the conclusion, where he asserts that everyone will bring funds by exchange and not in cash, upon which is based his other chief conclusion, that the high rate is the cause of the scarcity, I say that this conclusion, granting the truth of the parts of the argument, and that it follows from them necessarily, not conditionally, includes a necessary assumption:

that funds either came into the Kingdom in cash before exchange was resorted to, or must do so later, since otherwise
they would be paid into the Kingdom in some way.   If this
assumption is valid, then his argument or conclusion, though
true, does not prove anything or support his opinion that the
high rate of exchange is the cause of the scarcity of money in
the Kingdom; for the money had either been brought in
cash previously, or must have to come shortly afterwards;
whether before or after makes little or no difference. To this
the answer might be made that it is not necessary that these
funds should have come previously in cash, or have to come
later; since merchants, by understandings among themselves, will sell exchange to each other, thus keeping the
funds circulating in exchange without ever coming in cash;
or that the money will already be in the Kingdom, without
having to be sent, and so on. This reply involves the same
mistaking of appearances, since it does not meet the objection raised. For if the one who remitted by exchange, or
someone else, had not sent the funds previously in cash into
the Kingdom, or was not going to do so later, but expected
to draw them back by exchange again, and so on repeatedly,
this might go on for a time, but eventually the money would
have to come in cash and with a profit. For to say that it
would go on continually, would be to assume an indefinite
progression without any basis, than which no greater error
can befall the intellect, though it were for the money of only
one year; but as for continuing year after year, I will let him
who does not yet understand it consider the error and impossibility which this reply involves. And if it should be
said that he or others may have the funds already in the
Kingdom, without having sent any cash, in such a case it is
not the high exchange that should be held responsible for
money not coming in, but the other cause which put them
in possession of funds there. To demonstrate this truth
more clearly, to anyone who may not be convinced, I will
give an example.

Various citizens or foreigners wish to take out the commodities which are exported every year from the Kingdom, which according to de Santis amount to six millions a year; deducting the commodities which are imported and are needed in the Kingdom, and the incomes which foreigners draw from the country, there would remain five millions less two hundred thousand ducats, according to him. Exchange being high, those who wish to buy these goods will, because of the greater or less profit to be made, procure funds by selling exchange to various merchants in the Kingdom, who will pay for it with moneys of the Kingdom which they have there; and thus the commodities are exported without bringing in any cash, the exchange remaining the same; while the merchants who have paid will recoup themselves by exchanging from one to another, and thus no money will ever come into the Kingdom. This is all that could be said to maintain that the moneys paid in the Kingdom by the merchant who bought the exchange, if they had not previously been sent in cash, would not need to be.

To prove that this is false I ask: is this merchant who pays these moneys in the Kingdom a citizen or a foreigner? If he is a foreigner, with what money does he pay for this exchange? If he brought it in previously, I have proved my point that the funds had previously been brought in cash. If he has it because he receives revenues in the Kingdom or profit from industry, these should be held responsible for money not coming into the Kingdom, and the idleness of the inhabitants, as explained in the first part, not the high exchange; for with these incomes and profits from industry, commodities can be exported without sending any money, either by exchange or in cash.

And if it should be said that this merchant has these funds because he brought them in the form of exchange, this reply is rejected for the same reasons; since we have to find out how the one who bought this exchange got the money, which must be in the aforesaid way; and, to get on with the matter, we must finally come to this: either that the money came in previously, or that he had acquired it there in the same ways.

If the merchant is of the same Kingdom, how will he pay this money, unless it was sent previously? If it be said that it was remitted by exchange, the answer is as before. And if it should be said that he wishes to have credit by letters obtained from others, or accounts which they hold, or that it pleases him to do so, this credit will not last forever and keep him from sometime wishing to have his money back, with greater profit. And if it should be said that he will get it by selling exchange to others, receiving payment there or elsewhere, the same objection applies: that the one who gives him the money will get it back later, if he is of the Kingdom; and if he is a foreigner, we must find out how he got it, which is fully explained above. If it should be said that payment will be made elsewhere by means of commodities needed by the Kingdom, and so no cash will come, not import but export is to be expected from this, as does result; since these foreign goods needed by the Kingdom have to be offset by money due us; and it is this need of commodities that should be blamed for the scarcity of money, not the high rate of exchange. And if someone wished to maintain that he will draw it back by exchange through other places, and so on again, this may go on for some time, but eventually it must return whence it came and with a profit, as has been said; for to say that this transferring would go on forever appears to me ridiculous, and, as has been said, to give a progression into infinity, especially such an amount as five or six millions a year, not only for one year or two, but even ten or fifteen, and at present there would be twenty or twenty-two years. And so this transferring through the air would go on, to the extent of fifty or a hundred millions, and the real owners would never wish to possess or even see their money.

Moreover, if this were true, it would follow that the men of this Kingdom would at present have claims on foreigners in these twenty years alone amounting to a hundred millions; since at least five millions would have come every year in exchange to pay for the commodities exported, whether the merchants who have paid here for the exchange belong in the Kingdom or are foreigners; for in the end the money for these commodities belongs to the citizens of the Kingdom, according to de Santis' account. As it is well known, moreover, how many many times the extreme scarcity of money has caused the sovereign, the banks, and merchants, both foreign and local, to seek ways and means of getting money into the Kingdom, — I do not say sums as great as that, or a tenth, or even a hundredth, — and that it was necessary to resort to exchange in order to obtain even a very small sum: if what has been imagined were true, there would have been a flood of money in such an emergency. And this endless transferring is inconsistent with the other reason advanced by him for the extraction of funds from the Kingdom in cash, namely, the high exchange there, and the same profit to be made, both on imports from abroad and by the export of cash for the purpose of drawing it back afterwards by exchange, with a profit in less than a month of more than ten per cent; for if this reason were true, he who has bought exchange would wish to have his money in cash in order to make sure of this profit. And let no one say that he will remit it to others and have it returned by exchange to Naples, thus getting his money without any cash coming in, with the profit on the exchange besides, and making up the loss. For his returning it by exchange without any cash coming in is opposed by the same reasoning as above; and as for making good the loss, it is madness to exchange the certain for the uncertain, when to the uncertainty of profit on the exchange must be added the certainty of loss on the remittance. Nor will he ever make as much profit by exchanging for another place and exchanging back for Naples as he would by exporting cash, if his (de Santis) reasoning is correct. The same reasoning shows that his other assumption is not true, namely, that the high rate of exchange causes money to go out of the Kingdom in cash in order to be returned by exchange, with a profit of ten per cent in less than a month; for, as has been said, the funds must have been brought in previously in cash, since the exchange has to be paid for; and this export would have made, or would make, more cash come into the Kingdom. Of his other conclusion, namely, that the high rate in question causes funds to be sent in cash rather than by exchange to pay for the merchandise imported from abroad, I will speak later. Therefore the major conclusion of the aforesaid reasons is proved not to be true, that the high rate of exchange is the cause of the scarcity of money in the Kingdom, even though the other were true, that because of the profit from this high rate, everyone would remit by exchange, and would not bring cash into the Kingdom for the commodities which are to be exported; for the money must have come previously or would have to come. And although it might be transferred over and over a number of times, what is claimed is excessive. We have discussed it at such length because an error had been accepted as clear truth: wherefore, to remove this impression from the intellect more than one argument was necessary.

VIII

Of the remedy of prohibiting the export of money

The reason which apparently led to the adoption of this regulation of prohibiting the export of money was that in this way the money here and owed to us is preserved. For whether much or little comes in, no export being allowed, the total continually increases; and thus the Kingdom comes to abound in money, for it is assumed that five millions necessarily come every year, less two hundred thousand ducats, for the commodities exported. This reasoning has all the more weight, since it might be believed that profit was the reason why the money was exported; and such considerations have been so powerful, that they have led to its prohibition with very severe penalties. But the truth is quite the contrary, that the prohibition of the export of money is not expedient for States, and does not help to furnish them with an abundance of gold and silver, but is harmful rather; unless, through some disorder, the State was in such condition that the export might cause it harm. And in order that the truth of this conclusion may be recognized, I submit that he who wishes to export money must be assumed to have some purpose, since no agent operates without purpose; therefore, if money is exported for any purpose whatever, it must return with a profit into the Kingdom, from which it was sent. And in order that this may be more easily understood, let two causes be assumed, which are the most common and general ones leading to the export of money, namely, the desire to purchase goods abroad, and the carrying of money to other places where it is worth more or where there is a profit in drawing it back by exchange. If it is said that it will be exported to buy commodities abroad, there is no harm done, if these commodities are needed by the State from which the money is exported; for these commodities will certainly have to be paid for, if people wish to have them. Nor should any one object that they would be paid in exchange or by the barter of goods, which amount to the same thing, as has been proved; for if it is by exchange, the money must have been sent previously or subsequently in cash; if it is by the exchange of goods, the value and the funds received for them offset the money exported, nor is there any difficulty in this. If it is said that the commodities are not necessary for the State, but are carried elsewhere, I ask where they are carried. What will be done with these goods? Doubtless they will be sold at a higher price than was paid for them, and thus the money will return in greater quantity than was exported; and if new goods should be bought, it will return with all the more profit. And if it should be said that it will return by exchange and not in cash, this has already been answered above; if because the money of the State is worth more elsewhere than at home, the same reasoning applies: that it will return with a profit when commodities are bought with it, as has been said, and will be made clearer below. If it is exported because there is

a profit in returning it by exchange (which is the cause that
de Santis imagines is responsible for the export of money
from the Kingdom), it may be answered as above, that it returns with a profit; and so for the other causes of its export.
Hence the export can never work harm to the State, but
profit. Besides what has been said, freedom of export is a
cause of greater commerce and its prohibition of less; for
it is not always to the merchant's interest to remit by exchange, but more often it pays him to take cash; so if export
is prohibited, he refrains, because if he should need it later
elsewhere, he is impeded and cannot take it out. Hence he
will prefer to experience other loss, and will give up coming
there to trade. This is the harm that may be caused by prohibiting export, with no advantage. Nor is there need of
further argument to make this truth clear; not to mention
the example of other princes of Italy, who almost all permit
the export of their own money.

And since the signiory of Venice, though it permits the export of domestic money, forbids the export of foreign money,
I wish to explain why that is expedient; which is this, that
with such an arrangement she gains in every way; for by
the export of her own she acquires the advantage already
mentioned, while the prohibition on foreign cannot be a hin-
drance, since that city has plenty of her own money, however large sums may be wanted for export. Moreover, by
the prohibition against exporting foreign, she obtains the
profit of the mint, it being proper (as will be explained below) that the foreign money should go to the mint and not
circulate as money. Nor can this prohibition cause less commerce to come; for apart from many other reasons, it has already been said that this city has plenty of its own money,
and hence there is not the difficulty that, in bringing foreign
money there, one may not be able to obtain its equivalent
promptly from the mint, in the form of local money, which
may be exported, as has been said. And all this is to be
taken generally, where there is no disorder in the State, or
such a situation arising therefrom as would make export

harmful, as in our Kingdom. Not the reason which de Santis adduces, that when the Kingdom had been thus drained,
it would be in the power of one man to deprive it of money
entirely; as well as his other causes, which all have to do
with the low rate of exchange or the one just mentioned.
For under these conditions, export ought to be permitted;
since, there being no money there, and merchants wishing to
trade there on account of the freedom of export, they must
bring money in order to be able to get any; and what is obtained necessarily returns with a profit, generally speaking.
But the reason why export causes harm in our Kingdom is
the disorder which has been allowed to develop of foreigners
having such great incomes there, and having all the industries of the Kingdom in their hands; for which reasons, if
export were permitted, the money sent would not have to return again into the Kingdom. And they are such reasons
that for a part alone all the cash in the Kingdom would not
suffice, nor twice that much. Under these circumstances
alone, I say that it is a good thing to have export prohibited
in the Kingdom; all the more since it is true, as he says,
that, having occupied everything, foreigners cannot convert
their incomes into capital as formerly, there being nothing
left in the Kingdom to sell; so that, if it were possible, they
would certainly export money. Only in this respect does it
seem to me a good thing to prohibit export; for when this is
not the situation, it causes harm rather than benefit. Therefore let us conclude that the remedy of prohibiting export
can never make the Kingdom abound in money, but serves
only to control disorder as far as possible.

IX

*Of the remedy of making foreign money current or raising
its value*

Whether the second remedy, lowering the rate of exchange,
would suffice to make the Kingdom abound in gold and silver or not, has been fully discussed in the second part. Nor

is it necessary to discuss how this might help the factor of commerce; since it is the advantage of individuals that is chiefly concerned, conditions in the Kingdom being as described; and in this respect it is not necessary to take any measures apart from what is done by individuals themselves. We need to consider only the third remedy, namely, whether making foreign money current, allowing for the expense of coinage, or even raising its price, is an effective way to make money plentiful in the Kingdom; since with this object a regulation was issued making the silver *scudi* of Genoa current at the rate of thirteen *carlini* and a half. In this the opinion of de Santis was followed, who, after answering the twelfth objection to the regulation of exchange, goes on to argue that it was a mistake to issue a regulation that the Papal and Florentine *giulio*, which were formerly current in this Kingdom at ten *grana* and a half, should not be current at more than ten *grana*; since, as a result of this lowering of their price, all these moneys were removed from the Kingdom. He also points to the example of Mark Antony Colonna in Sicily, who, to cause money to come into that kingdom, where there was a scarcity of it, raised the price of the Neapolitan ducat by five per cent, which caused the money of the Kingdom to go to that island. He advises that the same be done here; and so as not to show that there is such a great scarcity of money in the Kingdom as to require the raising of foreign money, he proposes that no proclamation should be issued, but that the banks should be ordered to receive them at the raised price. This remedy was followed some years later with a public proclamation, since the remedy of lowering the exchange did not give any help, and the Kingdom became poorer and poorer; on the ground that, as it was expected to produce such a great good, it was not necessary to disguise it. At first sight this remedy seems excellent and sound, both by reason of its advantages and of the alleged experience of Sicily and of this Kingdom itself. But I reply that this appearance and experience contain only so much truth as was contained in the plan of lowering ex-

change; for making foreign money current and raising its
price cannot make the Kingdom abound in money, but will
impoverish it, and do harm to the real reasons and to individuals. And although the contrary seems true, that some
money really did come for a time, the more that comes the
more will it impoverish the Kingdom, and the more quickly.
These are regulations which we must consider carefully,
with a knowledge of the effects they can cause; looking
within and not being satisfied with appearances, only to find
ourselves mistaken at the end, having produced the opposite effect from what was desired.

It will be easy to show that appearances are deceiving in
raising foreign money in order to make it plentiful in the
Kingdom, or allowing it to circulate as money at a value
covering the expenses of coinage; but that it has the contrary effect, infringing the rights of the prince, and occa-
sioning, or rather causing, harm to his subjects and therefore generally, and is in every way unsuitable.

First, to show that appearances are deceiving, and that,
although money came for a time and to some extent, it must
eventually cause impoverishment, I ask for what purpose
this foreign money is brought into the Kingdom (because it
has been ordered that it should be current, and at a higher
rate than it is worth elsewhere, in order that the gain may
make it come here rather than elsewhere). What will be
done with this money in the Kingdom; for in any case,
though it were priced to yield ten or twenty per cent profit,
it is necessary to know what is done with it. If I am told
that commodities will be bought for export, this does not
cause plenty but scarcity; for as it was formerly necessary
that more money should come to buy these commodities,
now the same quantity is taken out by sending that much
less money. If it is said that goods will not be bought, but
there will be dealings in merchandise, or incomes will be
bought or other fixed property in the Kingdom, this is worse,
in that it makes all the greater scarcity. For, whereas it was
formerly necessary to bring more money for trading, now

less has to be brought, and as much is obtained; and it is the same in the purchase of incomes or real estate. But these are the very things that have caused scarcity in the Kingdom, and prevented the commodities produced in excess of our needs from being of any avail or bringing in any money, as explained at length above; the real reason why money does not come in return for the export of goods being the incomes drawn by foreigners from the Kingdom, and the industry they carry on there. Hence the more opportunity is given to foreigners to trade with greater advantage and profit in the Kingdom, and the more they are allowed to buy incomes and commodities, the more the scarcity of money will increase despite the export of goods. And that is the Kingdom's only hope.

And if it should be said that, if this were true, it would follow that princes ought to remove everything tending to bring foreigners into their States to trade, which is just the contrary of what seems to have been said in the first part, where we named commerce as one of the common factors which can make kingdoms abound in gold and silver, and said that in Venice this factor is very favorable and one of the causes of plenty, as it is a cause of the great amount of business there, wherefore what has been said above contradicts this: I answer that, well considered and understood, what I have said in the first part not only does not contradict what I have just said, but confirms it. For I said that great commerce is a cause of plenty for the place where it is, and when it is in connection with the commodities of other countries for other countries, that is, with trading; not with a country's own business alone, when it has the opposite effect. And in the same place it was proved that in our Kingdom there can be no commerce except in connection with its own business; which is a cause of scarcity, not of abundance, for this Kingdom; and that it is places like Venice to which it brings abundance, where it is carried on in connection with trading. And besides this reason showing that raising the value of money causes scarcity, not plenty, of money in the Kingdom, another stronger reason may be advanced, namely, that when foreign money is thus raised, domestic money will be exported with a very great profit by taking it to the place where the foreign money comes from, making it into that, and sending it back at a profit, and soon, over and over, till all there is has been extracted by means of a small amount.

It infringes the rights of the prince; for inasmuch as this all ought to go to the mint to be melted and made into local money, giving him the right and profit of the mint, he suffers loss, when it circulates as money; and, by permitting foreign money to circulate, a prince who has no mines of gold and silver in his State will have to suspend coinage. It may cause harm to his subjects generally, by making it possible for a foreign prince to cheat them, with malice or without; as, for example, when a prince, whose money circulates in another's country, lowers the fineness of his money, with malice or without. When the value is restored, — I do not say more than it was worth, but the just value, — the money of less fineness will doubtless circulate on a par with the former; so that damage to the extent of thousands and hundreds of thousands of ducats may easily be caused to the subjects and to the Kingdom in general. For this reason alone such money certainly ought not to circulate in the kingdoms of other princes, but should be carried to the mint and paid for according to the value of the silver. I shall not discuss how unfitting it is to allow foreign money to circulate in the State of a great prince. Therefore, it is proved that not in one way alone, which would suffice, but in every other channel of trade, this raising of money causes scarcity and not plenty; and so we find that, in the States of all intelligent princes, foreign money is always under- rather than overvalued.

VIII

THOMAS MUN

ENGLAND'S TREASURE BY FORRAIGN TRADE

NOTE

THOMAS MUN (1571–1641) was the son of a London mercer, and early engaged in trade, especially in Italy and the Levant. In this he was very successful, and he enjoyed a great reputation among London merchants. In 1615 he became a director of the East India Company, a position he held until his death. In defence of the Company he published in 1621 *A Discourse of Trade from England into the East Indies,* which occasioned a lively controversy. His *England's Treasure,* the most famous exposition of Mercantile principles, was written about 1630, but was not published till 1664. Six editions of it are known. It appears to be made up of several separate papers, the arrangement being that of his son, who first published the work. Though thoroughly Mercantilist in spirit, it contains several qualifications of the greatest significance.

ENGLAND'S TREASURE BY FORRAIGN TRADE

CHAPTER II

The means to enrich this Kingdom, and to encrease our Treasure.

ALTHOUGH a Kingdom may be enriched by gifts received, or by purchase taken from some other Nations, yet these are things uncertain and of small consideration when they happen. The ordinary means therefore to encrease our wealth and treasure is by *Forraign Trade*, wherein wee must ever observe this rule; to sell more to strangers yearly than wee consume of theirs in value. For suppose that when this Kingdom is plentifully served with the Cloth, Lead, Tinn, Iron, Fish and other native commodities, we doe yearly export the overplus to forraign Countries to the value of twenty two hundred thousand pounds; by which means we are enabled beyond the Seas to buy and bring in forraign wares for our use and Consumptions, to the value of twenty hundred thousand pounds; By this order duly kept in our trading, we may rest assured that the Kingdom shall be enriched yearly two hundred thousand pounds, which must be brought to us in so much Treasure; because that part of our stock which is not returned to us in wares must necessarily be brought home in treasure.

For in this case it cometh to pass in the stock of a Kingdom, as in the estate of a private man; who is supposed to have one thousand pounds yearly revenue and two thousand pounds of ready money in his Chest: If such a man through excess shall spend one thousand five hundred pounds *per annum*, all his ready mony will be gone in four years; and in the like time his said money will be doubled if he take a Frugal course to spend but five hundred pounds *per annum*; which rule never faileth likewise in the Commonwealth, but in some cases (of no great moment) which I will hereafter declare, when I shall shew by whom and in what manner this ballance of the Kingdoms account ought to be drawn up yearly, or so often as it shall please the State to discover how much we gain or lose by trade with forraign Nations. But first I will say something concerning those ways and means which will encrease our exportations and diminish our importations of wares; which being done, I will then set down some other arguments both affirmative and negative to strengthen that which is here declared, and thereby to shew that all the other means which are commonly supposed to enrich the Kingdom with Treasure are altogether insufficient and meer fallacies.

CHAPTER III

The particular ways and means to encrease the exportation of our commodities, and to decrease our Consumption of forraign wares.

The revenue or stock of a Kingdom by which it is provided of forraign wares is either *Natural* or *Artificial*. The Natural wealth is so much only as can be spared from our own use and necessities to be exported unto strangers. The Artificial consists in our manufactures and industrious trading with forraign commodities, concerning which I will set down such particulars as may serve for the cause we have in hand.

1. First, although this Realm be already exceeding rich by nature, yet might it be much encreased by laying the waste grounds (which are infinite) into such employments as should no way hinder the present revenues of other manured lands, but hereby to supply our selves and prevent the importations of Hemp, Flax, Cordage, Tobacco, and divers other things which now we fetch from strangers to our great impoverishing.

2. We may likewise diminish our importations, if we would soberly refrain from excessive consumption of forraign wares in our diet and rayment, with such often change

of fashions as is used, so much the more to encrease the waste and charge; which vices at this present are more notorious amongst us than in former ages. Yet might they easily be amended by enforcing the observation of such good laws as are strictly practised in other Countries against the said excesses; where likewise by commanding their own manufactures to be used, they prevent the coming in of others, without prohibition, or offence to strangers in their mutual commerce.

3. In our exportations we must not only regard our own superfluities, but also we must consider our neighbours necessities, that so upon the wares which they cannot want, nor yet be furnished thereof elsewhere, we may (besides the vent of the Materials) gain so much of manufacture as we can, and also endeavour to sell them dear, so far forth as the high price cause not a less vent in the quantity. But the superfluity of our commodities which strangers use, and may also have the same from other Nations, or may abate their vent by the use of some such like wares from other places, and with little inconvenience; we must in this case strive to sell as cheap as possible we can, rather than to lose the utterance of such wares. For we have found of late years by good experience, that being able to sell our Cloth cheap in Turkey, we have greatly encreased the vent thereof, and the *Venetians* have lost as much in the utterance of theirs in those Countreys, because it is dearer. And on the other side a few years past, when by the excessive price of Wools our Cloth was exceeding dear, we lost at the least half our clothing for forraign parts, which since is no otherwise (well neer) recovered again than by the great fall of price for Wools and Cloth. We find that twenty five in the hundred less in the price of these and some other Wares, to the loss of private mens revenues, may raise above fifty upon the hundred in the quantity vented to the benefit of the publique. For when Cloth is dear, other Nations doe presently practise clothing, and we know they want neither art nor materials to this performance. But when by cheapness we drive them

from this employment, and so in time obtain our dear price again, then do they also use their former remedy. So that by these alterations we learn, that it is in vain to expect a greater revenue of our wares than their condition will afford, but rather it concerns us to apply our endeavours to the times with care and diligence to help our selves the best we may, by making our cloth and other manufactures without deceit, which will encrease their estimation and use.

4. The value of our exportations likewise may be much advanced when we perform it ourselves in our own Ships, for then we get only not the price of our wares as they are worth here, but also the Merchants gains, the charges of ensurance, and fraight to carry them beyond the seas. As for example, if the *Italian* Merchants should come hither in their own shipping to fetch our Corn, our red Herrings or the like, in this case the Kingdom should have ordinarily but 25.s. for a quarter of Wheat, and 20.s. for a barrel of red herrings, whereas if we carry these wares ourselves into *Italy* upon the said rates, it is likely that wee shall obtain fifty shillings for the first, and forty shillings for the last, which is a great difference in the utterance or vent of the Kingdoms stock. And although it is true that the commerce ought to be free to strangers to bring in and carry out at their pleasure, yet nevertheless in many places the exportation of victuals and munition are either prohibited, or at least limited to be done onely by the people and Shipping of those places where they abound.

5. The frugal expending likewise of our own natural wealth might advance much yearly to be exported unto strangers; and if in our rayment we will be prodigal, yet let this be done with our own materials and manufactures, as Cloth, Lace, Imbroderies, Cutworks and the like, where the excess of the rich may be the employment of the poor, whose labours notwithstanding of this kind, would be more profitable for the Commonwealth, if they were done to the use of strangers.

6. The Fishing in his Majesties seas of *England*, *Scotland*

and *Ireland* is our natural wealth, and would cost nothing
but labour, which the *Dutch* bestow willingly, and thereby
draw yearly a very great profit to themselves by serving
many places of Christendom with our Fish, for which they
return and supply their wants both of forraign Wares and
Mony, besides the multitudes of Mariners and Shipping,
which hereby are maintain'd, whereof a long discourse might
be made to shew the particular manage of this important
business. Our Fishing plantation likewise in *New-England*,
Virginia, *Groenland*, the *Summer Islands* and the *New-
found-land*, are of the like nature, affording much wealth and
employments to maintain a great number of poor, and to encrease our decaying trade.

7. A Staple or Magazin for forraign Corn, Indico, Spices,
Raw-silks, Cotton wool or any other commodity whatsoever, to be imported will encrease Shipping, Trade, Treasure, and the Kings customes, by exporting them again where
need shall require, which course of Trading, hath been the
chief means to raise *Venice*, *Genoa*, the *low-Countreys*, with
some others; and for such a purpose *England* stands most
commodiously, wanting nothing to this performance but our
own diligence and endeavour.

8. Also wee ought to esteem and cherish those trades
which we have in remote or far Countreys, for besides the
encrease of Shipping and Mariners thereby, the wares also
sent thither and receiv'd from thence are far more profitable
unto the kingdom than by our trades neer at hand; As for
example; suppose Pepper to be worth here two Shillings the
pound constantly, if then it be brought from the *Dutch* at
Amsterdam, the Merchant may give there twenty pence the
pound, and gain well by the bargain, but if he fetch this Pepper from the *East-indies*, he must not give above three pence
the pound at the most, which is a mighty advantage, not
only in that part which serveth for our own use, but also for
that great quantity which (from hence) we transport yearly
unto divers other Nations to be sold at a higher price:
whereby it is plain, that we make a far greater stock by gain

upon these *Indian* Commodities, than those Nations doe where they grow, and to whom they properly appertain, being the natural wealth of their Countries. But for the better understanding of this particular, we must ever distinguish between the gain of the Kingdom, and the profit of the Merchant; for although the Kingdom payeth no more for this Pepper than is before supposed, nor for any other commodity bought in forraign parts more than the Stranger receiveth from us for the same, yet the Merchant payeth not only that price, but also the fraight, ensurance, customes and other charges which are exceeding great in these long voyages; but yet all these in the Kingdoms accompt are but commutations among our selves, and no Privation of the Kingdoms stock, which being duly considered, together with the support also of our other trades in our best Shipping to *Italy*, *France*, *Turkey*, the *East Countreys* and other places, by transporting and venting the wares which we bring yearly from the *East Indies*; It may well stir up our utmost endeavours to maintain and enlarge this great and noble business, so much importing the Publique wealth, Strength, and Happiness. Neither is there less honour and judgment by growing rich (in this manner) upon the stock of other Nations, than by an industrious encrease of our own means, especially when this later is advanced by the benefit of the former, as we have found in the *East Indies* by sale of much of our Tin, Cloth, Lead and other Commodities, the vent whereof doth daily encrease in those Countreys which formerly had no use of our wares.

9. It would be very beneficial to export money as well as wares, being done in trade only, it would encrease our Treasure; but of this I write more largely in the next Chapter to prove it plainly.

10. It were policie and profit for the State to suffer manufactures made of forraign Materials to be exported custome-free, as Velvets and all other wrought Silks, Fustians, thrown Silks and the like, it would employ very many poor people, and much encrease the value of our stock yearly is-

sued into other Countreys, and it would (for this purpose) cause the more forraign Materials to be brought in, to the improvement of His Majesties Customes. I will here remember a notable increase in our manufacture of winding and twisting only of forraign raw Silk, which within 35. years to my knowledge did not employ more than 300. people in the City and suburbs of London, where at this present time it doth set on work above fourteen thousand souls, as upon diligent enquiry hath been credibly reported unto His Majesties Commissioners for Trade. And it is certain, that if the said forraign Commodities might be exported from hence, free of custome, this manufacture would yet encrease very much, and decrease as fast in *Italy* and the *Netherlands*. But if any man allege the *Dutch* proverb, *Live and let others live;* I answer, that the Dutchmen notwithstanding their own Proverb, doe not onely in these Kingdoms, encroach upon our livings, but also in other forraign parts of our trade (where they have power) they do hinder and destroy us in our lawful course of living, hereby taking the bread out of our mouth, which we shall never prevent by plucking the pot from their nose, as of late years too many of us do practise to the great hurt and dishonour of this famous Nation; We ought rather to imitate former times in taking sober and worthy courses more pleasing to God and suitable to our ancient reputation.

11. It is needful also not to charge the native commodities with too great customes, lest by indearing them to the strangers use, it hinder their vent. And especially forraign wares brought in to be transported again should be favoured, for otherwise that manner of trading (so much importing the good of the Common wealth) cannot prosper nor subsist. But the Consumption of such forraign wares in the Realm may be the more charged, which will turn to the profit of the Kingdom in the *Ballance of the Trade*, and thereby also enable the King to lay up the more Treasure out of his yearly incomes, as of this particular I intend to write more fully in his proper place, where I shall shew how much

money a Prince may conveniently lay up without the hurt of his subjects.

12. Lastly, in all things we must endeavour to make the most we can of our own, whether it be *Natural* or *Artificial;* And forasmuch as the people which live by the Arts are far more in number than they who are masters of the fruits, we ought the more carefully to maintain those endeavours of the multitude, in whom doth consist the greatest strength and riches both of King and Kingdom: for where the people are many, and the arts good, there the traffique must be great, and the Countrey rich. The *Italians* employ a greater number of people, and get more money by their industry and manufactures of the raw Silks of the Kingdom of *Cicilia,* than the King of *Spain* and his Subjects have by the revenue of this rich commodity. But what need we fetch the example so far, when we know that our own natural wares doe not yield us so much profit as our industry? For Iron oar in the Mines is of no great worth, when it is compared with the employment and advantage it yields being digged, tried, transported, bought, sold, cast into Ordnance, Muskets, and many other instruments of war for offence and defence, wrought into Anchors, bolts, spikes, nayles and the like, for the use of Ships, Houses, Carts, Coaches, Ploughs, and other instruments for Tillage. Compare our Fleecewools with our Cloth, which requires shearing, washing, carding, spinning, Weaving, fulling, dying, dressing and other trimmings, and we shall find these Arts more profitable than the natural wealth, whereof I might instance other examples, but I will not be more tedious, for if I would amplify upon this and the other particulars before written, I might find matter sufficient to make a large volume, but my desire in all is only to prove what I propound with brevity and plainness.

CHAPTER IV

The Exportation of our Moneys in Trade of Merchandize is a means to encrease our Treasure.

This Position is so contrary to the common opinion, that it will require many and strong arguments to prove it before it can be accepted of the Multitude, who bitterly exclaim when they see any monies carried out of the Realm; affirming thereupon that wee have absolutely lost so much Treasure, and that this is an act directly against the long continued laws made and confirmed by the wisdom of this Kingdom in the High Court of Parliament, and that many places, nay *Spain* it self which is the Fountain of Mony, forbids the exportation thereof, some cases only excepted. To all which I might answer that *Venice, Florence, Genoa,* the *Low Countreys* and divers other places permit it, their people applaud it, and find great benefit by it; but all this makes a noise and proves nothing, we must therefore come to those reasons which concern the business in question.

First, I will take that for granted which no man of judgment will deny, that we have no other means to get Treasure but by forraign trade, for Mines wee have none which do afford it, and how this mony is gotten in the managing of our said Trade I have already shewed, that it is done by making our commodities which are exported yearly to over ballance in value the forraign wares which we consume; so that it resteth only to shew how our monyes may be added to our commodities, and being jointly exported may so much the more encrease our Treasure.

Wee have already supposed our yearly consumptions of forraign wares to be for the value of twenty hundred thousand pounds, and our exportations to exceed that two hundred thousand pounds, which sum wee have thereupon affirmed is brought to us in treasure to ballance the accompt. But now if we add three hundred thousand pounds more in ready mony unto our former exportations in wares,

what profit can we have (will some men say) although by
this means we should bring in so much ready mony more
than wee did before, seeing that wee have carried out the
like value.

To this the answer is, that when wee have prepared our
exportations of wares, and sent out as much of everything
as wee can spare or vent abroad: It is not therefore said
that then we should add our money thereunto to fetch in the
more mony immediately, but rather first to enlarge our
trade by enabling us to bring in more forraign wares, which
being sent out again will in due time much encrease our
Treasure.

For although in this manner wee do yearly multiply our
importations to the maintenance of more Shipping and Mariners, improvment of His Majesties Customs and other
benefits: yet our consumption of those forraign wares is no
more than it was before; so that all the said encrease of commodities brought in by the means of our ready mony sent
out as is afore written, doth in the end become an exportation unto us of a far greater value than our said moneys
were, which is proved by three several examples following.

1. For I suppose that 100000. *l.* being sent in our Shipping to the East Countreys, will buy there one hundred
thousand quarters of wheat cleer aboard the Ships, which
being after brought into *England* and housed, to export the
same at the best time for vent thereof in *Spain* or *Italy*, it
cannot yield less in those parts than two hundred thousand
pounds to make the Merchant but a saver, yet by this reck-
ning wee see the Kingdom hath doubled that Treasure.

2. Again this profit will be far greater when wee trade
thus in remote Countreys, as for example, if wee send one
hundred thousand pounds into the *East-Indies* to buy Pepper there, and bring it hither, and from hence send it for
Italy or *Turkey*, it must yield seven hundred thousand
pounds at least in those places, in regard of the excessive
charge which the Merchant disburseth in those long voyages in Shipping, Wages, Victuals, Insurance, Interest, Cus-

tomes, Imposts, and the like, all which notwithstanding the King and the Kingdom gets.

3. But where the voyages are short & the wares rich, which therefore will not employ much Shipping, the profit will be far less. As when another hundred thousand pounds shall be employed in *Turkey* in raw Silks, and brought hither to be after transported from hence into *France*, the *Low Countreys*, or *Germany*, the Merchant shall have good gain, although he sell it there but for one hundred and fifty thousand pounds: and thus take the voyages altogether in their *Medium*, the moneys exported will be returned unto us more than Trebled. But if any man will yet object, that these returns come to us in wares, and not really in mony as they were issued out,

The answer is (keeping our first ground) that if our consumption of forraign wares be no more yearly than is already supposed, and that our exportations be so mightily encreased by this manner of Trading with ready money as is before declared: It is not then possible but that all the over-ballance or difference should return either in mony or in such wares as we must export again, which, as is already plainly shewed will be still a greater means to encrease our Treasure.

For it is in the stock of the Kingdom as in the estates of private men, who having store of wares, doe not therefore say that they will not venture out or trade with their mony (for this were ridiculous) but do also turn that into wares, whereby they multiply their Mony, and so by a continual and orderly change of one into the other grow rich, and when they please turn all their estates into Treasure; for they that have Wares cannot want mony.

Neither is it said that Mony is the Life of Trade, as if it could not subsist without the same; for we know that there was great trading by way of commutation or barter when there was little mony stirring in the world. The *Italians* and some other Nations have such remedies against this want, that it can neither decay nor hinder their trade, for they transfer bills of debt, and have Banks both publick and private, wherein they do assign their credits from one to another daily for very great sums with ease and satisfaction by writings only, whilst in the mean time the Mass of Treasure which gave foundation to these credits is employed in Forraign Trade as a Merchandize, and by the said means they have little other use of money in those countreys more than for their ordinary expences. It is not therefore the keeping of our mony in the Kingdom, but the necessity and use of our wares in forraign Countries, and our want of their commodities that causeth the vent and consumption on all sides, which makes a quick and ample Trade. If wee were once poor, and now having gained some store of mony by trade with resolution to keep it still in the Realm; shall this cause other Nations to spend more of our commodities than formerly they have done, whereby we might say that our trade is Quickned and Enlarged? no verily, it will produce no such good effect: but rather according to the alteration of times by their true causes wee may expect the contrary; for all men do consent that plenty of mony in a Kingdom doth make the native commodities dearer, which as it is to the profit of some private men in their revenues, so is it directly against the benefit of the Publique in the quantity of the trade; for as plenty of mony makes wares dearer, so dear wares decline their use and consumption, as hath been already plainly shewed in the last Chapter upon that particular of our cloth; And although this is a very hard lesson for some great landed men to learn, yet I am sure it is a true lesson for all the land to observe, lest when wee have gained some store of mony by trade, wee lose it again by not trading with our mony. I knew a Prince in *Italy* (of famous memory) *Ferdinando the first*, great Duke of *Tuscanie*, who being very rich in Treasure, endevoured therewith to enlarge his trade by issuing out to his Merchants great sums of money for very small profit; I my self had forty thousand crowns of him *gratis* for a whole year, although he knew that I would presently send it away in *Specie* for the parts of *Tur-*

key to be employed in wares for his Countries, he being well assured that in this course of trade it would return again (according to the old saying) with a Duck in the mouth. This noble and industrious Prince by his care and diligence to countenance and favour Merchants in their affairs, did so encrease the practice thereof, that there is scarce a Nobleman or Gentleman in all his dominions that doth not Merchandize either by himself or in partnership with others, whereby within these thirty years the trade to his port of *Leghorn* is so much encreased, that of a poor little town (as I my self knew it) it is now become a fair and strong City, being one of the most famous places for trade in all Christendom. And yet it is worthy our observation, that the multitude of Ships and wares which come thither from *England*, the *Low Countreys*, and other places, have little or no means to make their returns from thence but only in ready money, which they may and do carry away freely at all times, to the incredible advantage of the said great Duke of *Tuscanie* and his subjects, who are much enriched by the continual great concourse of Merchants from all the States of the neighbour Princes, bringing them plenty of mony daily to supply their wants of the said wares. And thus we see that the current of Merchandize which carries away their Treasure, becomes a flowing stream to fill them again in a greater measure with mony.

There is yet an objection or two as weak as all the rest: that is, if wee trade with our Mony wee shall issue out the less wares; as if a man should say, those Countreys which heretofore had occasion to consume our Cloth, Lead, Tin, Iron, Fish, and the like, shall now make use of our monies in the place of those necessaries, which were most absurd to affirm, or that the Merchant had not rather carry out wares by which there is ever some gains expected, than to export mony which is still but the same without any encrease.

But on the contrary there are many Countreys which may yield us very profitable trade for our mony, which otherwise afford us no trade at all, because they have no use of our wares, as namely the *East-Indies* for one in the first beginning thereof, although since by industry in our commerce with those Nations we have brought them into the use of much of our Lead, Cloth, Tin, and other things, which is a good addition to the former vent of our commodities.

Again, some men have alleged that those Countries which permit mony to be carried out, do it because they have few or no wares to trade withall: but wee have great store of commodities, and therefore their action ought not to be our example.

To this the answer is briefly, that if we have such a quantity of wares as doth fully provide us of all things needful from beyond the seas: why should we then doubt that our monys sent out in trade, must not necessarily come back again in treasure; together with the great gains which it may procure in such manner as is before set down? And on the other side, if those Nations which send out their monies do it because they have but few wares of their own, how come they then to have so much Treasure as we ever see in those places which suffer it freely to be exported at all times and by whomsoever? I answer, *Even by trading with their Moneys;* for by what other means can they get it, having no Mines of Gold or Silver?

Thus may we plainly see, that when this weighty business is duly considered in his end, as all our humane actions ought well to be weighed, it is found much contrary to that which most men esteem thereof, because they search no further than the beginning of the work, which mis-informs their judgments, and leads them into error: For if we only behold the actions of the husbandman in the seed-time when he casteth away much good corn into the ground, we will rather accompt him a mad man than a husbandman: but when we consider his labours in the harvest which is the end of his endeavours, we find the worth and plentiful encrease of his actions.

CHAPTER X

The observation of the Statute of Imployments to be made by strangers, cannot encrease, nor yet preserve our Treasure.

To keep our mony in the Kingdom is a work of no less skill and difficulty than to augment our Treasure: for the causes of their preservation and production are the same in nature. The statute for employment of strangers wares into our commodities seemeth at the first to be a good and a lawful way leading to those ends; but upon th' examination of the particulars, we shall find that it cannot produce such good effects.

For as the use of forraign trade is alike unto all Nations, so may we easily perceive what will be done therein by strangers, when we do but observe our own proceedings in this waighty business, by which we do not only seek with the vent of our own commodities to supply our wants of forraign wares, but also to enrich our selves with treasure: all which is done by a different manner of trading according to our own occasions and the nature of the places whereunto we do trade; as namely in some Countrys we sell our commodities and bring away their wares, or part in mony; in other Countreys we sell our goods and take their mony, because they have little or no wares that fits our turns: again in some places we have need of their commodities, but they have little use of ours: so they take our mony which we get in other Countreys: And thus by a course of traffick (which changeth according to the accurrents of time) the particular members do accommodate each other, and all accomplish the whole body of the trade, which will ever languish if the harmony of her health be distempered by the diseases of excess at home, violence abroad, charges and restrictions at home or abroad: but in this place I have occasion to speak only of restriction, which I will perform briefly.

There are three ways by which a Merchant may make the returns of his wares from beyond the Seas, that is to say in mony, in commodities, or by Exchange. But the Statute of employment doth not only restrain mony (in which there is a seeming providence and Justice) but also the use of the Exchange by bills, which doth violate the Law of Commerce, and is indeed an Act without example in any place of the world where we have trade, and therefore to be considered, that whatsoever (in this kind) we shall impose upon strangers here, will presently be made a Law for us in their Countreys, especially where we have our greatest trade with our vigilant neighbours, who omit no care nor occasion to support their traffique in equal privileges with other Nations. And thus in the first place we should be deprived of that freedom and means which now we have to bring Treasure into the Kingdom, and therewith likewise we should lose the vent of much wares which we carry to divers places, whereby our trade and our Treasure would decay together.

Secondly, if by the said Statute we thrust the exportation of our wares (more than ordinary) upon the stranger, we must then take it from the *English*, which were injurious to our Merchants, Marriners and Shipping, besides the hurt to the Commonwealth in venting the Kingdoms stock to the stranger at far lower rates here than we must do if we sold it to them in their own Countrys, as is proved in the third Chapter.

Thirdly, whereas we have already sufficiently shewed, that if our commodities be over ballanced in value by forraign wares, our mony must be carried out. How is it possible to prevent this by tying the Strangers hands, and leaving the English loose? Shall not the same reasons and advantage cause that to be done by them now, that was done by the other before? or if we will make a statute (without example) to prevent both alike, shall we not then overthrow all at once? the King in his customes and the Kingdom in her profits; for such a restriction must of necessity destroy much trade, because the diversity of occasions and places which make an ample trade require that some men should both export and import wares; some export only, others import, some deliver out their monies by exchange, others take it up; some carry out mony, others bring it in, and this in a greater or lesser quantity according to the good husbandry or excess in the Kingdom, over which only if we keep a strict law, it will rule all the rest, and without this all other Statutes are no rules either to keep or procure us Treasure.

Lastly, to leave no Objection unanswered, if it should be said that a Statute comprehending the English as well as the stranger must needs keep our money in the Kingdom. What shall we get by this, if it hinder the coming in of money by the decay of that ample Trade which we enjoyed in the freedom thereof? is not the Remedy far worse than the Disease? shall we not live more like Irishmen than Englishmen, when the Kings revenues, our Merchants, Mariners, Shipping, Arts, Lands, Riches, and all decay together with our Trade?

Yea but, say some men, we have better hopes than so; for th' intent of the Statute is, that as all the forraign wares which are brought in shall be imployed in our commodities, thereby to keep our money in the Kingdom: So we doubt not but to send out a sufficient quantity of our own wares over and above to bring in the value thereof in ready money.

Although this is absolutely denied by the reasons afore written, yet now we will grant it, because we desire to end the dispute: For if this be true, that other Nations will vent more of our commodities than we consume of theirs in value, then I affirm that the overplus must necessarily return unto us in treasure without the use of the Statute, which is therefore not onely fruitless but hurtful, as some other like restrictions are found to be when they are fully discovered.

CHAPTER XI

*It will not increase our treasure to enjoyn the Merchant that
exporteth Fish, Corn, or Munition, to return all or part of
the value in Money.*

Victuals and Munitions for war are so pretious in a Commonwealth, that either it seemeth necessary to restrain the
exportation altogether, or (if the plenty permits it) to require the return thereof in so much treasure; which ap-
peareth to be reasonable and without difficulty, because
Spain and other Countries do willingly part with their
money for such wares, although in other occasions of trade
they straightly prohibit the exportation thereof: all which I
grant to be true, yet notwithstanding we must consider that
all the ways and means which (in course of trade) force
treasure into the Kingdom, do not therefore make it ours:
for this can be done onely by a lawful gain, and this gain is
no way to be accomplished but by the overballance of our
trade, and this overballance is made less by restrictions:
therefore such restrictions do hinder the increase of our
treasure. The Argument is plain, and needs no other reasons to strengthen it, except any man be so vain to think
that restrictions would not cause the less wares to be exported. But if this likewise should be granted, yet to enjoyn the Merchant to bring in money for Victuals and Munition carried out, wil! not cause us to have one peny the more
in the Kingdom at the years end; for whatsoever is forced in
one way must out again another way: because onely so
much will remain and abide with us as is gained and incorporated into the estate of the Kingdom by the overballance
of the trade.

This may be made plain by an example taken from an
Englishman, who had occasion to buy and consume the
wares of divers strangers for the value of six hundred
pounds, and having wares of his own for the value of one
thousand pounds, he sold them to the said strangers, and

presently forced all the mony from them into his own power;
yet upon cleering of the reckoning between them there remained onely four hundred pounds to the said Englishman
for overballance of the wares bought and sold; so the rest
which he had received was returned back from whence he
forced it. And this shall suffice to shew that whatsoever
courses we take to force money into the Kingdom, yet so
much onely will remain with us as we shall gain by the ballance of our trade.

CHAPTER XVII

*Whether it be necessary for great Princes to lay up
store of Treasure.*

Before we set down the quantity of Treasure which Princes
may conveniently lay up yearly without hurting the Common-wealth, it will be fit to examine whether the act it self of
Treasuring be necessary: for in common conference we ever
find some men who do so much dote or hope upon the Liberality of Princes, that they term it baseness, and conceive it
needless for them to lay up store of Treasure, accounting the
honour and safety of great Princes to consist more in their
Bounty, than in their Money, which they labour to confirm
by the examples of *Cæsar*, *Alexander*, and others, who hating covetousness, atchieved many acts and victories by lav-
ish gifts and liberal expences. Unto which they add also the
little fruit which came by that *great summ of money* which
King *David* laid up and left to his son *Solomon*, who notwithstanding this, and all his other rich Presents and wealthy
Traffique in a quiet reign, consumed all with pomp and vain
delights, excepting only that which was spent in building of
the Temple. Whereupon (say they) if so much treasure
gathered up by so just a King, effect so little, what shall we
hope for by the endeavours of this kind in other Princes?
Sardanapalus left ten millions of pounds to them that slew
him. *Darius* left twenty millions of pounds to *Alexander*
that took him; *Nero* being left rich, and extorting much

from his best Subjects, gave away above twelve millions of pounds to his base flatterers and such unworthy persons, which caused *Galba* after him to revoke those gifts. A Prince who hath store of mony hates peace, despiseth the friendship of his Neighbours and Allies, enters not only into unnecessary, but also into dangerous Wars, to the ruin and over-throw (sometimes) of his own estate: All which, with divers other weak arguments of this kind, (which for brevity I omit) make nothing against the lawful gathering and massing up of Treasure by wise and provident Princes, if they be rightly understood.

For first, concerning those worthies who have obtained to the highest top of *honour* and *dignity*, by their great gifts and expences, who knows not that this hath been done rather upon the spoils of their Enemies than out of their own Cofers, which is indeed a Bounty that causeth neither loss nor peril? Whereas on the contrary, those Princes which do not providently lay up Treasure, or do imoderately consume the same when they have it, will sodainly come to want and misery; for there is nothing doth so soon decay as Excessive Bounty, in using whereof they want the means to use it. And this was King *Solomons* case, notwithstanding, his infinite Treasure, which made him over-burthen his Subjects in such a manner, that (for this cause) many of them rebelled against his son *Rehoboam*, who thereby lost a great part of his dominions, being so grosly mis-led by his young Counsellors. Therefore a Prince that will not oppress his people, and yet be able to maintain his Estate, and defend his Right, that will not run himself into Poverty, Contempt, Hate, and Danger, must lay up treasure, and be thrifty, for further proof whereof I might yet produce some other examples, which here I do omit as needless.

Only I will add this as a necessary rule to be observed, that when more treasure must be raised than can be received by the ordinary taxes, it ought ever to be done with equality to avoid the hate of the people, who are never pleased except their contributions be granted by general consent: For which purpose the invention of Parliaments is an excellent policie of Government, to keep a sweet concord between a King and his Subjects, by restraining the Insolency of the Nobility, and redressing the Injuries of the Commons, without engaging a Prince to adhere to either party, but indifferently to favour both. There could nothing be devised with more judgment for the common quiet of a Kingdom, or with greater care for the safety of a King, who hereby hath also good means to dispatch those things by others, which will move envy, and to execute that himself which will merit thanks.

CHAPTER XVIII

How much Treasure a Prince may conveniently lay up yearly.

Thus far we have shewed the ordinary and extraordinary incomes of Princes, the conveniency thereof, and to whom only it doth necessarily and justly belong, to take the extraordinary contributions of their Subjects. It resteth now to examine what proportion of treasure each particular Prince may conveniently lay up yearly. This business doth seem at the first to be very plain and easy, for if a Prince have two millions yearly revenue, and spend but one, why should he not lay up the other? Indeed I must confess that this course is ordinary in the means and gettings of private men, but in the affairs of Princes it is far different, there are other circumstances to be considered; for although the revenue of a King should be very great, yet if the gain of the Kingdom be but small, this latter must ever give rule and proportion to that Treasure, which may conveniently be laid up yearly, for if he should mass up more mony than is gained by the overballance of his forraign trade, he shall not *Fleece*, but *Flea* his Subjects, and so with their ruin overthrow himself for want of future sheerings. To make this plain, suppose a Kingdom to be so rich by nature and art, that it may supply it self of forraign wares by trade, and yet advance yearly

200000 *l.* in ready mony: Next suppose all the Kings revenues to be 900000 *l.* and his expences but 400000 *l.* whereby he may lay up 300000 *l.* more in his Coffers yearly than the whole Kingdoms gain from strangers by forraign trade; who sees not then that all the mony in such a State, would suddenly be drawn into the Princes treasure, whereby the life of lands and arts must fail and fall to the ruin both of the publick and private wealth? So that a King who desires to lay up much mony must endeavour by all good means to maintain and encrease his forraign trade, because it is the sole way not only to lead him to his own ends, but also to enrich his Subjects to his farther benefit: for a Prince is esteemed no less powerful by having many rich and well affected Subjects, than by possessing much treasure in his Coffers.

But here we must meet with an Objection, which peradventure may be made concerning such States (whereof I have formerly spoken) which are of no great extent, and yet bordering upon mighty Princes, are therefore constrained to lay extraordinary taxes upon their subjects, whereby they procure to themselves very great incomes yearly, and are richly provided against any Forraign Invasions; yet have they no such great trade with Strangers, as that the overbalance or gain of the same may suffice to lay up the one half of that which they advance yearly, besides their own expences.

To this the answer is, that stil the gain of their Forraign Trade must be the rule of laying up their treasure, the which although it should not be much yearly, yet in the time of a long continued peace, and being well managed to advantage, it will become a great summe of money, able to make a long defence, which may end or divert the war. Neither are all the advances of Princes strictly tied to be massed up in treasure, for they have other no less necessary and profitable wayes to make them rich and powerfull, by issuing out continually a great part of the mony of their yearly Incomes to their subjects from whom it was first taken; as namely, by employ-

ing them to make Ships of War, with all the provisions thereunto belonging, to build and repair Forts, to buy and store
up Corn in the Granaries of each Province for a years use
(at least) aforehand, to serve in occasion of Dearth, which
cannot be neglected by a State but with great danger, to
erect Banks with their money for the encrease of their subjects trade, to maintain in their pay, Collonels, Captains,
Souldiers, Commanders, Mariners, and others, both by Sea
and Land, with good discipline, to fill their Store-houses (in
sundry strong places) and to abound in Gunpowder, Brim-
stone, Saltpeter, Shot, Ordnance, Musquets, Swords, Pikes,
Armours, Horses, and in many other such like Provisions
fitting War; all which will make them to be feared abroad,
and loved at home, especially if care be taken that all (as
neer as possible) be made out of the Matter and Manufacture of their own subjects, which bear the burden of the
yearly Contributions; for a Prince (in this case) is like the
stomach in the body, which if it cease to digest and distribute to the other members, it doth no sooner corrupt them,
but it destroyes it self.

Thus we have seen that a small State may lay up a great
wealth in necessary provisions, which are Princes Jewels, no
less precious than their Treasure, for in time of need they are
ready, and cannot otherwise be had (in some places) on the
suddain, whereby a State may be lost, whilest Munition is in
providing: so that we may account that Prince as poor who
can have no wares to buy at his need, as he that hath no
money to buy wares; for although *Treasure is said to be the
sinews of the War*, yet this is so because it doth provide, unite
& move the power of men, victuals, and munition where
and when the cause doth require; but if these things be
wanting in due time, what shall we then do with our mony?
the consideration of this, doth cause divers well-governed
States to be exceeding provident and well furnished of such
provisions, especially those Granaries and Storehouses with
that famous *Arsenal* of the *Venetians*, are to be admired for
the magnificence of the buildings, the quantity of the Muni-

tions and Stores both for Sea and Land, the multitude of the workmen, the diversity and excellency of the Arts, with the order of the government. They are rare and worthy things for Princes to behold and imitate; for Majesty without providence of competent force, and ability of necessary provisions is unassured.

CHAPTER XX

The order and means whereby we may draw up the ballance of our Forraign Trade.

Now, that we have sufficiently proved the Ballance of our Forraign Trade to be the true rule of our Treasure; It resteth that we shew by whom and in what manner the said ballance may be drawn up at all times, when it shall please the State to discover how we prosper or decline in this great and weighty business, wherein the Officers of his Majesties Customes are the onely Agents to be employed, because they have the accounts of all the wares which are issued out or brought into the Kingdome; and although (it is true) they cannot exactly set down the cost and charges of other mens goods bought here or beyond the seas; yet nevertheless, if they ground themselves upon the book of Rates, they shall be able to make such an estimate as may well satisfie this enquiry: for it is not expected that such an account can possibly be drawn up to a just ballance, it will suffice onely that the difference be not over great.

First therefore, concerning our Exportations, when we have valued their first cost, we must add twenty-five *per cent.* thereunto for the charges here, for fraight of Ships, ensurance of the *Adventure*, and the *Merchants* Gains; and for our Fishing Trades, which pay no Custome to his Majesty, the value of such Exportations may be easily esteem'd by good observations which have been made, and may continually be made, according to the increase or decrease of those affairs, the present estate of this commodity being valued at one hundred and forty thousand pounds issued yearly. Also we must add to our Exportations all the moneys which are carried out in Trade by license from his Majesty.

Secondly, for our Importations of Forraign Wares, the Custome-books serve onely to direct us concerning the quantity, for we must not value them as they are rated here, but as they cost us with all charges laden into our Ships beyond the Seas, in the respective places where they are bought: for the Merchants gain, the charges of Insurance, Fraight of Ships, Customes, Imposts, and other Duties here, which doe greatly indear them unto our use and consumption, are notwithstanding but Commutations amongst our selves, for the Stranger hath no part thereof: wherefore our said Importations ought to be valued at twenty five *per cent.* less than they are rated to be worth here. And although this may seem to be too great allowance upon many rich Commodities, which come but from the *Low Countreys* and other places neer hand, yet will it be found reasonable, when we consider it in gross Commodities, and upon Wares laden in remote Countreys, as our Pepper, which cost us, with charges, but four pence the pound in the *East Indies*, and it is here rated at twenty pence the pound: so that when all is brought into a *medium*, the valuation ought to be made as afore-written. And therefore, the order which hath been used to multiply the full rates upon wares inwards by twenty, would produce a very great errour in the Ballance, for in this manner the ten thousand bags of Pepper, which this year we have brought hither from the *East Indies*, should be valued at very near two hundred and fifty thousand pounds, whereas all this Pepper in the Kingdomes accompt, cost not above fifty thousand pounds, because the Indians have had no more of us, although we paid them extraordinary dear prices for the same. All the other charges (as I have said before) is but a change of effects amongst our selves, and from the Subject to the King, which cannot impoverish the Common-wealth. But it is true, that whereas nine thousand bags of the said Pepper are already shipped out for divers forraign parts; These and all other

Wares, forraign or domestick, which are thus transported Outwards, ought to be cast up by the rates of his Majesties Custome-money, multiplyed by twenty, or rather by twenty five (as I conceive) which will come neerer the reckoning, when we consider all our Trades to bring them into a *medium*.

Thirdly, we must remember, that all Wares exported or imported by Strangers (in their shipping) be esteemed by themselves, for what they carry out, the Kingdom hath only the first cost and the custom: And what they bring in, we must rate it as it is worth here, the Custom, Impost, and pety charges only deducted.

Lastly, there must be good notice taken of all the great losses which we receive at Sea in our Shipping either outward or homeward bound: for the value of the one is to be deducted from our Exportations, and the value of the other is to be added to our Importations: for to lose and to consume doth produce one and the same reckoning. Likewise if it happen that His Majesty doth make over any great sums of mony by Exchange to maintain a forraign war, where we do not feed and clothe the Souldiers, and Provide the armies, we must deduct all this charge out of our Exportations or add it to our Importations; for this expence doth either carry out or hinder the coming in of so much Treasure. And here we must remember the great collections of mony which are supposed to be made throughout the Realm yearly from our Recusants by Priests and Jesuits, who secretly convey the same unto their Colleges, Cloysters and Nunneries beyond the Seas, from whence it never returns to us again in any kind; therefore if this mischief cannot be prevented, yet it must be esteemed and set down as a cleer loss to the Kingdome, except (to ballance this) we will imagine that as great a value may perhaps come in from forraign Princes to their Pensioners here for Favours or Intelligence, which some States account good Policy, to purchase with great Liberality; the receipt whereof notwithstanding is plain Treachery.

There are yet some other petty things which seem to have reference to this Ballance, of which the said Officers of His Majesties Customs can take no notice, to bring them into the accompt. As namely, the expences of travailers, the gifts to Ambassadors and Strangers, the fraud of some rich goods not entred into the Custom-house, the gain which is made here by Strangers by change and re-change, Interest of mony, ensurance upon English mens goods and their lives: which can be little when the charges of their living here is deducted; besides that the very like advantages are as amply ministred unto the English in forraign Countreys, which doth counterpoize all these things, and therefore they are not considerable in the drawing up of the said Ballance.

IX

SIR WILLIAM PETTY

A TREATISE OF TAXES & CONTRIBUTIONS

NOTE

Sir William Petty (1623–1687) was educated for the profession of medicine, and pursued studies in that field at various
continental universities and at Oxford. After a short term as
professor of anatomy at Oxford, he spent several years in Ireland, directing the survey and distribution of the lands for-
feited after the rebellion. He then resumed his scientific
studies in London, devoting much time to ship-building experiments, and helping to found the Royal Society. In 1666 he
returned to Ireland where he spent most of the remaining years
of his life, managing his large estates, writing, and working for
administrative reforms. All his works show an intensely practical bent and a keen spirit of inquiry. None of them is very
systematically arranged, and even taken as a whole they do not
present a unified economic philosophy; but they contain many
passages of the greatest interest. Especially important are his
writings on "political arithmetic," in which he sought to deal
with political and economic matters "in terms of Number,
Weight, or Measure," thus anticipating modern statistical
methods. His chief works are *A Treatise of Taxes and Contributions* (1662), *Discourses on Political Arithmetic* (1691), *Quantu-
lumcunque concerning Money* (1682), and *Political Anatomy of
Ireland* (1672).

A TREATISE OF TAXES &
CONTRIBUTIONS[1]

CHAPTER III

How the Causes of the unquiet bearing of Taxes may be lessened.

WE have slightly gone through all the six Branches of the Publick Charge, and have (though imperfectly and in haste) shewn what would encrease, and what would abate them.

We come next to take away some of the general Causes of the unquiet bearing of Taxes, and yielding to Contributions, *viz.*

1. That the people think, the Sovereign askes more then he needs. To which we answer, 1. That if the Sovereign were sure to have what he wanted in due time, it were his own great dammage to draw away the money out of his Subjects hands, who by trade increase it, and to hoard it up in his own Coffers, where 'tis of no use even to himself, but lyable to be begged or vainly expended.

2. Let the Tax be never so great, if it be proportionable unto all, then no man suffers the loss of any Riches by it. For men (as we said but now) if the Estates of them all were either halfed or doubled, would in both cases remain equally rich. For they would each man have his former state, dignity and degree; and moreover, the Money leavied not going out of the Nation, the same also would remain as rich in comparison of any other Nation; onely the Riches of the Prince and People would differ for a little while, namely, until the money leavied from some, were again refunded upon the same, or other persons that paid it: In which case every

---

[1] Reprinted, with the consent of the publishers, from Hull's edition of Petty's Economic Works (Cambridge University Press).

man also should have his chance and opportunity to be made the better or worse by the new distribution; or if he lost by one, yet to gain by another.

3. Now that which angers men most is to be taxed above their Neighbours. To which I answer, that many times these surmizes are mistakes, many times they are chances, which in the next Tax may run more favourable; and if they be by design, yet it cannot be imagined, that it was by design of the Sovereign, but of some temporary Assessor, whose turn it may be to receive the *Talio* upon the next occasion from the very man he has wronged.

4. Men repine much, if they think the money leavyed will be expended on Entertainments, magnificent Shews, triumphal Arches, &c. To which I answer, that the same is a refunding the said moneys to the Tradesmen who work upon those things; which Trades though they seem vain and onely of ornament, yet they refund presently to the most useful; namely, to Brewers, Bakers, Taylours, Shoe-makers, &c. Moreover, the Prince hath no more pleasure in these Shews and Entertainments then 100000. others of his meanest Subjects have, whom, for all their grumbling, we see to travel many miles to be spectators of these mistaken and distasted vanities.

5. The people often complain, that the King bestows the money he raises from the people upon his Favourites: To which we answer; that what is given to Favourites, may at the next step or transmigration, come into our own hands, or theirs unto whom we wish well, and think do deserve it.

Secondly, as this man is a Favourite to day, so another, or our selves, may be hereafter; favour being of a very slippery and moveable nature, and not such a thing as we need much to envy; for the same way that —— leads up an hill, leads also down the same. Besides, there is nothing in the Lawes or Customes of *England*, which excludes any of the meanest mans Childe, from arriving to the highest Offices in this Kingdom, much less debars him from the Personall kindness of his Prince.

All these imaginations (whereunto the vulgar heads are subject) do cause a backwardness to pay, and that necessitates the Prince to severity. Now this lighting upon some poor, though stubborn, stiffnecked Refuser, charged with Wife and Children, gives the credulous great occasion to complain of Oppression, and breeds ill blood as to all other matters; feeding the ill humours already in being.

6. Ignorance of the Number, Trade and Wealth of the people, is often the reason why the said people are needlessly troubled, *viz.* with the double charge and vexation of two, or many Levies, when one might have served: Examples whereof have been seen in late Poll-moneys; in which (by reason of not knowing the state of the people, *viz.* how many there were of each Taxable sort, and the want of sensible markes whereby to rate men, and the confounding of Estates with Titles and Offices) great mistakes were committed.

Besides, for not knowing the Wealth of the people, the Prince knows not what they can bear; and for not knowing the Trade, he can make no Judgment of the proper season when to demand his Exhibitions.

7. Obscurities and doubts, about the right of imposing, hath been the cause of great and ugly Reluctancies in the people, and of Involuntary Severities in the Prince; an eminent Example whereof was the Ship-money, no small cause of twenty years calamity to the whole Kingdom.

8. Fewness of people, is real poverty; and a Nation wherein are Eight Millions of people, are more then twice as rich as the same scope of Land wherein are but Four; For the same Governours which are the great charge, may serve near as well, for the greater, as the lesser number.

Secondly, If the people be so few, as that they can live, *Ex sponte Creatis*, or with little labour, such as is Grazing, &c. they become wholly without Art. No man that will not exercise his hands, being able to endure the tortures of the mind, which much thoughtfulness doth occasion.

9. Scarcity of money, is another cause of the bad payment of Taxes; for if we consider, that of all the wealth of this Nation, *viz.* Lands, Housing, Shipping, Commodities, Furniture, Plate, and Money, that scarce one part of an hundred is Coin; and that perhaps there is scarce six millions of Pounds now in *England*, that is but twenty shillings a head for every head in the Nation. We may easily judge, how difficult it is for men of competent estates, to pay a Summe of money on a sudden; which if they cannot compass, Severities, and Charges ensue; and that with reason, though unluckie enough, it being more tolerable to undoe one particular Member, then to endanger the whole, notwithstanding indeed it be more tolerable for one particular Member to be undone with the whole, then alone.

10. It seems somewhat hard, that all Taxes should be paid in money, that is, (when the King hath occasion to Victual his Ships at *Portsmouth*) that Fat Oxen, and Corn should not be received in kind, but that Farmers must first carry their Corn perhaps ten Miles to sell, and turn into money; which being paid to the King, is again reconverted into Corn, fetcht many miles further.

Moreover, the Farmer for haste is forced to under-sell his Corn, and the King for haste likewise, is forced to over-buy his provisions. Whereas the paying in kinde, *Pro Hic & Nunc*, would lessen a considerable grievance to the poor people.

The next consideration shall be of the consequences, and effects of too great a Tax, not in respect of particular men, of which we have spoken before, but to the whole people in general: To which I say, that there is a certain measure, and proportion of money requisite to drive the trade of a Nation, more or less then which would prejudice the same. Just as there is a certain proportion of Farthings necessary in a small retail Trade, to change silver money, and to even such reckonings, as cannot be adjusted with the smallest silver pieces. For money, (made of Gold and silver) is to the τὰ χρήζα (that is to the matter of our Food and Covering) but as Farthings, and other local extrinsick money, is to the Gold and Silver species.

Now as the proportion of the number of Farthings requisite in comerse is to be taken from the number of people, the frequency of their exchanges; as also, and principally from the value of the smallest silver pieces of money; so in like maner, the proportion of money requisite to our Trade, is to be likewise taken from the frequency of commutations, and from the bigness of the payments, that are by Law or Custome usually made otherwise. From whence it follows, that where there are Registers of Lands, whereby the just value of each mans interest in them, may be well known; and where there are Depositories of the τὰ χρήζα, as of Metals, Cloth, Linnen, Leather, and other Usefuls; and where there are Banks of money also, there less money is necessary to drive the Trade. For if all the greatest payments be made in Lands, and the other perhaps down to ten pound, or twenty pound be made by credit in Lombars or Money-Banks: It follows, that there needs onely money to pay sums less than those aforementioned; just as fewer Farthings are requisite for change, where there be plenty of silver two Pences, then where the least silver piece is six Pence.

To apply all this, I say, that if there be too much money in a Nation, it were good for the Commonalty, as well as the King, and no harm even to particular men, if the King had in his Coffers, all that is superfluous, no more then if men were permitted to pay their Taxes in any thing they could best spare.

On the other side, if the largeness of a publick Exhibition should leave less money then is necessary to drive the Nations Trade, then the mischief thereof would be the doing of less work, which is the same as lessening the people, or their Art and Industry; for a hundred pound passing a hundred hands for Wages, causes a 10000 l. worth of Commodities to be produced, which hands would have been idle and useless, had there not been this continual motive to their employment.

Taxes if they be presently expended upon our own Domestick Commodities, seem to me, to do little harm to the whole Body of the people, onely they work a change in the Riches and Fortunes of particular men; and particularly by transferring the same from the Landed and Lazy, to the Crafty and Industrious. As for example, if a Gentleman have let his Lands to Farm for a hundred pound *per annum*, for several years or lives, and he be taxed twenty pound *per annum*, to maintain a Navy; then the effect hereof will be, that this Gentlemans twenty pound *per annum*, will be distributed amongst Seaman, Ship-Carpenters, and other Trades relating to Naval matters; but if the Gentleman had his Land in his own hands, then being taxed a Fifth part, he would raise his Rents near the same proportion upon his under Tenants, or would sell his Cattle, Corn, and Wooll a Fifth part dearer; the like also would all other subdependents on him do; and thereby recover in some measure, what he paid. Lastly, but if all the money levied were thrown into the Sea, then the ultimate effect would onely be, that every man must work a fifth part the harder, or retrench a fifth part of his consumptions, *viz.* the former, if forreign Trade be improveable, and the latter, if it be not.

This, I conceive, were the worst of Taxes in a well policyed State; but in other States, where is not a certain prevention of Beggary and Theevery, that is a sure livelihood for men wanting imployment; there, I confess, an excessive Taxe, causes excessive and insuperable want, even of natural necessities, and that on a sudden, so as ignorant particular persons cannot finde out what way to subsist by; and this, by the law of Nature, must cause sudden effects to relieve it self, that is, Rapines, Frauds; and this again must bring Death, Mutilations, and Imprisonments, according to the present Laws which are Mischiefs, and Punishments, as well unto the State, as to the particular sufferers of them.

CHAPTER IV

*Of the several wayes of Taxe, and first, of setting a part, a
proportion of the whole Territory for Publick uses, in the
nature of Crown Lands; and secondly, by way of Assess-
ment, or Land-Taxe.*

But supposing, that the several causes of Publick Charge are
lessened as much as may be, and that the people be well
satisfied, and contented to pay their just shares of what is
needful for their Government and Protection, as also for
the Honour of their Prince and Countrey: It follows now to
propose the several wayes, and expedients, how the same
may be most easily, speedily, and insensibly collected. The
which I shall do, by exposing the conveniencies and inconveniences of some of the principal wayes of Levyings, used of
later years within the several States of *Europe*: unto which
others of smaller and more rare use may be referred.

Imagine then, a number of people, planted in a Territory,
who had upon Computation concluded, that two Millions of
pounds *per annum*, is necessary to the publick charges. Or
rather, who going more wisely to work, had computed a
twenty fifth part of the proceed of all their Lands and Labours, were to be the *Excisum*, or the part to be cut out,
and laid aside for publick uses. Which proportions perhaps
are fit enough to the affairs of *England*, but of that hereafter.

Now the question is, how the one or the other shall be
raised. The first way we propose, is, to Excize the very
Land it self in kinde; that is, to cut out of the whole twenty
five Millions, which are said to be in *England* and *Wales*, as
much Land *in specie*, as whereof the Rack-rent would be two
Millions, *viz.* about four Millions of Acres, which is about a
sixth part of the whole; making the said four Millions to be
Crown Lands, and as the four Counties intended to be reserved in *Ireland* upon the forfeitures were. Or else to excize
a sixth part of the rent of the whole, which is about the proportion, that the Adventures and Souldiers in *Ireland* retri-

bute to the King, as Quit Rents. Of which two wayes, the latter is manifestly the better, the King having more security, and more obligees; provided the trouble and charge of this universal Collection, exceed not that of the other advantage considerably.

This way in a new State would be good, being agreed upon, as it was in *Ireland*, before men had even the possession of any Land at all; wherefore whosoever buyes Land in *Ireland* hereafter, is no more concerned with the Quit Rents wherewith they are charged, then if the Acres were so much the fewer; or then men are, who buy Land, out of which they know Tythes are to be paid. And truly that Countrey is happy, in which by Original Accord, such a Rent is reserved, as whereby the Publick charge may be born, without contingent, sudden, superadditions, in which lies the very *Ratio* of the burthen of all Contributions and Exactions. For in such cases, as was said before, it is not onely the Landlord payes, but every man who eats but an Egg, or an Onion of the growth of his Lands; or who useth the help of any Artisan, which feedeth on the same.

But if the same were propounded in *England*, *viz.* if an aliquot part of every Landlords Rent were excinded or retrenched, then those whose Rents were settled, and determined for long times to come, would chiefly bear the burthen of such an Imposition, and others have a benefit thereby. For suppose *A*. and *B*. have each of them a parcel of Land, of equal goodness and value; suppose also that *A*. hath let his parcel for twenty one years at twenty pound *per annum*, but that *B*. is free; now there comes out a Taxe of a fifth part; hereupon *B*. will not let under 25 l. that his remainder may be twenty, whereas *A*. must be contented with sixteen neat; nevertheless the Tenants of *A*. will sell the proceed of their bargain at the same rate, that the Tenants of *B*. shall do. The effect of all this is; First, that the Kings fifth part of *B*. his Farm shall be greater then before. Secondly, that the Farmer to *B*. shall gain more then before the Taxe. Thirdly, that the Tenant or Farmer of *A*. shall gain as much as the King and Tenant to *B*. both. Fourthly, the Tax doth ultimately light upon the Landlord *A*. and the Consumptioners. From whence it follows, that a Land-taxe resolves into an irregular Excize upon consumptions, that those bear it most, who least complain. And lastly, that some Landlords may gain, and onely such whose Rents are predetermined shall loose; and that doubly, *viz*. one way by the raising of their revenues, and the other by enhansing the prices of provisions upon them.

Another way is an *Excisium* out of the Rent of Houseing, which is much more uncertain then that of Land. For an House is of a double nature, *viz*. one, wherein it is a way and means of expence; the other, as 'tis an Instrument and Tool of gain: for a Shop in *London* of less capacity and less charge in building then a fair Dining-Room in the same House unto which both do belong, shall nevertheless be of the greater value; so also shall a Dungeon, Sellar, then a pleasant Chamber; because the one is expence, the other profit. Now the way [of a] Land-taxe rates housing, as of the latter nature, but the Excize, as of the former.

We might adde hereunto, that housing is sometimes disproportionately taxed to discourage Building, especially upon new Foundations, thereby to prevent the growth of a City, suppose *London;* such excessive and overgrown Cities being dangerous to Monarchy, though the more secure when the supremacy is in Citizens of such places themselves, as in *Venice*.

But we say, that such checking of new Buildings signifies nothing to this purpose; forasmuch as Buildings do not encrease, until the People already have increased: but the remedy of the above mentioned dangers is to be sought in the causes of the encrease of People, the which if they can be nipt, the other work will necessarily be done.

But what then is the true effect of forbidding to build upon new foundations? I answer to keep and fasten the City to its old seat and ground-plot, the which encouragement for new Buildings will remove, as it comes to pass almost in all great Cities, though insensibly, and not under many years progression.

The reason whereof is, because men are unwilling to build new houses at the charge of pulling down their old, where both the old house it self, and the ground it stands upon do make a much dearer ground-plot for a new house, and yet far less free and convenient; wherefore men build upon new free foundations, and cobble up old houses, until they become fundamentally irreparable, at which time they become either the dwelling of the Rascality, or in process of time return to waste and Gardens again, examples whereof are many even about *London*.

Now if great Cities are naturally apt to remove their Seats, I ask which way? I say, in the case of *London*, it must be Westward, because the Windes blowing near ¾ of the year from the West, the dwellings of the West end are so much the more free from the fumes, steams, and stinks of the whole Easterly Pyle; which where Seacoal is burnt is a great matter. Now if it follow from hence, that the Pallaces of the greatest men will remove Westward, it will also naturally follow, that the dwellings of others who depend upon them will creep after them. This we see in *London*, where the Noblemens ancient houses are now become Halls for Companies, or turned into Tenements, and all the Pallaces are gotten Westward; Insomuch, as I do not doubt but that five hundred years hence, the King's Pallace will be near *Chelsey*, and the old building of *Whitehall* converted to uses more answerable to their quality. For to build a new Royal Pallace upon the same ground will be too great a confinement, in respect of Gardens and other magnificencies, and withall a disaccommodation in the time of the work; but it rather seems to me, that the next Palace will be built from the whole present contignation of houses at such a distance as the old Pallace of *Westminster* was from the City of *London*, when the Archers began to bend their bowes just without *Ludgate*, and when all the space between the *Thames*, *Fleet-street*, and *Holborn* was as *Finsbury-Fields* are now.

This digression I confess to be both impertinent to the business of Taxes, and in it self almost needless; for why should we trouble our selves what shall be five hundred years hence, not knowing what a day may bring forth; and since 'tis not unlikely, but that before that time we may be all transplanted from hence into *America*, these Countreys being overrun with Turks, and made waste, as the Seats of the famous Eastern Empires at this day are.

Onely I think 'tis certain, that while ever there are people in *England*, the greatest cohabitation of them will be about the place which is now *London*, the *Thames* being the most commodious River of this Island, and the seat of *London* the most commodious part of the *Thames*; so much doth the means of facilitating Carriage greaten a City, which may put us in minde of employing our idle hands about mending the High-wayes, making Bridges, Cawseys, and Rivers navigable: Which considerations brings me back round into my way of Taxes, from whence I digrest.

But before we talk too much of Rents, we should endeavour to explain the mysterious nature of them, with reference as well to Money, the rent of which we call usury; as to that of Lands and Houses, afore-mentioned.

Suppose a man could with his own hands plant a certain scope of Land with Corn, that is, could Digg, or Plough, Harrow, Weed, Reap, Carry home, Thresh, and Winnow so much as the Husbandry of this Land requires; and had withal Seed wherewith to sowe the same. I say, that when this man hath subducted his seed out of the proceed of his Harvest, and also, what himself hath both eaten and given to others in exchange for Clothes, and other Natural necessaries; that the remainder of Corn is the natural and true Rent of the Land for that year; and the *medium* of seven years, or rather of so many years as makes up the Cycle, within which Dearths and Plenties make their revolution, doth give the ordinary Rent of the Land in Corn.

But a further, though collaterall question may be, how much English money this Corn or Rent is worth? I answer, so much as the money, which another single man can save, within the same time, over and above his expence, if he imployed himself wholly to produce and make it; *viz.* Let another man go travel into a Countrey where is Silver, there Dig it, Refine it, bring it to the same place where the other man planted his Corn; Coyne it, &c. the same person, all the while of his working for Silver, gathering also food for his necessary livelihood, and procuring himself covering, &c. I say, the Silver of the one, must be esteemed of equal value with the Corn of the other: the one being perhaps twenty Ounces and the other twenty Bushels. From whence it follows, that the price of a Bushel of this Corn to be an Ounce of Silver.

And forasmuch as possibly there may be more Art and Hazzard in working about the Silver, then about the Corn, yet all comes to the same pass; for let a hundred men work ten years upon Corn, and the same number of men, the same time, upon Silver; I say, that the neat proceed of the Silver is the price of the whole neat proceed of the Corn, and like parts of the one, the price of like parts of the other. Although not so many of those who wrought in Silver, learned the Art of refining and coining, or out-lived the dangers and diseases of working in the Mines. And this also is the way of pitching the true proportion, between the values of Gold and Silver, which many times is set but by popular errour, sometimes more, sometimes less, diffused in the world; which errour (by the way) is the cause of our having been pestred with too much Gold heretofore, and wanting it now.

This, I say, to be the foundation of equallizing and ballancing of values; yet in the superstructures and practices hereupon, I confess there is much variety, and intricacy; of which hereafter.

The world measures things by Gold and Silver, but principally the latter; for there may not be two measures, and consequently the better of many must be the onely of all; that is, by fine silver of a certain weight: but now if it be hard to measure the weight and fineness of silver, as by the different reports of the ablest Saymasters I have known it to be; and if silver granted to be of the same fineness and weight, rise and fall in its price, and be more worth at one place then another, not onely for being farther from the Mines, but for other accidents, and may be more worth at present, then a moneth or other small time hence; and if it differ in its proportion unto the several things valued by it, in several ages upon the increase and diminution thereof, we shall endeavour to examine some other natural Standards and Measures, without derogating from the excellent use of these.

Our Silver and Gold we call by severall names, as in *England* by pounds, shillings, and pence, all which may be called and understood by either of the three. But that which I would say upon this matter is, that all things ought to be valued by two natural Denominations, which is Land and Labour; that is, we ought to say, a Ship or garment is worth such a measure of Land, with such another measure of Labour; forasmuch as both Ships and Garments were the creatures of Lands and mens Labours thereupon: This being true, we should be glad to finde out a natural Par between Land and Labour, so as we might express the value by either of them alone as well or better then by both, and reduce one into the other as easily and certainly as we reduce pence into pounds. Wherefore we would be glad to finde the natural values of the Fee simple of Land, though but no better then we have done that of the *usus fructus* abovementioned, which we attempt as followeth.

Having found the Rent or value of the *usus fructus per annum*, the question is, how many years purchase (as we usually say) is the Fee simple naturally worth? If we say an infinite number, then an Acre of Land would be equal in value to a thousand Acres of the same Land; which is absurd, an infinity of unites being equal to an infinity of thousands. Wherefore we must pitch upon some limited number, and that I apprehend to be the number of years, which I conceive one man of fifty years old, another of twenty eight, and another of seven years old, all being alive together may be thought to live; that is to say, of a Grandfather, Father, and Childe; few men having reason to take care of more remote Posterity: for if a man be a great Grandfather, he himself is so much the nearer his end, so as there are but three in a continual line of descent usually co-existing together; and as some are Grandfathers at forty years, yet as many are not till above sixty, and *sic de cæteris*.

Wherefore I pitch the number of years purchase, that any Land is naturally worth, to be the ordinary extent of three such persons their lives. Now in *England* we esteem three lives equal to one and twenty years, and consequently the value of Land, to be about the same number of years purchase. Possibly if they thought themselves mistaken in the one, (as the observator on the Bills of Mortality thinks they are) they would alter in the other, unless the consideration of the force of popular errour and dependance of things already concatenated, did hinder them.

This I esteem to be the number of years purchase where Titles are good, and where there is a moral certainty of enjoying the purchase. But in other Countreys Lands are worth nearer thirty years purchase, by reason of the better Titles, more people, and perhaps truer opinion of the value and duration of three lives.

And in some places, Lands are worth yet more years purchase by reason of some special honour, pleasures, priviledge or jurisdiction annexed unto them.

On the other hand, Lands are worth fewer years purchase (as in *Ireland*) for the following reasons, which I have here set down, as unto the like whereof the cause of the like cheapness in any other place may be imputed.

First, in *Ireland*, by reason of the frequent Rebellions, (in which if you are conquered, all is lost; or if you conquer, yet you are subject to swarms of thieves and robbers) and the envy which precedent missions of English have against the subsequent, perpetuity it self is but forty years long, as within which time some ugly disturbance hath hitherto hap-

pened almost ever since the first coming of the English
thither.

2. The Claims upon Claims which each hath to the others
Estates, and the facility of making good any pretence whatsoever by the favour of some one or other of the many Governours and Ministers which within forty years shall be in
power there; as also by the frequency of false testimonies,
and abuse of solemn Oaths.

3. The paucity of Inhabitants, there being not above the
$\frac{1}{5}$th part so many as the Territory would maintain, and of
those but a small part do work at all, and yet a smaller work
so much as in other Countreys.

4. That a great part of the Estates, both real and personal in *Ireland*, are owned by Absentees, and such as draw
over the profits raised out of *Ireland* refunding nothing; so
as *Ireland* exporting more then it imports doth yet grow
poorer to a paradox.

5. The difficulty of executing justice, so many of those in
power being themselves protected by Offices, and protecting
others. Moreover, the number of criminous and indebted
persons being great, they favour their like in Juries, Offices,
and wheresoever they can: Besides, the Countrey is seldom
[rich] enough to give due encouragement to profound Judges
and Lawyers, which makes judgements very casual; ignorant men being more bold to be apt and arbitrary, then such
as understand the dangers of it. But all this a little care
in due season might remedy, so as to bring *Ireland* in a few
years to the same level of values with other places; but of
this also elsewhere more at large, for in the next place we
shall come to Usury.

CHAPTER V

Of Usury

What reason there is for taking or giving Interest or Usury
for any thing which we may certainly have again whenso-
ever we call for it, I see not; nor why Usury should be
scrupled, where money or other necessaries valued by it, is

lent to be paid at such a time and place as the Borrower chuseth, so as the Lender cannot have his money paid him back where and when himself pleaseth, I also see not. Wherefore when a man giveth out his money upon condition that he may not demand it back until a certain time to come, whatsoever his own necessities shall be in the mean time, he certainly may take a compensation for this inconvenience which he admits against himself: And this allowance is that we commonly call Usury.

And when one man furnisheth another with money at some distant place, and engages under great Penalties to pay him there, and at a certain day besides; the consideration for this, is that we call Exchange or local Usury.

As for example, if a man wanting money at *Carlisle* in the heat of the late Civil Wars, when the way was full of Souldiers and Robbers, and the passage by Sea very long, troublesome, and dangerous, and seldom passed; why might not another take much more then an 100 l. at *London* for warranting the like Summe to be paid at *Carlisle* on a certain day?

Now the Questions arising hence are; what are the natural Standards of Usury and Exchange? As for Usury, the least that can be, is the Rent of so much Land as the money lent will buy, where the security is undoubted; but where the security is casual, then a kinde of ensurance must be enterwoven with the simple natural Interest, which may advance the Usury very conscionably unto any height below the Principal it self. Now if things are so in *England*, that really there is no such security as abovementioned, but that all are more or less hazardous, troublesome, or chargeable to make, I see no reason for endeavoring to limit Usury upon time, any more then that upon place, which the practice of the world doth not, unless it be that those who make such Laws were rather Borrowers then Lenders: But of the vanity and fruitlessness of making Civil Positive Laws against the Laws of Nature, I have spoken elsewhere, and instanced in several particulars.

As for the natural measures of Exchange, I say, that in times of Peace, the greatest Exchange can be but the labour of carrying the money *in specie*, but where are hazards [and] emergent uses for money more in one place then another, &c. or opinions of these true or false, the Exchange will be governed by them.

Parallel unto this, is something which we omitted concerning the price of Land; for as great need of money heightens Exchange, so doth great need of Corn raise the price of that likewise, and consequently of the Rent of the Land that bears Corn, and lastly of the Land it self; as for example, if the Corn which feedeth *London*, or an Army, be brought forty miles thither, then the Corn growing within a mile of *London*, or the quarters of such Army, shall have added unto its natural price, so much as the charge of bringing it thirty nine miles doth amount unto: And unto perishable Commodities, as fresh fish, fruits, &c. the ensurance upon the hazard of corrupting, &c. shall be added also; and finally, unto him that eats these things there (suppose in Taverns) shall be added the charge of all the circumstancial appurtenances of House-rent, Furniture, Attendance, and the Cooks skill as well as his labour to accompany the same.

Hence it comes to pass, that Lands intrinsically alike near populous places, such as where the perimeter of the Area that feeds them is great, will not onely yield more Rent for these Reasons, but also more years purchase then in remote places, by reason of the pleasure and honour extraordinary of having Lands there; for

Omne tulit punctum qui miscuit utile dulci.

. . . .

The TABLE [1]

But to make nearer approaches to the perfection of this Work, 'twould be expedient to know the Content of Acres of every Parish, and withal, what quantity of Butter, Cheese, Corn, and Wooll, was raised out of it for three years conse-

---

[1] From *The Political Anatomy of Ireland.* — ED.

quent; for thence the natural Value of the Land may be known, and by the number of People living within a Market-days Journey, and the Value of their housing, which shews the Quality and Expence of the said People; I would hope to come to the knowledg of the Value of the said Commodities, and consequently the Value of the Land, by deducting the hire of Working-People in it. And this brings me to the most important Consideration in Political Oeconomies, *viz.* how to make a *Par* and *Equation* between Lands and Labour, so as to express the Value of any thing by either alone. To which purpose, suppose two Acres of Pasture-land inclosed, and put thereinto a wean'd Calf, which I suppose in twelve Months will become 1 *C.* heavier in eatable Flesh; then 1 *C.* weight of such Flesh, which I suppose fifty days Food, and the Interest of the Value of the Calf, is the value or years Rent of the Land. But if a mans labour —— for a year can make the said Land to yield more than sixty days Food of the same, or of any other kind, then that overplus of days food is the Wages of the Man; both being expressed by the number of days food. That some Men will eat more than others, is not material, since by a days food we understand $\frac{1}{100}$ part of what 100 of all Sorts and Sizes will eat, so as to Live, Labour, and Generate. And that a days food of one sort, may require more labour to produce, than another sort, is also not material, since we understand the easiest-gotten food of the respective Countries of the World.

As for example, I suppose a pint of Oatmeal equal to half a pint of Rice, or a quart of Milk, or a pound of Bread, or a pound and quarter of Flesh, *&c.* each, in the respective place where each is the easiest gotten food. But if Rice be brought out of *India* into *Ireland*, or Oatmeal carried from *Ireland* thither; then in *India* the pint of Oatmeal must be dearer than half a pint of Rice, by the freight and hazard of Carriage, *& vice-versa, & sic de cæteris*. For, as for pleasant tast, I question whether there be any certainty, or regularity of the same in Nature, the same depending upon Novelty, opinion of Virtue, the recommendation of others, *&c.*

Wherefore the days food of an adult Man, at a Medium, and not the days labour, is the common measure of Value, and seems to be as regular and constant as the value of fine Silver. For an ounce, suppose, of Silver in *Peru* is equivalent to a days food, but the same in *Russia* is equivalent to four days food, by reason of the Freight, and hazard in carrying the same from *Peru* to *Russia*; and in *Russia* the price of Silver shall grow to be worth more days labour, if a Workman can by the esteem and request of Silver Utensils earn more than he can on other materials. Wherefore I valued an *Irish* Cabbin at the number of days food, which the Maker spent in building of it.

By the same way we must make a Par and Equation between Art and Simple Labour; for if by such Simple Labour I could dig and prepare for Seed a hundred Acres in a thousand days; suppose then, I spend a hundred days in studying a more compendious way, and in contriving Tools for the same purpose; but in all that hundred days dig nothing, but in the remaining nine hundred days I dig two hundred Acres of Ground; then I say, that the said Art which cost but one hundred days Invention is worth one Mans labour for ever; because the new Art, and one Man, perform'd as much as two Men could have done without it.

By the same way we make an Equation between Art and Opinion. For if a Picture-maker, suppose, make Pictures at 5 *l.* each; but then, find that more Persons would employ him at that rate than his time would extend to serve them in, it will certainly come to pass that this Artist will consider whether as many of those who apply to him at 5 *l.* each Picture, will give 6 *l.* as will take up his whole time to accommodate; and upon this Computation he pitcheth the Rate of his Work.

By the same way also an Equation may be made between drudging Labour, and Favour, Acquaintance, Interest, Friends, Eloquence, Reputation, Power, Authority, &c. All which I thought not amiss to intimate as of the same kind with finding an Equation between Land and Labour, all these not very pertinent to the Proportionation of the several Counties of *Ireland*.

Wherefore to return to the matter in hand, I say, that the Quantity of Commodity produced, and the Quantity of the —— shews the effects of the Land; and the number of People living thereupon, with the Quality of their housing, shews the Value of the Commodity; for one days delicate and exquisite Food may be worth ten of ordinary. Now the Nature of Peoples feeding may be estimated by the visible part of their Expence, which is their housing. But such helps of knowing the Value of Lands, I am not yet able to furnish.

X

PHILIPP W. VON HORNICK

OESTERREICH ÜBER ALLES, WANN ES NUR NUR WILL

NOTE

PHILIPP WILHELM VON HORNICK (1638–1712) was the son of Hofrat Ludwig von Hornick. He studied law at Ingolstadt, and received his doctorate in 1661. Returning to Vienna, he followed his profession for some years, and in 1682 published two tracts on public law, in which he vigorously attacked the French claims to German territory. This was followed two years later by his famous *Oesterreich über Alles*, a thoroughly typical Mercantile production, which he published anonymously. It was very popular for a generation or more and went through twelve editions. In 1690 he entered the service of the Cardinal of Passau, by whom he was later appointed privy councillor. His last publication was the *Historische Anzeigen von den Privilegien des Erzhauses Oesterreich* (1708).

AUSTRIA OVER ALL IF SHE ONLY WILL

I

NINE PRINCIPAL RULES OF NATIONAL ECONOMY

IF the might and eminence of a country consist in its surplus of gold, silver, and all other things necessary or convenient for its *subsistence*, derived, so far as possible, from its own resources, without *dependence* upon other countries, and in the proper fostering, use, and application of these, then it follows that a general national *economy* (*Landes-Oeconomie*) should consider how such a surplus, fostering, and enjoyment can be brought about, without *dependence* upon others, or where this is not feasible in every respect, with as little *dependence* as possible upon foreign countries, and sparing use of the country's own cash. For this purpose the following nine rules are especially serviceable.

First, to inspect the country's soil with the greatest care, and not to leave the agricultural possibilities or a single corner or clod of earth unconsidered. Every useful form of *plant* under the sun should be experimented with, to see whether it is adapted to the country, for the distance or nearness of the sun is not all that counts. Above all, no trouble or expense should be spared to discover gold and silver.

Second, all commodities found in a country, which cannot be used in their natural state, should be worked up within the country; since the payment for *manufacturing* generally exceeds the value of the raw material by two, three, ten, twenty, and even a hundred fold, and the neglect of this is an abomination to prudent managers.

Third, for carrying out the above two rules, there will be need of people, both for producing and cultivating the raw materials and for working them up. Therefore, attention should be given to the population, that it may be as large as the country can support, this being a well-ordered state's most important concern, but, unfortunately, one that is often neglected. And the people should be turned by all possible means from idleness to remunerative *professions;* instructed and encouraged in all kinds of *inventions,* arts, and trades; and, if necessary, instructors should be brought in from foreign countries for this.

Fourth, gold and silver once in the country, whether from its own mines or obtained by *industry* from foreign countries, are under no circumstances to be taken out for any purpose, so far as possible, or allowed to be buried in chests or coffers, but must always remain in *circulation;* nor should much be permitted in uses where they are at once *destroyed* and cannot be utilized again. For under these conditions, it will be impossible for a country that has once acquired a considerable supply of cash, especially one that possesses gold and silver mines, ever to sink into poverty; indeed, it is impossible that it should not continually increase in wealth and property. Therefore,

Fifth, the inhabitants of the country should make every effort to get along with their domestic products, to confine their luxury to these alone, and to do without foreign products as far as possible (except where great need leaves no alternative, or if not need, wide-spread, unavoidable abuse, of which Indian spices are an example). And so on.

Sixth, in case the said purchases were indispensable because of necessity or *irremediable* abuse, they should be obtained from these foreigners at first hand, so far as possible, and not for gold or silver, but in exchange for other domestic wares.

Seventh, such foreign commodities should in this case be imported in unfinished form, and worked up within the country, thus earning the wages of *manufacture* there.

Eighth, opportunities should be sought night and day for selling the country's superfluous goods to these foreigners in manufactured form, so far as this is necessary, and for gold and silver; and to this end, *consumption,* so to speak, must be sought in the farthest ends of the earth, and developed in every possible way.

Ninth, except for important considerations, no importation should be allowed under any circumstances of commodities of which there is a sufficient supply of suitable quality at home; and in this matter neither sympathy nor compassion should be shown foreigners, be they friends, kinsfolk, *allies*, or enemies. For all friendship ceases, when it involves my own weakness and ruin. And this holds good, even if the domestic commodities are of poorer quality, or even higher priced. For it would be better to pay for an article two dollars which remain in the country than only one which goes out, however strange this may seem to the ill-informed.

There is no need of further elucidating these fundamental rules of a general national *economy*. Their reasonableness is obvious to every man of intelligence. I do not mean to exclude all exceptions. The circumstances of each country may allow them now and then, but only rarely. If countries and their way of looking after things are considered according to these rules, it will be easy to judge their general *economy*. I do not presume to instruct anyone; but, in all modesty, I venture to say that any manager and administrator of a general national *economy*, whether of high or low degree, who judges himself according to these rules, will be able to tell easily whether he has properly administered his duties or not. They are not the *invention* of a *speculative* mind. They follow from the nature of things, reason confirms them, and in every place where riches flourish all or part of them are applied. Therefore my reader will not resent my delaying him somewhat with this bit of *theory*; and if he has intelligence, which I do not doubt, he will easily discover its purpose. I believe that he will gradually see the light, if he has not already done so, and realize whether the well-known scarcity of money in Austria is to be ascribed to nature, or to indolence and carelessness, that is, to human will alone. "This is an old story," many perhaps will say, "a sort of commercial or *cameral primer*, which we have known a long time." But why is such a primer in so many places unfortunately so little practised, or even learned? By this standard, then, and this touch-stone we wish to test our Austria: to investigate her natural gifts as far as possible, and then to consider how they can be developed.

II

HOW TO INSTITUTE REFORMS IN THE NATIONAL ECONOMY PROPERLY

"Good preaching," some one will reproach me. "He may well cry the loudest over the pain of a sick man who can help least. Show us what to do about it." Now I have already said that I did not intend to explain how to *apply* our rules, but to leave that to those who have general oversight of the Austrian realm, and who are in charge of its administration. If my unauthoritative ideas are desired, however, I should like to begin with the above-mentioned fifth rule, and advise the Austrians TO BE CONTENT FOR A WHILE WITH THEIR OWN GOODS, WITH THEIR OWN MANUFACTURES, HOWEVER BAD THEY MAY BE AT FIRST, AND TO REFRAIN FROM FOREIGN ONES, KEEPING THEIR GOOD GOLD AND SILVER IN THEIR POCKETS. This would fit in with all the other rules, and everything else would follow from this alone. For the ninth rule is practically included in this fifth one; and if people would use nothing but domestic *manufactures*, the children and inhabitants of the country would be compelled (most of them gladly) to turn their hands to their own *manufactures*, and to work up the domestic raw materials. In this way the second rule would be greatly furthered. And since artisans go where they can get a living, and many foreigners would necessarily be out of work as a result of the prohibition of their *products*, and sometimes even lack our raw materials, they would be compelled to come to Austria, in order to seek work, necessary raw materials, and their living, and to settle there; thus furthering the principal part of the third rule, namely, the development of a population engaged in *manu-*

factures. Then foreigners, having little more of their own to give, would lose the magnet with which they attract away our gold and silver. And thus the fourth rule would be *observed*, and the money would remain in the country. Since we could not do without a few things, however, such as Indian spices, fish products, and, for a time, raw silk, &c., we would have cause, opportunity, and material to exchange our surplus domestic products with our neighbors and others, without giving the most indispensable goods for them, according to the advice of the sixth rule. We would be able to do without these all the more easily, since the erection of domestic *factories*, immigration of foreign artisans, and growth of the country's population would increase domestic *consumption;* whereby the eighth rule would be greatly furthered. And once the country had acquired a supply of cash in this way (as must certainly happen in a very few years, even if we kept only the annual product of our mines), then with the means would come the spirit, the desire, and the *perseverance* to apply the first rule, by developing *plants* hitherto lacking, and abandoned or otherwise neglected mines; the seventh, in working up foreign raw materials; and to take such further measures as may be needed under the first rule for the improvement of hitherto uncultivated tracts of land, under the third for populating the country with peasantry, under the sixth for doing our own transporting both of foreign and domestic goods, and under the eighth in various ways. Indeed I may say without shyness, and surely without joking, that Austria has certain hidden resources, which will raise the first, third, and eighth rules to a degree impossible for the other countries of Europe to attain, and will, in all probability, win for Austria a wealth and splendor such as she has never had in her history or even dared to hope for.

III

Now we come to the big question, how to go about it to induce the inhabitants of Austria to content themselves with
their own domestic *manufactures;* for according to my own
admission, there are very few such available, and one can
hardly advise people to clothe themselves as in primitive
times in untanned sheepskin. *Hic opus, hic labor est!* and
my only concern is that I shall have to prescribe a bitter pill
for my Austrians, who like to dress trimly and expensively,
and live for their physical *comfort.* But to make some con-
cession, I must admit that I did not mean the *abstinence*
from foreign goods to be taken in a *general* sense at the beginning, intending for the time being to put only those
things on our black-list, the neglect of which can bring
greatest harm to the country, the proper cultivation of
which will bring the greatest, quickest, and most obvious
advantage, and the lack of which from abroad will be easiest
to bear or most readily replaced. In this category I place
first woolen *manufactures,* both woven and knit goods, with
the single exception of millers' bolting-cloth, as interfering
too much with the pantry, for a year, until it is supplied
within the country. Second, all linen goods of all kinds.
Third, silk *manufactures* of all *stages.* Fourth, everything
included under the name French *manufactures* and not included in the three classes mentioned above, whether made
in France itself or in Italy, or in Switzerland, or elsewhere.
Quite an undertaking! but I think that even according to
our description it is the right solution. For it is certain that
these four *sorts* of foreign goods are the real leeches which
rob us of the inmost strength of our body and suck the best
blood from our veins. Certain it is that these four *manufactures* are the beasts of prey which alone take every year up-

wards of sixteen million *gulden* from our pockets, just as if they had never been there. I was present when it was estimated, by distinguished men well acquainted with the country, that our annual loss of money through French wares alone amounts to three million *gulden* and more. If, moreover, as the above-mentioned *Survey of Manufactures in Germany* makes certain, fifteen thousand dollars are exported every year for bolting-cloth from Saxony alone, so that at least a hundred thousand dollars must yearly take flight from Austria as a whole for it, and bolting-cloth makes up hardly a fiftieth part of the foreign wool *manufactures* imported by us: then it must follow that at least seven million *gulden* leave Austria every year for these wool *manufactures*. What I have said above about the six and a half million dollars of mere wages and business-men's *profits*, which remain every year in the city of Leyden alone, according to clear reckoning, for woolen *manufactures* in cloth, small-wares, &c. will make credible what I here allege concerning the seven million *gulden* which annually go out of Austria for such *manufactures*. Now silk *manufactures* are probably not much inferior to the woolen.

Indeed, if more than nine thousand dollars are exported annually for silk from Saxony alone, again according to the statement in the *Survey of Manufactures in Germany*, and the *author* is afraid of appearing unreasonable in placing the total at such a modest sum, should we not likewise consider a man unreasonable who put the Austrian consumption thereof only about four times higher? And yet that would make six million *gulden*. If, however, everything made of linen be added, which is also not inconsiderable, we can reckon up and see whether less than eighteen or twenty millions are sacrificed annually, simply to satisfy the unnecessary desire for display in dress, and poured into the coffers of strangers, mostly our enemies. I might say that in Vienna before the siege there were two hundred thousand men over twelve years old, each of whom on the average spent ten *gulden* a year (most of them, indeed, thirty and more, many even a hundred, and not a few several hundred and even thousands) for foreign articles of clothing. Now it is easy to show that the other capital cities of the Austrian states, also very splendid, as well as other substantial and fine towns, besides the great and lesser nobility, together with their servants and officials, the whole kingdom of Hungary, the great and lesser clergy, besides all those under twelve years of age and yet having their share of foreign goods, and finally what is spent on other forms of personal property from abroad, all taken together, must, if Vienna amounts to at least eight, reveal a loss of eighteen millions. Let no one be offended at this, or be astonished at the huge sum, as if we were only playing with millions. For a neighboring state, which is only one sixth as large as Austria, exports annually, according to clear reckoning, three million dollars, according to the above-cited *Survey of Manufactures*. We know where all this money comes from, yet the country remains in the same condition as before, and consequently is exporting just as much again. How much more credible is it, then, that Austria lets foreigners have eleven or twelve million dollars.

To guard, nevertheless, against all doubts, reasonable or unreasonable: I will reduce the figures almost a half, leaving the total ten millions net, which are thrown out the door like a penny, without any hope of their return, simply for four kinds of *manufactures*. If these ten millions were kept in Austria for only a single year, how this lifeless body would begin to move and to revive! How it would recover and gain strength! And if, as would follow anyway, these ten millions made their way into *circulation*, in addition to what is in general use even under the present bad conditions, and, like the human blood by the power of the heart, passed every year to a large extent through the prince's treasury, in a gentle, practical, and tolerable way (which is the duty of the exchequer): How all the members of the German-Austrian state would suddenly rejoice and feel strong! If, however, this were kept up ten or twenty years, or longer, and if a suitable watch were kept over these four *manufactures* and also over the other trades in this way, and in each branch as far as practicable, and if finally the foreign *consumption* of domestic raw and *manufactured* products were increased in the course of time as much as possible; what in all Europe would then equal our Austria? And what sort of *manufactures* are these, the dispensing with which from foreign sources could make us so prosperous? They would, it is true, require some oversight and pains for their development, but nowhere would they be easier to introduce than in Austria, as I will demonstrate below. We could well do without the French trumpery, without special difficulty either, and in a few years imitate them more easily and more readily than others. I will also explain that in its place.

IV

WHY NOT ADOPT OTHER MORE MODERATE MEANS THAN THE COMPLETE PROHIBITION OF FOREIGN MANUFACTURES?

Now we come to the question how to enable Austria to be content with her own domestic *products* in the often-cited four branches of *manufacture*, giving up foreign ones, and this is the real crux of the matter. Following the general course hitherto adopted, people will immediately conclude: First of all, *manufactures* should be introduced in Austria, privileges granted for this purpose, companies established; and when they have been introduced, either heavy taxes and import duties should be put upon foreign goods coming in, so that they may not be as cheap as the domestic ones, and so will have to stay outside; or *magazines* should be established, in which foreign as well as domestic goods shall be deposited, with instructions that merchants shall not proceed to the sale of the foreign, until the domestic have all been sold; finally, in order that progress may be made with the domestic *manufactures*, foreign goods should then be forbidden through the Bank. But these ways are, in my opinion, uncertain, slow, and, in view of our German temperament, sure to come to nothing. For, in the first place, capitals will be lacking, because rich people will not want to let them out of their strong-boxes, because of lack of confidence in the project. In the second place, no spirit or *resolution* will be forthcoming, on account of equal lack of confidence in the result, and this not unreasonably. For, in the third place, because of the slowness of such *introduction*, merchants and others not well disposed toward the plan, especially foreign *factors*, will have ample opportunity to *ruin* the beginnings by a thousand kinds of devices. The desire to become rich quickly, and impatience at waiting for gains, which, on account of the uncertainty of *consumption*, are bound to be uncertain, will, in the fourth place, do a good deal of damage by itself; the long time, in the fifth place, will also take away our energy and cool our enthusiasm. Besides, in the sixth place, there would be endless smuggling under such easy and careless *administration*. The domestic goods, in the seventh place, will have to bear reproaches for this or that pretended defect, and so fall into disrepute and *discredit*. *Luxury*, the raging *beast*, would, in the eighth place, not be repelled by the high prices of foreign goods, but would develop all the greater passion for them. The domestic *manufactures* would, in the ninth place, never attain complete development, as long as there was hope of getting the foreign ones. To sum up: The eventual prohibition and exclusion of foreign *products* would never be achieved in this way. For our illness is too great and too dangerous to yield to such weak and slow treatment.

I therefore deal with the problem in a very different way. Other people wish to introduce domestic *manufactures*, in order to exclude foreign ones later. I, however, advise the prohibition of foreign ones, in order to introduce domestic ones later. A big program! How much *opposition* is doubtless already being *formulated* against it, almost before it has left my hand! I shall not allow myself to be misled thereby, but remain convinced that foreign *manufactures* must be *banned* in order to promote domestic ones. I only wish to restrain premature judgment, until I have set forth the arguments for my proposal, and have disposed of the objections which may be urged against it. All my life I have preferred the simplest, most effective, and most certain, though apparently somewhat strong means to over-refined methods, neither cold nor warm, and therefore subject to all sorts of attacks, and in the end to much more inconvenience than those which work rigorously. Now there is nothing simpler in *execution* than the complete prohibition of all foreign goods in our four branches of *manufacture*. For smuggling cannot take place, if only those assigned to supervise it remain faithful, through fear and hope, punishment and reward; and if domestic goods are protected against violators of the public faith by the strict taboo. Nothing easier; for a bit of paper and ink, some decrees at the custom-houses and passes, *instruction* of some officials, arrangements for inspection and paying duties, and the unavoidable and inescapable punishing of the first or second who are caught red-handed, as well as the criminal's helpers and the receivers of the smuggled goods, be they great or small, will fix everything. Nothing prompter; for in twenty-four hours, so to speak, everything can be put into operation, and within a year the *effect* will be felt throughout Austria, both in the *Treasury* of the prince and in the coffers of his subjects. Nothing surer and more vigorous; for necessity itself and the sure profit resulting from the certainty of *consumption*, will teach the country's inhabitants to devote themselves to their own *manufactures*. When the money no longer goes to foreigners, at least ten millions will remain in the country annually, and go to increase our business capital. And the above-mentioned assurance of *consumption*, and the resulting sure profit, will encourage the capitalists to release their cash. Foreign artisans will be compelled by lack of work and bread to come into Austria to seek both. A hundred other advantages besides, which may not now be thought of, are likely to appear in the course of the *execution*.

.   .   .   .

V

OBJECTIONS TO THE PROHIBITION OF FOREIGN
GOODS ANSWERED

I now have to answer the objections. I will take them up briefly, in order that this work may not be expanded to undue proportions. Enough is said for the sensible, and more detail would be wasted on the others. The first is: HOW COULD WE GET ALONG WITH DOMESTIC GOODS, IF FOREIGN ONES WERE SO SUDDENLY BANNED, AND HOW PROVIDE SUBSTITUTES? Answer: To tell the truth, we do not need the so-called French wares at all. Hence we shall be able to do without them merely until they gradually come to be *produced* in the country, as there is already a beginning in many of them; and other branches also cannot long fail to be *stabilized*, even more promptly than the other three much more important *manufactures*. In the case of silk goods the situation is about the same. Moreover, it is only for two or three years that there will be any shortage of them in the country; in five or six years there will be plenty. In the case of linen *manufactures*, Austria would have plenty already, as far as quantity goes, if only the good people who make that their *profession*, could find enough work. And as for variety and quality, it would probably not take long to supply that. Silesia alone would suffice, where this weaving has almost no gild, and everywhere, both in distinguished and peasant houses, the loom is found in rooms and chambers, upon which everybody works, and everyone is taught, just as in spinning. In the case of cloth-making the circumstances are not much different, and I know that in many an otherwise little known town there has been almost incredible progress. If only the domestic *consumption* were assured to them, and they were provided with, say, a half-year's stock of wool, how soon the cloth-making industry, as well as wool-spinning, which is not very badly off anyway, on account of the *continual* sales to foreign countries, would expand to five or six times what it now is. The thinner stuffs might, in case of necessity, have to bear the same fate as silk-making, namely, to slow down for a short time, meanwhile replacing the wanted linings with something else, until their *fabrication* is introduced in the country. To sum up: Linen and cloth, the most necessary, we should have in sufficient supply immediately, the small-wares would be supplementary to them. With light woolens, silks, and French wares we could, in case of necessity, dispense altogether forever, as our ancestors did, and hence all the more readily for a time only.

.   .   .   .

WHAT IS TO BE DONE ABOUT THOSE MERCHANTS WHO ARE ENGAGED SOLELY IN THE IMPORTING BUSINESS? THEY WILL BE RUINED. — An advantage! For they are the very fellows who are impoverishing the country. It is therefore better that they should collapse than the commonwealth. They will be able to hold out, however, until they obtain *commissions* from domestic wholesalers or financiers, or *credit* from them, or book-keeping with the *manufacturers*, or some other position or service (of which there will then be a hundred times as many as there are ruined merchants), or invest any *capital* they may have in domestic *manufactures*. If they do not wish to be employed by the domestic *factories*, however, and they have no *capital* to invest, then such worthless rascals, who act only to the advantage of foreigners and to the harm of Austria, and who have not been able to do any more than earn their daily bread, are no more worthy of sympathy than downright fools.

OUR AUSTRIAN MANUFACTURES WILL NOT BE AS GOOD AS THE FOREIGN ONES. — Such a claim is in many cases a delusion of the Devil, who is hostile to the prosperity of Austria. Granted, however, that this would be an unavoidable evil, still it would not be unendurable. I will cite the prohibition of Hungarian wine in Austria, Styria, and elsewhere. If you ask why wines are prohibited which are better than the domestic ones, and even cheaper, the answer will be: That the domestic gifts of Providence may be utilized and prudently *consumed*, not despised, thrown away, or ruined;

that the highlands may be *benefited*, and the limited cultivation of vineyards, an important source of regalian revenue, may not be abandoned; that thereby so much more money may stay in our pockets. It is the same with Hungarian salt, to which the Austrian is inferior. And yet the former is kept out and the latter retains control of the field. It is quite the proper thing, however, and can be applied *ad literam* to domestic *manufactures*. For if we have such *principles* in a few things, why do we not *extend* them to the great and many? If we use them on two such necessary articles as wine and salt, why do we not apply them the more readily to the unnecessary abuse in matters of clothing? If my proposal aimed at restricting the subsistence of Austria, and cutting down her food or drink by prohibiting commodities, there might be some reason to complain that this was too hard; that the body could not suddenly give up the nourishment to which it had become accustomed; that it would be an injury to health. But there is no question here of eating and drinking, or of health and long life, or of fasting and abstaining, but whether the body should be decked with Silesian or foreign cloth, with Upper Austrian linen or Indian *bombazine*, with domestic or foreign-made silks or stockings, with Austrian or French ribbons, which has nothing to do with health or palate or stomach, but merely things of fancy, and not even becoming to the proud spirit of display. As to how domestic wares may be made as good as foreign in quality, that is, in durability as well as beauty, I will undertake to set forth my views somewhat more fully below.

.   .   .   .

We cannot make our products as good as foreign ones, since we have neither silk nor the Spanish wool which is indispensable for fine cloths. — On that point people may well ask advice of the English and Dutch, who not only have no silk at home, but have no hope of ever having any; and have little of the long wool for cloth, besides having no Spanish wool, the same as we. Where they procure such raw materials, we shall find them too. Indeed, we shall obtain Milanese and Sicilian silk and Spanish wool all the more easily, since the Spaniards will prefer to grant this to their kinsfolk and most faithful *allies* rather than to others. As for long wool, it is not only easy to develop an ample supply of that in Bohemia, as pointed out above, but our neighbors will be as glad to sell it to us for our money or other goods as to anyone else.

BUT WHAT WILL DAME FASHION, THE SOLE ARBITER OF MANUFACTURES IN MATTERS OF DRESS, SAY TO THAT: SURELY ONE MUST DRESS LIKE OTHER NATIONS. — It would be a good thing if we sent Dame Fashion to the Devil, her father. There are incomparably more *nations* in the world that keep to one kind of clothing, than vary it. Why should we, then, imitate the few and not the many? Or if we can not do without this foolish *variety*, we should be free, anyway, to be as foolish as the French, and to *invent* such things from time to time out of our own fancy, in order to remain masters of our *manufactures*. If this would not do either, then samples, both of clothing styles and cloth patterns, might be brought from France and *fabricated* here; thus remedying this misfortune also. Indeed, it would be an advantageous change for the merchants. For now, when a new fashion comes in, the goods have to be ordered from a distance. Before they arrive, the style often changes again, and the merchant suffers a loss. If the *factories* are in the country itself, however, no more will be made in the new styles than just enough, so to speak, to supply the daily demand.

WHERE ARE OUR GERMANS TO GET CLEVERNESS ENOUGH TO INVENT A NEAT CLOTH-PATTERN OR FANCY JEWELRY-DESIGN, OR EVEN TO IMITATE ONE? THEY HAVEN'T BRAINS ENOUGH. — Such sarcasm should be retracted by the lips that uttered it. For the contrary is amply demonstrated above, and there is no other reason for the backwardness of our people except that the best artists are not honored among us. So they go off to France and Holland. The artisans who stay among us are not encouraged, and know,

moreover, that even if they did make something good, foreign wares would always be esteemed more highly. Nevertheless there are such people here and there. I should like to
have defied the one who displayed before the old King in
Augsburg a foreign-made ribbon, which he could not imitate. And even in Dresden I know a young man whose first
trade was that of ribbon-maker, later, as this did not give
him a living, a lackey, still later a silk weaver in the new
royal silk *manufactory;* who, in everything to which he
chooses to *apply* himself, equals, where he does not surpass,
foreigners, and has already given so many proofs of it that
he can not be accused of presumption when he says, according to his habit, that he will undertake to imitate any *lessons*
given him; and to give *lessons* to others which they would
not imitate.

· · · · · · · · · · · ·

WHERE IS THE CAPITAL FOR DOMESTIC INVESTMENT TO BE
OBTAINED? — If I should answer that it is for the Prince to
see to that, I should be right, perhaps, but the times will not
endure it. If I should therefore pass it on to the provinces, it
might not be a mistake, either, but it might nevertheless not
encounter the same *sentiment.* Therefore let it remain as
suggested above, that if ten millions stay in the country
every year more than now, and the *consumption* of domestic
products is well assured, then there will be an abundance of
capital. Moreover, I hear of a new strange proposal for obtaining *Credit* to make a big *Capital* without any; of which
it will be possible to judge, when it has been given out.

· · · · · · · · · · · ·

IT IS TO BE FEARED THAT WE SHALL HAVE TO LIVE AT THE
MERCY OF DOMESTIC ARTISANS AND BUSINESS-MEN, SINCE
THEY WILL RAISE THEIR PRICES EXCESSIVELY WHEN THEY
ARE NOT RESTRAINED BY FOREIGNERS. — If the government
supervises things as it should, and checks wantonness, this
will not have to be feared. And if manufactures eventually
become extensive, the people themselves will strive for

money and bread, and make goods cheap through their plentifulness. Where foodstuffs, house-rent, and wages of servants, as well as raw materials or goods, are inexpensive, as with us, and where wares are not brought from a distance and consequently are subject to no heavy charges for freight, tolls, or risk, it is hardly possible that they should be higher-priced than foreign ones (especially if the market is certain, and the goods do not have to lie long at *interest*). It might even be said that strangers do not make us gifts of these things, either; and it would be better, after all, if something must be sacrificed, to be a victim to one's own countryman rather than to a stranger, and to console one's self with the fact, already alluded to above, that it is better, although not every peasant can understand it, to pay two dollars for a domestic article, which remains in the country, than only one for a foreign one, which is exported. For what once goes out stays out. But what remains in domestic *circulation* involves no loss to the *public*, but is an advantage in several ways. The merchant himself, who invested it, can profit by it again. The state is to be thought of as a rich man, who has his money in many purses. If he takes something out of one and puts it into the other, he becomes no poorer thereby. For, although one purse becomes lighter, the other becomes that much heavier. He is master, however, of one as well as of the other. And this must be a leading *principle* of national *economy*, or things will not go well.

But those nations whose manufactures we propose to prohibit will be angry, and cut us off from such things as we may still need from them; our domestic goods hitherto taken by them will be left on our hands; our alliances and we ourselves will be deserted in time of need. — Let them be angry who will. If they are enemies, we do not need to spare their feelings; if they are friends, they will excuse us if we, by eventually developing a good *economy*, get into a *position* not only to help ourselves, but also in case of need to be of more *real* service to them. We see how France is angry at the way England consigns to the flames all French wares that are discovered. And after all, let him who stands behind Job take a friendship which really aims only at plundering our purse. We have learned how much friends give us for nothing in an emergency. And other *nations* are not so foolish, either, as to refuse us their unprohibited wares out of spite on account of the prohibited ones, and to avenge and increase the forced loss by a voluntary one. The free commerce of many places, such as Hamburg, Amsterdam, &c., does not allow any buyer to be excluded. And even if all others should treat us that way, the Spaniards, at any rate, for the reasons pointed out above, and because they have almost as much interest in our prosperity as we, would be for us rather than for anyone else, and not leave us in the lurch for the best Spanish wool and Italian silk; which are the two things which we still need to import. And, after all, we could get silk through Turkey. The nations, however, from whom we must get long wool, are not among those to whom our prohibition will cause any damage. They will therefore have no reason to prohibit our buying it; and in an emergency Bohemia, as already pointed out, would have to devote herself more to the production of this long wool. So there is no danger that our goods intended for export will be left on our hands. These are: wine, grain, oxen, copper, iron, quicksilver, hides, linen, all kinds of *minerals*, &c. For those who buy these things of us are either not among those who are injured by our prohibition, or are not able to do without such goods of ours. When we have become somewhat stronger financially as a result of our *economy*, we will not only have no need of foreign alliances and assistance, but they would even offer themselves of their own accord. For much money, many *alliances*, as France shows well enough. And on the contrary: *Point d'argent, point de Suisses.* Doubtless those who will not like our good order, because hitherto they have had good fishing in troubled waters, will try all sorts of tricks in order to lead us astray. *Mais fin contre fin, ne fait point de fourrure.*

VI

HOW TO RAISE THE QUALITY OF DOMESTIC MANUFACTURES, SO THAT THEY MAY NOT BE INFERIOR TO FOREIGN ONES

Here we have to consider briefly how the quality of domestic *manufactures* is to be raised, in order that they may equal foreign ones. This reminds me of that humorous or, at any rate, strange chemical saying: *Accipe quod debes, & operare sicuti debet, tunc eveniet tibi, quod debet.* I mean: We have the materials for work like others, hands and heads like others, tools like others. If then the *effect* is not produced, as with others, it is certainly a willful wantonness, or at least a wanton awkwardness, which the government will know how to restrain, if it understands its duties. And it has been pointed out already that foreigners take our woven cloths and linen to their countries, finish them there, and thereby *transform* them into foreign goods; which finishing, God willing, we should also be able to imitate. They likewise take out our Silesian yarns and make their linen out of them. They take out our flax, hackle it again, and prepare it in a special way; then spin it in their way. In this connection it is to be noted that they make two kinds of linen, the best for themselves, the poorer for us and other foreigners; and indeed for the reason that they think we do not pay for theirs according to its value. The first is made of Silesian weft, but the warp is of Dutch or similar yarns, made, however, of Silesian or other high-German flax. In the other, both warp and weft are high-German and Silesian. I have been informed, moreover, that they take our woven Silesian linen and full it in butter-milk. For let no one be surprised at the fulling of linen, since Leipzig also understands that. In this way must high-German goods be made into good foreign ones. There is nothing in all this which we Austrians could not imitate. If our minds were too dull to find it out for ourselves, then have artists from other places come here; and spare no expense, for they will pay for themselves, though they had to be bought for their weight in gold. If this is not satisfactory, then send some of our native sons thither, and have them learn it. If the Germans, as soon as they reach France or Holland, equal or even surpass the inhabitants there, as long as they are among them, they can also bring the art back with them, and do a service to their fatherland, to which they owe everything anyway. It is of no consequence that the tools may not be brought to us from France or Holland. For even if that were not possible, either whole or in pieces, it would be a simple thing for an alert *mathematical* head to grasp them and later set them up here, though it required more than one journey. I also hear from the Swiss that they now know how to make their hemp as good as the best Dutch linen. I praise them, not only for such diligence, but also because they plant their land with big high hemp rather than small flax, and yet know how to make use of it as well as the latter. Now if the Swiss can do this, why not the Austrians too? These very Swiss also furnish us with a notable example of diligence in the wool manufacture. All the world a while ago procured its bolting-cloth from France, and long believed that it would never be brought from anywhere else. But now it is made as well in Switzerland as in France, and the greater part of what is used in Germany comes from there, although the Calwische Company in Würtemberg does something along that line. How much the silk *Manufacture* is growing in Switzerland is well known, moreover. And sometimes we are so absurd as to tax these people with being a little too *materialistic*, when we doubt all the while whether we also have intelligence and cleverness enough to do what is an easy matter for them.

It would also be no small assurance of the goodness of domestic wares to erect halls, warehouses, and inspecting rooms, requiring all finished pieces of cloth of any kind, or other things, to be brought there and pass an examination. Only those passing it would be current in the warehouses and honest merchants' shops; those which did not pass it would be *excluded* from other upright wares and remain mere peddler's goods. The falsifying or misuse of the stamps put on the good wares after inspection should, on account of the great *consequences*, be punished as a *violation* of general confidence and a weakening of the general *credit* of the community; not much less severely than the counterfeiting of money and government documents and seals, even with capital punishment in some cases, like grand larceny. In this way Austrian goods would not only be kept up to proper quality and workmanship, but in a short time would also acquire great *credit* and *reputation* at home and abroad, which would promote sales greatly, since every buyer could feel assured he was not being cheated.

Furthermore, there might be established in Austria certain annual *competitions*, no master or journeyman being excluded who is either a native of the country or who plans to settle there; and providing that whoever won there should be rewarded with certain *privileges*, emoluments, or in money and other prizes, which would be easy to arrange in such a way that it would not cost the *public* anything. This would not only be an impetus to the arts among the inhabitants, but would also attract the best workmen from abroad.

XI

RICHARD CANTILLON

ESSAI SUR LA NATURE DU COMMERCE EN GÉNÉRAL

NOTE

RICHARD CANTILLON (c. 1680–1734) was a wealthy British merchant of Irish descent, with houses in most of the leading centers of Europe. Little is known about his life. In 1716 we find him established in Paris, but he was forced to leave three years later, having incurred the ill-will of John Law, and returned to London. Although he is said to have written a good deal, all that has come down to us is the remarkable *Essai sur le Commerce*, the most important work on economics before the *Wealth of Nations*. This appears to have been written some time between 1730 and 1734, and to have been translated into French by the author himself. It circulated quite widely in manuscript, but was not published till 1755. Although its closely reasoned, abstract discussions had no very wide appeal, many able men recognized its merits, and it was twice reprinted. The Physiocrats, in particular, were considerably influenced by Cantillon, and he is one of the few authors mentioned by Adam Smith.

ON THE NATURE OF COMMERCE
IN GENERAL

I

*The number of Laborers, Artisans, & other people working in
a state adjusts itself naturally to the need of them.*

IF all the Laborers [1] in a Village bring up several Sons in
the same work, there will be too many Laborers to cultivate the land belonging to this Village, & the Superfluous
adults will have to seek their living somewhere else, ordinarily in the Cities: if some stay with their Fathers, since
they will not find enough work, they will live in great poverty, & will not marry, not having the means to raise children, or if they marry, the children born soon die of misery
along with the Father & the Mother, as we see every day in
France.

Thus if working conditions remain the same in the Village,
& it gets its living by working the same amount of land, it
will not increase in population in a thousand years.

It is true that the Wives & Daughters of this Village may,
while not working in the fields, busy themselves with spinning, knitting, or work to be sold in the Cities; but that is
rarely enough to rear the superfluous children, who leave the
Village to seek their fortune elsewhere.

We may reason in the same way about the Artisans of a
Village. If a single Tailor makes all the clothing there, & he
brings up three Sons to the same trade, since there is only
work enough for one who will succeed him, the other two
will have to seek their living elsewhere: if they do not find
work in the next Village, they will have to go farther, or
change trades to earn their living, becoming Lackeys, Soldiers, Sailors, &c.

[1] This is always used to refer to farm laborers. — ED.

It is easy to see from the same line of reasoning that the Laborers, Artisans & others, who earn their living by work, must adjust their numbers to the employment & to the need of them in the Towns & Cities.

But if four Tailors are enough to make all the clothes of a Town, & a fifth Tailor comes in, he may attract some business at the expense of the other four; with the result that if the work comes to be divided among the five Tailors, none of them will have enough work, & each will get a poorer living out of it.

It often happens that the Laborers & Artisans have not enough employment, when there are too many of them to share the work. It also happens that they are deprived of the employment they had, by accidents & by a variation in consumption; it will also happen that they have too much work, according to circumstances: in any case, when they lack employment, they leave the Villages, Towns, or Cities where they live, in such numbers that the number left is always adjusted to the employment which suffices to give them a living; & when a permanent increase of work develops, it is profitable, & enough others come to share the work.

From this reasoning it is easy to understand that the charity Schools in England & the projects in France for increasing the number of Artisans are quite useless. If the King of France sent a hundred thousand of his Subjects to Holland at his expense, to learn the Shipping trade, they would be useless when they returned, if no more Ships were sent to Sea than formerly. It is true that it would be a great advantage for a State to teach its Subjects to make the Manufactures which it is customary to import from Abroad, & all the products bought there; but I am now considering only a State by itself.

Since the Artisans earn more than the Laborers, they are in a better position than the latter to have their children learn a trade; & there can never be a lack of Artisans in a State, when there is enough work to give them regular employment.

II

The price & intrinsic value of a thing in general is the measure of the land & the labor which enters into its production.

One Acre of land produces more wheat, or supports more Sheep, than another Acre: the labor of one man is dearer than that of another man, according to skill & circumstances, as has already been explained. If two Acres of land are of the same quality, one will support as many Sheep & will produce the same quantity of wool as the other Acre, assuming the same labor; & the wool produced by the one will sell for the same price as that which is produced by the other.

If the Wool in one case is worked up into a suit of coarse cloth, & the Wool in the other into a suit of fine cloth; since this last suit will require more labor & more expensive labor than is put into the coarse cloth, it will sometimes be ten times dearer, although both suits contain the same amount of Wool & of the same quality. The quantity of the produce of land, & the quantity as well as the quality of the labor, will necessarily enter into the price.

A pound of Flax worked up into fine Brussels Lace, requires the labor of fourteen persons for a year, or the work of one person for fourteen years, as may be seen from a calculation of the different parts of the work in the Supplement.[1] It may also be seen from these figures that the price paid for this lace suffices to pay for the support of one person for fourteen years, & to pay in addition the profits of all the Entrepreneurs & Merchants involved.

The Spring of fine steel, which regulates an English Watch, ordinarily sells at a price which makes the ratio between the material & the work or between the steel & the Spring as one to one, with the result that the labor here makes almost the entire value of this Spring; see the calculation in the Supplement.

[1] This supplement has not been preserved. — ED.

On the other hand, the price of the Hay from a Meadow, brought to market, or of a Wood which you desire to cut down, depends upon the material, or upon the produce of the land, according to its quality.

The price of a jar of water from the river Seine is nothing, because it is an immense supply which never dries up; but people give a penny for it in the streets of Paris, which is the price or measure of the labor of the water Carrier.

From these arguments & examples, I think it will be understood that the price or the intrinsic value of a thing is the measure of the amount of land & of labor which enters into its production, taking into account the quality or produce of the land & the quality of the labor.

But it often happens that several things which now have this intrinsic value do not sell in the Market according to this value: that will depend upon the whims & fancies of men, & upon the amount they consume.

If a Lord cuts canals & builds terraces in his Garden, their intrinsic value will be in proportion to the land & labor; but the price in fact will not always follow this proportion: if he offers to sell this Garden, it may happen that nobody will give him half as much as he has spent on it; & it may also happen, if several persons desire it, that he will be paid twice its intrinsic value, that is, the value of the land & of the amount he has spent on it.

If the Farmers in a State sow more wheat than ordinarily, that is to say, much more wheat than is needed for the year's consumption, the intrinsic & real value of the wheat will correspond to the land & labor which enter into its production: but since there is too great an abundance of it, & more Sellers than Buyers, the price of wheat in the Market will necessarily fall below the intrinsic price or value. If, on the contrary, the Farmers sow less wheat than is needed for the consumption, there will be more Buyers than Sellers, & the price of wheat in the Market will rise above its intrinsic value.

There is never any variation in the intrinsic value of

things; but the impossibility of adjusting the production of merchandise & commodities to the consumption of them in a State causes a daily variation, & a perpetual flux & reflux in the prices of the Market. However, in well regulated Societies, the Market prices of commodities & merchandise of which the consumption is fairly constant & uniform do not vary greatly from the intrinsic value; & when there do not happen to be too sterile or too abundant years, the Magistrates of the Cities are always in a position to fix the Market price of many things, such as bread & meat, without giving anyone cause for complaint.

Land is the material, & labor is the form, of all commodities & merchandise; & since those who work must necessarily live on the produce of the Land, it seems as if we could find a relation between the value of labor & that of the produce of Land: that will be the subject of the following Chapter.

III

Of the par or ratio between the value of land and the value of labor.

It does not seem that Providence gave the right of possessing Land to one Man rather than another. The most ancient Titles are founded upon violence & conquests. The Lands of Mexico now belong to Spaniards, & those of Jerusalem to Turks. But however the ownership & possession of Lands is acquired, we have already remarked that they always eventually fall to a small number of persons in proportion to the whole population.

If the Proprietor of a great Estate undertakes to exploit it himself, he will employ Slaves, or free People, to work on it: if he employs several Slaves, he will need Inspectors to make them work; he will also have to have Slave Artisans, to provide all the conveniences & comforts of life for himself, & for those whom he employs; he will have to have trades taught to others to continue the work.

In this economy, he will have to furnish a simple subsist-

252 EARLY ECONOMIC THOUGHT

ence to his slave Laborers & the wherewithal to bring up their Children. He will have to give their Inspectors advantages in proportion to the trust & authority they have; he will have to maintain the Slaves, to whom he is having Trades taught, during the time of their Apprenticeship without return, & to grant the Slave artisans who work, & to their Inspectors, who have to be experienced in the Trades, a more nourishing subsistence compared with that of the Slave laborers, &c., because the loss of an Artisan would be greater than that of a Laborer, & because they ought to be given better care, seeing that it is always an expense to have a trade taught to replace them.

On this assumption, the work of the humblest adult slave, is worth at least & corresponds to the amount of land which the Proprietor is obliged to employ for his food & other necessaries, & also to twice as much land as it takes to bring up a Child till old enough to work, inasmuch as half of the Children born die before the age of seventeen years, according to the calculations & observations of the famous Doctor Halley: thus it is necessary to bring up two Children in order that one may reach working age, & it would seem that this reckoning would not suffice to keep up the supply of labor, since adult Men die at all ages.

It is true that the half of the Children born who die before the age of seventeen years, die for the most part during the first years of their life rather than later, since a full third of those born die during the first year. This circumstance appears to diminish the expense required to bring up a Child till old enough to work: but as the Mothers lose a good deal of time in taking care of their Children in sickness & childhood, & since even the adult Daughters do not equal the work of the Males, & earn barely enough to keep them; it seems that to bring up one of two Children to manhood or working age, it is necessary to employ as much produce of Land as for the subsistence of an adult Slave, whether the Proprietor raises these Children in his own house or has them brought up, *or the slave Father brings them up in a sep-*

arate House or Hamlet. Thus I conclude that the daily work of the humblest Slave, corresponds in value to twice the produce of Land on which he subsists, whether the Proprietor gives it to him for his own subsistence & that of his Family; or has him supported with his Family in his own House. It is a matter which does not admit of exact calculation, & in which precision is not even very necessary; it suffices if we do not get too far from reality.

If the Proprietor employs Vassals or free Peasants on his work, he will probably support them somewhat better than Slaves, & this according to the custom of the place; but again, on this supposition, the work of the free Laborer should correspond in value to twice the produce of land required for his support; but it would always be more advantageous for the Proprietor to support Slaves, rather than free Peasants, since, when he has raised too many of them for his work, he will be able to sell the superfluous ones like cattle, & will be able to get a price for them in proportion to the amount he has expended to bring them up to manhood or working age; except in cases of old age & infirmity.

We can likewise estimate the work of Artisan slaves at twice the produce of land which they consume; that of the Inspectors of work likewise, according to the favors & advantages which are given them over & above those who work under their direction.

The Laborers or Artisans, when they have their double portion in their proper degree, if they are married employ one portion for their own support, & the other for that of their Children.

If they are Bachelors, they will put aside a small part of their double portion, to get into a position where they can marry, & to collect a little fund for house-keeping; but the greater number will consume the double portion for their own support.

For example, the married Peasant will be satisfied to live on bread, cheese, vegetables, &c., will rarely eat meat, will drink little wine or beer, will have only old & rough clothes, which he will wear as long as he can: he will employ the surplus of his double portion in bringing up & supporting his Children; while the bachelor Peasant will eat meat as often as he can, & will buy himself new clothes, &c., & consequently will employ his double portion for his own support; thus he will consume twice as much produce of land on his person as the married Peasant does.

I do not consider here the expenses of the Wife, I assume that her work is barely enough for her own support, & when a great number of little Children are seen in one of those poor households, I assume that some charitable persons are contributing something to their subsistence, without which the Husband & the Mother have to deprive themselves of a part of their necessaries to support their Children.

In order to understand this better, it is necessary to know that a poor Peasant can support himself, at the lowest calculation, on the produce of an Acre & a half of land, living on bread & vegetables, wearing clothes of Hemp, & wooden shoes, &c., whereas, if he can buy himself wine & meat, clothes of broadcloth, &c., he will be able to spend, without drunkenness or gluttony, & without any excess, the produce of from four to ten Acres of land of average quality, taking the greater part of the lands of Europe, one with another; I have had some calculations made, which will be found in the Supplement, to show the quantity of land of which a Man can consume the produce in each kind of food, clothing, & other necessaries of life, in a year, according to the standards of living in our Europe, where the Peasants of the different Countries often live in rather different styles.

This is why I did not specify how much Land corresponds in value to the work of the humblest Peasant or Laborer, when I said that it is worth twice the produce of the Land which serves to support him; for that varies according to the standard of living in the different Countries. In some southern Provinces of France, the Peasant lives on the produce of an acre & a half of Land, & there his labor may be estimated as equal to the produce of three acres. But in

Middlesex County, the Peasant ordinarily spends the produce of 5 to 8 acres of Land, & thus his work may be estimated at twice that.

In the Country of the Iroquois, where the Inhabitants do not cultivate the land, & where people live solely on the fruits of the chase, the humblest hunter can consume the produce of 50 acres of Land, since it probably requires that many acres to support the animals which he eats during the year, all the more since these Savages do not know the art of making plants grow by cutting down timber, & leave all to the will of nature.

It may therefore be estimated that the work of this hunter is equal in value to the produce of a hundred acres of Land. In the southern Provinces of China, the Land produces as much as three crops of Rice per year, & yields up to a hundred times the amount sown, each time, as a result of the great care they bestow on Agriculture & the excellence of the land, which never rests. The Peasants, who work there almost naked, live only on Rice, & drink only Rice water; & it seems that one acre supports more than ten Peasants: hence it is not astonishing that the Inhabitants are prodigiously numerous there. However that may be, it appears from these examples, that it makes little difference to nature, whether Lands produce grass, woods, or grain, & whether she supports a great or a small number of Plants, Animals, or Men.

The Farmers of Europe seem to correspond to the Inspectors of Slave laborers in other Countries, & the Master Artisans who employ several Journeymen, to the Inspectors of Slave artisans.

These Master Artisans know about how much work a Journeyman artisan can do in a day in each Trade, & often pay them in proportion to the work they do; hence these Journeymen do as much work as they can, for the sake of their own interest, without other inspection.

Since the Farmers & Master artisans in Europe are all Entrepreneurs & work subject to risk (*au hasard*), some become rich & earn more than a double subsistence, others are ruined & become bankrupt, as will be explained in greater detail when we come to discuss Entrepreneurs; but the greater number support themselves from hand to mouth with their Families, & we might estimate their work or inspection at about three times the produce of Land which serves for their support.

.   .   .   .

The Silver or Coin, which finds in exchange the proportions between values, is the most certain measure for judging the par between Land & Labor, & the relation of one to the other in the different Countries where this Par varies according to the greater or less produce of Land which is attributed to those who labor.

For example, if one Man earns an ounce of silver every day by his labor, & if another earns only half an ounce in the same place; it may be concluded that the first has once again as much produce of Land to spend as the second.

Sir William Petty, in a little Manuscript of the year 1685, considers this par, as an Equation between Land & Labor, the most important consideration in political Arithmetic; but the analysis which he made of it in passing is bizarre & not in accord with the rules of nature, simply because he did not keep to causes & principles, but only to effects; as Messrs. Locke & d'Avenant, & all the other English Authors who have written upon this subject, have done since.

IV

The circulation & exchange of commodities & merchandise, as well as their production, are carried on in Europe by Entrepreneurs, & subject to risk.

The Farmer is an Entrepreneur who promises to pay the Proprietor, for his Farm or Land, a definite sum of money (which is ordinarily assumed to be equal in value to a third of the produce of the Land), without having any assurance as to the profit he will make from this enterprise. He employs a part of this Land to pasture Herds, to produce grain, wine, hay, &c. according to his ideas, without being able to foresee which of these kinds of commodities will bring the best price. This price of the commodities will depend in part upon the Seasons, & in part upon consumption; if there is an abundance of wheat in relation to consumption, it will be cheap; if there is a scarcity, it will be dear. Who can foresee the number of births & deaths among the Inhabitants of the State in the course of the year? Who can foresee the increase or diminution of expenditure which may arise among the Families? Yet the price of the Farmer's commodities naturally depends upon these events which he cannot foresee, & consequently he carries on the enterprise of his Farm with uncertainty.

The City consumes more than half of the Farmer's commodities. He takes them to Market there, or he sells them in the Market of the nearest Town, or some even set up as Entrepreneurs to do this transporting. The latter undertake to pay the Farmer a definite price for his commodities, which is that of the Market that day, to get an uncertain price in the City, which must nevertheless repay them the expenses of carriage, & leave them a profit for their enterprise; yet the daily variation in the prices of commodities in the City, though not considerable, renders their profit uncertain.

The Entrepreneur or Merchant who transports commodities from the Country to the City, cannot remain there to sell them at retail when they come to be consumed: not one Family in the City will undertake to buy all at once the commodities it might consume; since each Family may increase or decrease in number as well as in consumption, or at least vary in the kinds of commodities which it will consume: Families lay in stocks of wine alone. In any case, the greater number of the Inhabitants of the City, who live only from hand to mouth, & who nevertheless are the largest consumers, will not be able to lay in stocks of commodities from the Country.

As a result, several persons in the City set up as Merchants or Entrepreneurs, to buy the commodities of the Country from those who bring them in, or to have them brought in on their own account: they pay a fixed price for them according to that of the place where they buy, to resell them in large or small quantities at an uncertain price.

These Entrepreneurs are the wholesale Merchants of wool and grain, the Bakers, Butchers, Manufacturers, & all Merchants of all kinds who buy the commodities & materials of the Country, to work them up & resell them as the Inhabitants need to consume them.

These Entrepreneurs can never know the volume of consumption in their City, nor even how long their Customers will buy of them, seeing that their Rivals will try in every way to get away their Business: all this causes so much uncertainty among all these Entrepreneurs that we see failures among them every day.

The Manufacturer who has purchased the wool of the Merchant, or of the Farmer directly, cannot know what profit he will make from his enterprise, in the sale of his cloths & stuffs to the Merchant draper. If the latter has not a fairly good market, he will not load up with the cloths & stuffs of the Manufacturer, still less if these stuffs go out of style.

The Draper is an Entrepreneur who buys cloths & stuffs from the Manufacturer at a fixed price, to resell them at an uncertain price, because he can not foresee the volume of consumption; it is true that he can fix a price & refuse to sell unless he gets it, but if his Customers leave him to buy cheaper of somebody else, he will run up expenses while waiting to sell at the price he proposes, & that will ruin him as much or more than if he sold without profit.

Merchants in shops & Retailers of all kinds are Entrepreneurs who buy at a definite price & resell in their Shops or in the public Squares at an uncertain price. What encourages & maintains Entrepreneurs of these kinds in a State is the fact that the Consumers, who are their Customers, prefer to pay a little more in order to find at hand what they need in small quantities, rather than to lay in a stock of it, & that the greater part of them have not the means to lay in such a stock, buying at first hand.

All these Entrepreneurs become consumers & Customers of each other; the Draper, of the wine Merchant; the latter, of the Draper: they adjust their numbers in the State to their Customers or to their market. If there are too many Hatters in a City or in a street for the number of persons who buy hats there, those having the fewest customers will have to become bankrupt; if there are too few, it will be a profitable enterprise, which will encourage some new Hatters to open shop there, & it is thus that Entrepreneurs of all kinds, at their own risk, adjust their numbers in a State.

All other Entrepreneurs, such as those who undertake Mining operations, Spectacles, Building, &c., Merchants on sea & on land, &c., Cook-shop keepers, Pastry-cooks, Tavern-keepers &c., as well as Entrepreneurs of their own work, who have no need of funds to establish themselves, such as Journeymen, artisans, Coppersmiths, Menders, Chimney-sweeps, Water carriers, get an uncertain living, & adjust their numbers according to their Customers. Master artisans, such as Shoe-makers, Tailors, Carpenters, Hairdressers &c., who employ Journeymen in proportion to the work they have, live in the same uncertainty, since their Customers may leave them any day: Entrepreneurs of their own work in the Arts & Sciences, such as Painters, Physicians, Lawyers, &c., are subject to the same uncertainty. If one Solicitor or Barrister earns 5000 pounds sterling a year serving his Clients or customers, & another earns only 500, we may regard them as having just as uncertain incomes as those who employ them.

It might perhaps be argued that all the Entrepreneurs seek to secure all they can in their state, & to cheat their Customers, but that is outside my subject.

From all these arguments & an infinity of others which might be advanced upon a question which concerns all the Inhabitants of a State, we may conclude that, with the ex-

ception of the Prince & the Proprietors of Lands, all the
Inhabitants of a State are dependent; that they may be
divided into two classes, namely, Entrepreneurs & Wage-
earners; & that the Entrepreneurs work for uncertain
wages, so to speak, & all others for certain wages while they
have them, although their functions & their rank are very
disproportionate. The General who has a salary, the Cour-
tier who has a pension, & the Domestic who has wages, are
in the latter class. All the others are Entrepreneurs,
whether they establish themselves with a capital to carry on
their enterprise, or are Entrepreneurs of their own work
without any capital, & they may be considered as living subject to uncertainty; even Beggars & Robbers are Entrepreneurs of this class. Finally, all the Inhabitants of a State
draw their subsistence & their benefits from the fund of the
Proprietors of Lands, & are dependent.

It is true, however, that if some Inhabitant receiving high
wages, or some Entrepreneur of importance, has saved up
some property or wealth, that is, if he has stores of wheat, of
wool, of copper, of gold or silver, or of some commodity or
merchandise having a stable use or sale in a State & having a
real or intrinsic value, he may properly be regarded as independent to the extent of this fund. He can dispose of it to
buy a mortgage, & a rent upon Lands, & upon the funds of
the State when it makes loans secured by lands: he may
even live much better than the Proprietors of small estates,
& even buy some of these.

But commodities & merchandise, even gold & silver, are
much more subject to accidents & losses than landed property; & however they have been earned or saved, they
have always been drawn from the fund of the existing Proprietors, either by profit, or by savings of wages destined for
one's subsistence.

The number of Proprietors of money, in a great State, is
often pretty considerable; & although the value of all the
money which circulates in the State does not exceed the
ninth or tenth part of the value of the commodities derived

from the land at the present time, nevertheless since the Proprietors of money lend considerable sums from which they draw interest, either by mortgages on land, or by the commodities & merchandise itself of the State, the sums owed them generally exceed all the actual money of the State, & they often become such a powerful group that they would in certain cases rival the Proprietors of lands, if the latter were not often likewise Proprietors of money, & if the Proprietors of large sums of money were not always seeking also to become Proprietors of lands.

It is always true, however, that all the sums which they have earned or saved have been drawn from the fund of the existing Proprietors; but since several of the latter ruin themselves every day in a State, & since the others who acquire ownership of their lands take their place, the independence which is given by the ownership of lands pertains only to those who retain possession of them; & since all lands always have an existing Master or Proprietor, I always assume that it is from the fund of the latter that all the Inhabitants of the State draw their subsistence & all their riches. If these Proprietors all limited themselves to living on their rents, this would not be doubtful, and in that case it would be much more difficult for the other Inhabitants to enrich themselves at their expense.

I shall establish as a principle, therefore, that the Proprietors of lands are alone naturally independent in a State; that all the other orders are dependent, either as Entrepreneurs, or as wage-earners, & that all the exchange & circulation in the State is carried on by the intervention of these Entrepreneurs.

V

Of Market Prices

Suppose the Butchers on the one hand & the Buyers on the other. The price of meat will be determined after some altercations; & a pound of Beef will bear about the same ratio to a piece of money, that all the Beef offered for sale in the Market bears to all the money brought thither to buy Beef.

This proportion is settled by altercation. The Butcher holds out for a price according to the number of buyers he sees; the Buyers, on their part, offer less according as they believe that the Butcher will have less market: the price settled upon by some is ordinarily followed by the others. Some are more skillful in getting good prices for their merchandise, others more adroit in discrediting it. Though this method of fixing the prices of things in the Market has no just or geometrical basis, since it often depends upon the eagerness or the facility of a small number of Buyers or of Sellers; yet it does not seem possible to arrive at it in any other more suitable way. It remains true that the quantity of commodities or of merchandise offered for sale, compared with the demand or with the number of Buyers, is the basis upon which people fix, or always think they fix, the prevailing Market prices; & that in general these prices do not differ much from the intrinsic value.

Another supposition. Several Stewards have received orders, at the beginning of the season, to buy green Peas. One Master has given orders for the purchase of ten quarts at 60 *livres*, another for ten quarts at 50 *livres*, & a fourth ten at 30 *livres*. In order to fill these orders, there would have to be forty quarts of green peas in the Market. Suppose there are only twenty: the Sellers, seeing many Buyers, will keep up their price, & the Buyers will raise their offers as high as instructed; with the result that those who offer 60 *livres* for ten quarts will be the first served. The Sellers, seeing then that nobody will go above 50 *livres*, will let the other ten quarts go at this price, but those who had instructions not to go above 40 & 30 *livres* will go back empty-handed.

If instead of forty quarts, there are four hundred, not only will the Stewards get the green peas for much less than the prices to which they were limited, but the Sellers, to be preferred over each other by the small number of Buyers, will lower their green peas, to about their intrinsic value, &

in this case several Stewards who had no orders will buy some.

It often happens that the Sellers, desiring to keep their prices too high in the Market, lose the opportunity to sell their commodities or merchandise on good terms, & suffer a loss. It also happens that by keeping up these prices they will often be able to sell to better advantage another day.

Distant Markets may always have an influence on the prices of the Market where one happens to be: if wheat is extremely dear in France, its price will rise in England & in the other neighboring Countries.

VI

Of the increase & the decrease in the quantity of Money in a State

If mines of gold or silver are discovered in a State, & if considerable quantities of material are taken from them, the Proprietor of these Mines, the Entrepreneurs, & all those who work in them will not fail to increase their expenditures in proportion to the riches & the profits which they will make: they will also lend at interest the sums of money which they have over and above what they need for their expenses. All this money, lent as well as spent, will enter into circulation, & will not fail to raise the price of commodities & merchandise in all the channels of circulation which it enters. The increase of money will bring about an increase of expenditure, & this increase of expenditure will bring about an increase of Market prices in the years of most active trade, & by degrees in the least active.

Everybody agrees that the abundance of money, or its increase in trade, raises the price of all things. The quantity of money brought from America to Europe during the last two centuries demonstrates this truth by experience.

Mr. Locke lays it down as a fundamental Maxim that the quantity of commodities & merchandise, as compared with the quantity of money, determines Market price. I have tried to explain his idea in the preceding Chapters: he realized well that the abundance of money makes everything dear, but he did not analyze how that takes place. The great difficulty of this analysis consists in discovering by what path & in what proportion the increase of money raises the price of things.

I have already remarked that an acceleration, or a greater speed, in the circulation of money in trade amounts to the same thing as an increase in standard money, up to a certain degree. I have also remarked that an increase or decrease in the prices of a distant Market, whether in the State or Abroad, has an influence upon the current prices of the Market. On the other hand, money circulates in detail through such a great number of channels, that it seems impossible not to lose sight of it; for after having been collected to make large sums, it is distributed in the tiny streams of trade, & subsequently is gradually accumulated again to make large payments. For those operations it is necessary to exchange coins of gold, silver, & copper constantly, according to the briskness of this trade. It therefore happens ordinarily that people do not notice the increase or decrease in the money supply in a State, because it slips away to foreign countries, or is introduced into the State, by paths & in proportions which are so imperceptible that it is impossible to determine exactly the quantity which comes into the State, or which goes out of it.

However, all these operations take place before our eyes, & everyone has a direct part in them. Hence I think I may venture some reflections upon this subject, though I cannot treat it in an exact & precise manner.

I hold that in general an increase in the monetary stock causes in a State a proportional increase in consumption, which by degrees produces the rise of prices.

If the increase in the money supply comes from Mines of gold or silver in a State, the Proprietor of these Mines, the Entrepreneurs, the Smelters, the Refiners, & in general all those working in them will not fail to increase their expenditures in proportion to their gains. They will consume in their households more meat & more wine or beer than they used to, they will acquire the habit of wearing better clothes, finer linen, of having better furnished Houses, & other refinements. Consequently they will give employment to several Artisans who did not have so much work formerly, & who for the same reason will increase their expenditures also; all this increase of expenditures on meat, wine, wool, &c., necessarily diminishes the share of the other Inhabitants of the State who do not participate at first in the riches from the Mines in question. The altercations of the Market, or the demand for meat, wine, wool, &c., being stronger than usual, will not fail to raise their price. These high prices will induce the Farmers to employ more land to produce these things another year: these same Farmers will profit from this increase of price, & will increase the expenditures of their families like the others. Those, therefore, who will suffer from this dearness, & from the increased consumption, will be at first the Proprietors of lands, during the term of their Leases, then their servants, & all the workmen or people working for fixed wages who support their families thereby. All these will have to diminish their expenditures in proportion to the new consumption; which will oblige a great many of them to leave the State to seek their fortunes elsewhere. The Proprietors will dismiss many of them, & the others will eventually demand an increase in wages in order to be able to live according to their customary standard. This, roughly, is how a considerable increase of money from Mines increases consumption; & while diminishing the number of inhabitants, brings about a greater expenditure among those who remain.

If more money is taken from the Mines, the prices of all things will be increased by this abundance of money to such an extent, that not only will the Proprietors of lands increase their Rents considerably at the expiration of their Leases, & resume their former standard of living, increasing proportionately the wages of those who serve them; but the Artisans & Workmen will ask such high prices for their products that it will be quite profitable to bring them from Abroad, where they are made much cheaper. This will naturally induce several people to import quantities of Manufactured goods made in foreign Countries, where they may be had cheaply: which will imperceptibly ruin the Artisans & Manufacturers of the State who could not live on such low wages, in view of the high prices.

When the too great abundance of money from the Mines has diminished the population of a State, accustomed those who remain to excessive expenditure, carried the produce of land & the work of Artisans to excessive prices, ruined the Manufacturers of the State, through the use made by the Proprietors of land & those who work in the Mines of goods from foreign countries, the money produced by the Mines will necessarily be transferred to Foreigners to pay for what we import from them: which will imperceptibly impoverish this State, & render it in some ways dependent upon foreign countries to which money has to be sent every year, as it is drawn from the Mines. The great circulation of money, which at first was general, ceases; poverty & misery follow, & the working of the Mines appears to be only for the advantage of those employed in them, & for the Foreigners who profit from it.

This is about what has happened to Spain since the discovery of the Indies. As for the Portuguese, since the discovery of the gold Mines of Brazil, they have almost always used the products and the Manufactures of Foreigners; & it seems as if they work the Mines only for the account & advantage of these same Foreigners. All the gold & silver which these two States draw from the Mines furnishes them no more in circulation than it does others. England & France even have more of it ordinarily.

Now if the increase of money in the State is derived from a balance of trade with Foreigners (that is, by sending them products & Manufactures of greater value & quantity than we import from them & consequently receiving the surplus in money), this annual increase of money will enrich a great number of Merchants & Entrepreneurs in the State, & will give employment to many Artisans & Workmen who furnish the products which are sent Abroad whence this money is obtained. This will gradually increase the consumption of these industrious inhabitants, & will raise the prices of land & labor. But the industrial Classes, who are eager to accumulate property, will not increase their expenditures at first; they will wait until they have accumulated a good fortune, from which they can obtain a sure interest independently of their trade. When a great number of inhabitants have acquired considerable fortunes from this money which enters constantly & annually into the State, they will not fail to increase their consumption & to make all things dear. Although this dearness involves them in even greater expenditures than they had at first intended to make, they will not for the most part give them up, as long as they have any capital left; since nothing is easier or more agreeable than to increase the expenditures of families, but nothing is more difficult or more disagreeable than to reduce them.

If an annual & constant balance has caused a considerable increase of money in a State, it will not fail to increase consumption, to raise the price of everything, & even to diminish the number of inhabitants, unless an additional amount of commodities is obtained from Abroad in proportion to the increase of consumption. Moreover, States which have acquired a considerable abundance of money ordinarily import many things from neighboring countries where money is scarce, & where everything is consequently cheap: but since money has to be sent for that, the balance of trade will become smaller. The cheapness of land & labor in foreign countries where money is scarce will naturally cause Manufactures & other industries to be set up there like those of the State, but which will not at first be as perfect or as well liked.

In this situation, the State can subsist amid an abundance of money, consume all its produce & even much of the produce of foreign countries, & still over & above all that keep a small balance of trade over Foreign Countries, or at least keep this balance many years at par; that is, to import in exchange for its products & its Manufactures, as much money from these foreign countries as it has to send them in exchange for commodities or the produce of land which it imports from them. If this State is a maritime State, the facility & cheapness of its shipping for the transport of its products & its Manufactures into foreign countries may compensate in some measure for the dearness of labor which the excessive supply of money causes there; with the result that the products & the Manufactures of the State, dear as they are, will not cease to be sold in distant foreign countries, at lower prices sometimes than the Manufactures of another State where labor is cheaper.

The expenses of carriage increase considerably the prices of things transported into distant countries; but these expenses are rather moderate in maritime States, where there is regular transportation to all Ports abroad, so that Ships ready to sail are almost always to be found there, which load with all the merchandise entrusted to them, for a very reasonable freight charge.

It is not so in States where navigation is not flourishing; there it is necessary to build ships expressly for the transport of merchandise, which sometimes wipes out all the profit; & the expenses of operation are always high, which discourages commerce altogether.

England consumes nowadays not only the greater part of her scanty produce, but also much of the produce of other countries; such as silks, wines, fruits, considerable amounts of linen &c., while she sends Abroad only the output of her Mines, her Products, & her Manufactures for the most part, & however dear labor is there, as a result of the plenty of money, she does not cease selling her products in distant countries, as a result of the advantage of her navigation, at prices as reasonable as in France, where these same goods are much less expensive.

The increase in the quantity of money in a State may also be caused, without any balance of commerce, by subsidies paid to this State by foreign Powers; by the expenses of numerous Ambassadors, or Travellers, who may be led to go there for political reasons, or by curiosity, or for pleasure; by the transfer of the property & fortunes of Families, who from motives of religious liberty, or for other reasons, leave their native land to take up their residence in this State. In all these cases, the sums which come into the State always cause an increase of expenditures & consumption there, & consequently raise the prices of everything in the channels of trade which the money enters.

Let us suppose that a quarter of the inhabitants of the State consume meat, wine, beer, &c. daily, & buy themselves clothing, linen, &c. frequently, before the introduction of the increase of money, but that after this introduction, a third or a half of the inhabitants consume these same things; the prices of these commodities & of this merchandise will not fail to rise, & the dearness of meat will induce several of the inhabitants who made up the quarter of the State to consume less than ordinarily. A Man who eats three pounds of meat per day will still get along on two pounds, but he feels this retrenchment; while the other half of the inhabitants, who used to eat almost none, will not feel it. Bread will become dearer, indeed, by degrees, as a result of this increase in consumption, as I have often pointed out, but it will be less dear in proportion than meat. The increase in the price of meat causes a diminution in the share of a small part of the inhabitants, which makes it perceptible; but the increase in the price of bread diminishes the share of all the inhabitants, which renders it less perceptible. If a hundred thousand additional persons come to live in a State which contains ten million inhabitants, their extra consumption of bread will amount to only one pound in a hundred, which will have to be taken from the former inhabitants; but when a man, instead of a hundred pounds of bread, consumes ninety-nine pounds for his subsistence, he hardly feels this retrenchment.

When the consumption of meat increases, the Farmers increase their meadows in order to raise more meat, which decreases the quantity of arable fields, consequently the amount of wheat. But what causes meat to rise proportionately more in price than bread, ordinarily, is that the importation of wheat from foreign countries into the State is usually permitted freely, while the importation of cattle is strictly forbidden, as in England, or is subject to considerable import duties, as is the case in other States. This is the reason why the rents of meadows & pastures rise in England, when money is plentiful, three times as much as the rents of arable lands. . . .

VII

Continuation of the same subject of the increase & diminution of the amount of money in a State

Since gold, silver, & copper have an intrinsic value in proportion to the land & labor which enter into their production, in the localities where they are mined, & also to the expenses of importing or introducing them into States which have no Mines, the quantity of money, like that of all other commodities, determines its value in the altercations of Markets as compared with all other things.

If England begins to use gold, silver & copper for the first time in barter, money will be esteemed, according to the amount of it in circulation, in proportion to its value compared with all other commodities & merchandise, & this valuation will be arrived at roughly by the altercations of the Markets. Upon the basis of these valuations, Proprietors of lands & Entrepreneurs will fix the wages of the Servants & Workmen they employ, at so much per day or per year, in such a way that they & their families may be able to live on the wages given them.

Let us suppose, now, that as a result of the residence of Ambassadors & foreign Travellers in England, as much money has been introduced into that country's circulation as there was originally; this money will pass at first into the hands of numerous Artisans, Domestics, Entrepreneurs, & others who will have taken part in the work on the equipages, entertainments, &c. of these Foreigners: the Manufacturers, Farmers & other Entrepreneurs will be aware of this increase of money which will accustom many persons to making greater expenditures than in the past, which will consequently raise the prices in the Markets. Even the Children of these Entrepreneurs & these Artisans will begin to make new expenditures: their Fathers amid this plenty will give them some money for their small pleasures, with which they will buy cakes, tarts, &c., & this new amount of money will be distributed in such a way that several persons who used to live without ever handling any money will not fail to have some in the present case. Many exchanges which formerly took place by barter will now be made with the help of ready money, & consequently there will be more rapidity in the circulation of money than there was at the beginning in England.

I conclude from all this that as a result of the introduction of a double quantity of money into a State, the prices of commodities & merchandise are not always doubled. A River which follows a winding course will not flow twice as fast, if the volume of its waters is doubled.

The proportion of dearness, which the increase & the quantity of money introduce into the State, will depend on the effect produced by this money on consumption & on circulation. Through whatever hands the money introduced passes, it will naturally increase consumption; but this increase will be greater or less according to circumstances; it will affect certain kinds of commodities or merchandise more or less, according to the tastes of those who acquire the money. The prices in the Markets will rise more for some kinds than for others, however plentiful money may be. In England, the price of meat might triple, without the price of wheat rising more than a quarter.

It is always permitted in England to import grain from foreign countries, but the importation of cattle is not allowed. As a result, however considerable the increase of money may be in England, the price of wheat can never rise higher there than in other countries where money is scarce, except by the amount of the expenses & risks involved in importing wheat from these same foreign countries.

It is not the same with the price of cattle, which will necessarily be in proportion to the quantity of money offered for meat, as compared with the amount of this meat & the number of cattle raised there.

An ox weighing eight hundred pounds sells nowadays in Poland & in Hungary for two or three ounces of silver, while in the London Market it is generally sold for more than forty ounces of silver. However, a quarter of grain does not sell in London for twice as much as in Poland & in Hungary.

The increase of money increases the price of commodities & merchandise only by the cost of transportation, when this transportation is permitted. But in many cases this transportation would cost more than the value of the article; which makes forests useless in many places. This same transportation is the reason why milk, fresh butter, fresh vegetables, game, &c. are worth almost nothing in the Provinces at a distance from the Capital.

I conclude that an increase of money in a State always leads to an increase of consumption there & the habit of making greater expenditures. But the dearness caused by this money does not affect all kinds of commodities & merchandise equally, in proportion to the quantity of this money; unless what is introduced is continued in the same channels of circulation as the original money; that is, unless those who offered one ounce of silver in the Markets are the same & the only ones who now offer two ounces there, since the doubling of the weight of the money in circulation, which never happens. I take it that when a substantial addition is made to the money of a State, the new money gives a new turn to consumption, & even a rapidity to circulation; but it is not possible to determine the exact degree.

VIII

Of the interest of money & its causes

As the prices of things are determined in the altercations of the markets by the quantity of things offered for sale in proportion to the amount of money offered for them, or, what is the same thing, by the numerical proportion between the Sellers & the Buyers; similarly the interest of money in a State is determined by the numerical proportion between the Lenders & the Borrowers.

Although money passes as a pledge in exchange, yet it does not multiply, & does not produce any interest by merely circulating. The necessities of Men seem to have introduced the practice of interest. A Man who lends his money upon good security, or upon land mortgages, runs at least the risk of the enmity of the Borrower, or that of the expenses of law suits & losses; but when he lends without security, he runs the risk of losing all. Because of these reasons, Men in need must have at first tempted the Lenders by the attraction of a profit; & this profit must have been in proportion to the needs of the Borrowers & to the fear & the avarice of the Lenders. This, it seems to me, was the original source of interest. But its constant practice in States appears to be founded upon the profits which Entrepreneurs can make out of it.

Land produces naturally, aided by the labor of Man, four, ten, twenty, fifty, a hundred, a hundred & fifty times the quantity of wheat sown, according to the quality of the land & the industry of the Inhabitants. It multiplies fruits & Cattle. The Farmer who cultivates it ordinarily has two thirds of the produce, of which one third pays his expenses & his support, the other remains to him as the profit on his enterprise.

If the Farmer has enough funds to carry on his enterprise, if he has all the tools & the equipment necessary, the horses for cultivating, the cattle needed to develop the land, &c., he will take for himself, all expenses paid, a third of the produce of the Farm. But if an experienced Laborer, living by his labor at wages from hand to mouth, & having no land, can find someone willing to lend him land, or money to buy some, he will be in a position to give this Lender all of the third rent, or a third of the produce of a Farm of which he will become the Farmer or Entrepreneur. However, he will consider his position better than formerly, seeing that he will find his subsistence in the second rent, & will become a Master, whereas before he was a Servant: so that if, through his great economy, & by depriving himself of certain necessaries, he can gradually accumulate a small capital, he will have to borrow less & less every year, & will succeed in time in appropriating all the third rent for himself.

If this new Entrepreneur finds an opportunity to buy wheat or cattle on credit, to pay for them after a considerable time & when he will be in a position to make money by the sale of the produce of his Farm, he will readily pay a higher price for them than that of the market for cash: & this method will be the same as if he borrowed money to buy the wheat for cash, paying as interest the difference between the price for cash & for credit: but in whatever way he borrows, whether cash or merchandise, he has to have something left to live on from his enterprise, or else he will be bankrupt. This risk will cause people to demand of him twenty to thirty per cent profit or interest upon the amount of money or upon the value of the commodities or merchandise lent to him.

In another case, a master Hatter, who has some capital to carry on his hat Manufacture, either to hire a house, buy beavers, wool, dye, &c., or to pay every week the subsistence of his Workmen, must not only obtain his living out of this enterprise, but also a profit similar to that of the Farmer, who has the third part for himself. This living, like this profit, must be derived from the sale of the hats, of which the price must pay not only for the materials but also for the support of the Hatter & of his Workmen, & also the profit in question.

But a Journeyman Hatter, experienced, but without capital, can undertake the same Manufacture, borrowing money
& materials, & giving up the profit to anyone willing to lend
him money, or to anyone willing to entrust him with beaver,
wool, &c., for which he will pay only after considerable time
& when he has sold his hats. If, at the maturity of his notes,
the Lender of the money calls for his capital again, or if the
wool Merchant & the other Lenders do not wish to trust him
any longer, he will have to give up his enterprise; in which
case he will perhaps prefer to become bankrupt. But if he is
steady & industrious, he will be able to make his creditors
see that he has, in money or in hats, approximately the
value of the capital he borrowed, & they will probably prefer to continue to trust him & to be satisfied, for the present,
with their interest or profit. Which will enable him to continue, & perhaps he will gradually accumulate some capital
by depriving himself of a few necessaries. With this help he
will have to borrow less & less every year, & when he has
accumulated sufficient capital to carry on his Manufacture,
which will always be in proportion to the market he has, the
profit will all remain to him, & he will grow rich, if he does
not increase his expenditures.

It is well to note that the living expenses of such a Manufacturer are of relatively small value, compared to that of
the sums he borrows in his business, or of the materials entrusted to him; & consequently the Lenders do not run a
great risk of losing their capital, if he is an honest & industrious man: but as it is very possible that he may not be,
the Lenders will always demand of him a profit or interest
of twenty to thirty per cent of the value of the loan: besides
it will be only those who have a good opinion of him who will
trust him. We can reason in the same way with respect to
all Masters, Artisans, Manufacturers, & other Entrepreneurs
in the State, who conduct enterprises of which the capital
exceeds considerably the value of their annual subsistence.

But if a water Carrier in Paris sets up as an Entrepreneur
of his own work, all the capital he will need will be the price

of two buckets, which he will be able to buy for an ounce of silver, after which all that he earns becomes profit. If he earns by his labor fifty ounces of silver per year, the sum of his capital or loan will be to that of his profit as one to fifty. That is, he will make five thousand per cent, while the Hatter will not make fifty per cent, & will even be obliged to pay twenty to thirty per cent of it to the Lender.

However, a Lender of money will prefer to lend a thousand ounces of silver to a Hatter at twenty per cent interest, rather than to lend a thousand ounces to a thousand water Carriers at five hundred per cent interest. The water Carriers will soon spend on their subsistence not only the money they earn by their daily work, but all that is lent to them. These capitals that are lent to them are small in proportion to the sum they need for their subsistence: whether they have much or little employment, they can easily spend all they earn. Thus the earnings of these humble Entrepreneurs cannot be determined. One might well say that a water Carrier makes five thousand per cent of the value of the buckets which constitute the capital of his enterprise, & even ten thousand per cent, if by strenuous work he earned a hundred ounces a year. But since he can spend the hundred ounces on his living expenses, as well as the fifty, it is only by knowing how much he does spend for his living that one can tell how much clear profit he has.

It is always necessary to deduct the subsistence & living expenses of the Entrepreneurs before deciding about their profit. That is what we did in the example of the Farmer, & in that of the Hatter: & this is what cannot be determined for the humble Entrepreneurs: & so they generally become bankrupt, if they have any debts.

It is customary for the Brewers of London to lend some barrels of beer to the Entrepreneurs of Taverns, & when the latter pay for the first barrels, more are lent to them. If the consumption in these Taverns becomes large, these Brewers sometimes make a profit of five hundred per cent per year; & I have heard it said that the big Brewers do not fail to

make money, as long as only half of the Taverns go bankrupt on them in the course of the year.

All the Merchants in the State make a regular practice
of entrusting merchandise or commodities to Retailers on
credit, & adjust their rate of profit, or their interest, to the
risk they run. This risk is always great on account of the
great proportion which the living expenses of the borrower
bear to the amount lent. For if the borrower or retailer has
not a prompt sale in small trade, he will soon be ruined &
will spend all that he has borrowed upon his subsistence,
& consequently will be obliged to become bankrupt. The
Hucksters who buy fish at Billingsgate, in London, to resell
it in the other sections of the City, ordinarily pay by a contract drawn by a Notary, one shilling per guinea, or per
twenty-one shillings, interest per week; which amounts to
two hundred sixty per cent per year. The Hucksters in the
Market at Paris, whose enterprises are less considerable, pay
five *sous* interest per week per *ecu* of three *livres*, which is
more than four hundred thirty per cent per year; however,
there are few Lenders who make a fortune from such high
interest rates.

These high interest rates are not only tolerated, but are
even in a way useful & necessary in a State. Those who buy
fish in the streets pay this heavy interest in the increased
price which they give; this is a convenience to them, & they
do not feel the loss of it. Similarly an Artisan who drinks a
mug of beer, & pays a price for it which allows the Brewer a
profit of five hundred per cent, enjoys this convenience, &
does not feel the loss at all on such small transactions. . . .

XII

FERDINANDO GALIANI

DELLA MONETA

NOTE

FERDINANDO GALIANI (1728–1787) was a native of Chieti. He was educated for the church and attained the rank of monsignore, but most of his life was spent in the service of the state. He published his brilliant *Della Moneta* anonymously in 1751, and did not acknowledge the authorship till some thirty years later. In the meantime he had established a reputation as a wit and a scholar by various other publications, and had been sent to Paris as secretary of the Neapolitan legation, of which he was later made the head. He also spent considerable time in London, being there when his *Dialogues sur le Commerce des Blés* was published (1770). This able work, in which he attacked the doctrines of the Physiocrats, and argued against all attempts at system building in economic matters, attracted much attention, and was probably a factor in the author's appointment as a member of the supreme board of trade at Naples, and later minister of the royal domains. His works are marked by great dialectic skill and unusual powers of analysis but he is not always an entirely fair critic.

MONEY

I

EXPLANATION OF THE PRINCIPLES WHICH GOVERN THE VALUE
OF ALL THINGS — OF UTILITY AND SCARCITY, THE FUNDA-
MENTALS OF VALUE — REPLIES TO MANY OBJECTIONS

THE acquisition of gold and silver, from which the most
valuable money is made, has always been, and still is,
the ultimate goal of the desires of the multitude, the disdain
and scorn of those few who claim the honorable name of
"philosophers." Of these two opposed opinions, the one is
often base or ill-regulated, while the other is for the most
part unjust or not very sincere. Thus, with some valuing
them too high, and the others too low, there is no one left to
judge and reason sanely about the value of these metals.
Very many people, I believe, are convinced that their price
is purely chimerical and arbitrary, and that it results from a
popular error, developed in us along with our education; and
hence these people always give it such uncomplimentary
names as "madness," "delirium," "error," and "folly."
Some, more discrete, believe that the consent of men, after
they had decided to use money, originally gave to the metals
chosen for the purpose this merit, which they do not possess
in themselves. There are very few who realize that these
have their just price and value always fixed and settled in
their nature itself, and in the constitution of human minds.
How important it is to demonstrate this truth, before going
on, the reader will understand, when he considers that at
every step, whether discussing extrinsic value, raising, interest, exchange, or the ratio between moneys, we always
have to do with a definite intrinsic and natural value.

Aristotle, a man of very great and extraordinary genius,
in the fifth book of his *Ethics*, the seventh chapter, where he

has developed many fine ideas, expresses the following opinion about the nature of money: *Money is derived from convention, and for this reason is called* νόμισμα, *that is, from law, because its value depends not upon nature but upon law, and because it is in our power to change it and render it useless.*[1] And in his *Politics,* in the first book, the sixth chapter, he says the same thing. Now if this philosopher has been followed in his teachings more than he deserved, to our loss, there is no better example of it than this. Hence we see that Bishop Covarruvias follows his master's argument thus: *If money receives its value, not from nature but from the prince, and can be rendered useless by his revoking the law, surely the material itself of gold or silver is not valued as high as the money itself; since, if it were valued as high, it would have its price from nature itself, not from law.* This line of reasoning is followed by the Aristotelians, who may be said to make up the body of moralists and juriconsults. How correct such conclusions are, assuming this premise to be true, is plain. How fatal they may be and productive of misfortunes for a people, I would that our own experience never had to demonstrate to us. But these opinions cannot be refuted without destroying their basis. Hence I do not know, nor can I understand, how John Locke, Davanzati, Broggia, the author of the work *On Commerce,* and the author of the one *On the Spirit of Laws,* and several others, not denying the first principle, have had contrary opinions and built solidly upon a false foundation, without recognizing the weakness of the one or the unsteadiness of the other. Therefore I shall make every effort, first of all, to demonstrate what I have long believed, that not only the metals of which money is made, but everything else in the world, without exception, has its natural value, derived from definite, general, and constant principles; that neither caprice, nor law, nor the prince, nor anything else can violate these principles and their effects; and finally that in valuing things men, as the scholastics say,

---

[1] Galiani quotes in Latin, which I have rendered literally. Cf. p. 27, above. — Ed.

are passive factors. Whatever edifice may be raised upon these foundations will be durable and eternal. The reader will pardon me for some length, in view of the importance of the subject; and, if he should wish to blame me, let him blame rather that infinite number of writers, who have either not recognized so great a truth, or have not wished to demonstrate it, as they ought.

The value of things (since I am reasoning about all in general) is defined by many as the esteem which men have for them; but perhaps these words do not arouse a clearer and more distinct idea than the first ones did. Hence one might say that esteem, or value, is AN IDEA OF PROPORTION BETWEEN THE POSSESSION OF ONE THING AND THAT OF ANOTHER IN THE MIND OF A MAN. Thus, when we say that ten bushels of grain are worth as much as a cask of wine, there is an expression of equality between having one thing or the other; hence it is that men, always very careful not to be defrauded of their pleasures, exchange one thing for the other, since in equality there is no loss or gain.

From what I have said, it is evident that, since the constitutions of human minds are varied and needs are varied, the value of things varies. Hence it is that some things, being more generally relished and sought, have a value called current; while others are valued only by the desire on the part of the one who wishes to have them and the one who gives them up.

Value, then, is a ratio; and this is compounded of two ratios, expressed by the names UTILITY and SCARCITY. I will explain what I mean by giving examples, so that there may be no dispute over the words. It is evident that air and water, which are elements very useful for human life, have no value, because they lack scarcity; and, on the other hand, a bag of sand from the shores of Japan would be a rare thing, but, assuming that it had no special utility, it would have no value.

But here I realize someone will ask me what great utility I find in many things which bring a very high price. And, since this natural and frequent difficulty seems to make men out to be foolish and unreasonable, and at the same time destroys the foundations of the science of money, it will be necessary to discuss the utility of things, and its measurement, more fully. If it does not depend upon definite principles, the price of things will not have any either; and then there will be no more science of money; for there is no science where there is no proof and certainty.

By utility I mean a thing's capacity to bring happiness. Man is made up of passions, which move him with unequal force. The satisfaction of them is pleasure. The acquisition of pleasure is happiness. Wherein (since I, being no epicurean, do not even wish to seem one), may I be permitted to explain my meaning, and to make a digression. It is to be noted that the satisfaction of one passion which vexes and irritates another is not complete happiness; but if the vexation it causes is greater than the pleasure, it is to be avoided as a real evil and pain. If the pain is less than the pleasure, it will be a good, but imperfect and curtailed. This holds good both with respect to the pleasures of this life considered absolutely, and when they are viewed in conjunction with the life eternal. To us it is manifest (thanks to Providence) that after this life we shall live another, the pleasures or pains of which are strictly connected with the actions of the present. Therefore, without changing what I have said, the pleasures of this life which do not harm those of the other are true and perfect; but those which in that life will produce pain (the difference between the pleasures and the pains of the one life and those of the other being infinite), however great may be the pleasure in the one case, and however small the evil in the other, will always be deceptive and false pleasures. If this explanation, occupying but few lines, were made by everyone, the old conflict between the Epicureans and the Stoics, between sensuality and virtue, would not have been heard, and either the Stoics would have been wrong, or it would have been seen that they were only disputing foolishly over words. I return now to the argument.

Everything is useful that can produce a true pleasure, that is, which satisfies the desire aroused by a passion. Now our passions are not merely the desire for food, drink, and sleep. These are merely the primary ones; and when they are satisfied, others equally strong arise. For man is so constituted that he has scarcely satisfied one desire, when another shows itself, which is always as powerful a stimulus as the first; and so he is kept perpetually active, and never manages to satisfy himself entirely. Hence it is not true that the only useful things are those required for the first needs of life; nor can any boundary be found between what is necessary and what is not; it being very true that, as soon as the need of one thing ceases, because we have obtained it, we begin to feel a need of something else.

But among all the passions which appear in the human mind, after those are satisfied which we share with animals, and which are designed for the preservation of the individual or the species, none has more power to move man than the desire for distinction and superiority over others. This, being the eldest child of self-love, that is, of our chief impulse, surpasses every other passion, and causes the things which help to satisfy it to have the greatest value, every other pleasure and often the safety of life itself being subordinated to the acquisition of them. Whether men act justly in thinking and deciding thus, let each one judge for himself: it is certain that men act no more reasonably in buying food when they have none, than a title of nobility when they are provided with food; for if life is miserable and unhappy when I am hungry, it is just as unhappy when I am not esteemed or regarded; and sometimes this unhappiness is so much greater, that we would rather die or expose ourselves to obvious danger of death than live unhappily without the respect of other men. What is more just, then, than to procure, even with great and long toil and labor, a thing which is very useful, since it produces many great pleasures? For if anyone scoffs at this deriving pleasure from the esteem and respect of others, this is a criticism of our nature, which has endowed us with this mental make-up, not of ourselves, who have received it without being able to get rid of it, and who neither must nor can account for it to anyone, any more than for hunger, thirst, or sleep. For if certain philosophers have shown disdain for this esteem of others, and have scorned riches and rank; if they say they did this because the respect of others did not give them pleasure, they lie: for they were impelled to make such assertions by no other motive than the certainty they felt of being liberally applauded and commended by the people for such beliefs and actions.

Thus those things which win respect deservedly have the greatest value. Such are rank, titles, honors, nobility, authority, which are for the most part intangible things. Next come certain objects which, on account of their beauty, have always been eagerly sought by men; and those who have chanced to possess them and use them as ornaments have been esteemed and envied. These are gems, rare stones, certain skins, the most beautiful metals, namely, gold and silver, and some works of art embodying much labor and beauty. On account of the concern which all men feel about the adornment of their persons, these objects have become adapted to conferring on some people the superiority which, as I have said, is the source of the keenest pleasure. Hence their value is deservedly great; it being only too true that kings themselves owe the greater part of the veneration of their subjects to the exterior trappings which always surround them, and they have realized that without these, though they retained the same endowments of mind and power as before, the reverence toward them has greatly decreased. And therefore those powers which have less real force and authority resort to greater outward display to control the ideas of men, among whom the august and the magnificent is often no more than a glorified nothing called formality, a word drawn from the schools and rather suitable, meaning: that which does not exist, neither nothing nor something.

But if among men the desire to make a good appearance

arouses a love for these more rare and beautiful products of nature, among women and children the ardent desire to appear beautiful makes these objects of the utmost value. Women, who constitute a half of the human race, and all or most of whom appear destined solely for our propagation and education, have no other price and merit but the love they awaken among the males; and this being almost wholly a result of beauty, they have no greater concern than to appear beautiful to the eyes of man. How much ornaments contribute to this is a matter of common agreement: hence, if value among women results from love, and this from beauty, which is increased by ornaments, there is all too good reason why they should value these very high.

As for children, they are the most tender care of their parents; and men know no way to show this tenderness of love except by rendering the object loved attractive and pretty to their eyes. Now what will man not do when he is actuated by the desire to satisfy woman and to adorn his children? Thus it has come about that the most beautiful metals have been gathered with great effort, at first in the sands of rivers, later in the bowels of the earth. And hence it is that the very peoples that are considered rich in these metals, such as the Mexicans and the Peruvians, next to gems value nothing higher than gold and silver. And if they esteem our trifles of glass and steel more, that confirms rather than destroys what I have said above; for the beauty of our workmanship was what enchanted them. The fact that this beauty of glass and crystal is the product of art rather than of nature does not alter the price, except by altering the scarcity; which being unknown to the Americans, cannot be used as an argument against what I have shown.

But most men, including Bernardo Davanzati, reason thus: A natural calf is nobler than a golden calf, but how much less its value is. I answer, that if a natural calf were as rare as one of gold, its price would be as much more than that of the golden calf as the utility and need of the one exceeds that of the other. These people imagine that value depends on a single factor, rather than on many which unite to form a compound ratio. Others, I believe, say that a pound of bread is more useful than a pound of gold. I answer that this is a shameful fallacy, due to not knowing that "more useful" and "less useful" are relative terms, which are measured according to the varying condition of individuals. If we are speaking of one who lacks bread and gold, the bread is certainly more useful; but the facts correspond to this and are not contrary, for no one will be found who would leave the bread and die of hunger, taking gold instead. Those who dig in the mines never forget to eat and sleep. But to a man who is satiated, is anything more useless than bread? Hence it is well if he satisfies other passions then. Therefore these metals are companions of luxury, that is, of that state in which the first needs are already satisfied. Therefore, if Davanzati says that an egg, worth half a grain of gold, was able to keep Count Ugolino in the dungeon from starving ten days, which all the gold in the world could not do, he is badly confusing the price given an egg by a man not in danger of death, if he does not get it, and the needs of Count Ugolino. Who told him that the count would not have paid even a thousand grains of gold for the egg? The proof of this error is shown us by Davanzati himself a little later, without realizing it, when he says: A rat is a disgusting thing; but during the siege of Casilino one was sold for two hundred florins, on account of famine; and it was not dear, for the one who sold it died of hunger, and the other was saved. Here for once, thanks to heaven, he has admitted that dear and cheap are relative terms.

Now if anyone is astonished that precisely all the most useful things are of low value, while the less useful ones are of high and exorbitant value, he should note that, with marvelous providence, this world is so constituted for our good that utility, generally speaking, is never found with scarcity; but the more primary utility increases, the greater abundance is found with it, and therefore the value cannot be great. The things needed to sustain life are so plentifully spread over the whole earth, that they have no, or fairly little, value. Hence no false accusations against our judgment can be derived from such considerations as these, or unjust disdain for what we value, as so many think; but always sentiments of humility and gratitude to the beneficent hand of God, blessing it at every instant, which very few do.

. . . .

By scarcity I mean the proportion between the quantity of a thing and the use made of it. By use I mean not only the destruction of a thing, but such occupation as prevents it from satisfying the desires of another, while one person is using it. Suppose, for example, there are a hundred pictures offered for sale; if a gentleman buys fifty of them, pictures become about twice as scarce, not because they are consumed, but because fifty are no longer for sale; which in such a case may be called dropping out of commerce. It is true, however, that destruction makes things dearer than does this removal from commerce; for the former takes away all hope entirely, while the latter is rated according to the probability that the thing occupied and out of circulation will return to market and commerce; and this deserves some reflection.

Going on now to discuss the quantity of a thing, I say that there are two classes of objects. In some it depends upon the varying abundance with which nature produces them; in others only upon the varying amount of toil and work bestowed upon them. The first class is composed of those things which may be reproduced after a short time, and which are destroyed in consumption, such as the fruits of the earth and animals. In these, according to the changes in the seasons, about the same labor may produce a yield eight or ten times greater one year than the year before. Hence it is that the abundance of these does not depend upon the human will but upon climate and weather conditions. In the other class are to be included certain objects, such as minerals, stones, marbles, which are not produced in varying amounts every year, but are scattered in deposits over the world, and the output of which depends upon our will; because, if more people devote themselves to these things, more can be obtained from the bowels of the earth. Thus, when we wish to make calculations concerning objects of this class, we need only compute the labor of procuring them, the quantity of the material always corresponding to this. Not that I think that new metals and gems are not produced by nature in her great laboratories; but, as this production is very slow, it should not be taken into account on a par with consumption.

Now I come to the question of labor, which is the sole source of value, not only in all things which are entirely works of art, such as pictures, sculptures, engravings, etc., but also in many objects such as minerals, rocks, the spontaneous plants of the forests, etc. The amount of material enters into the value of these objects only insofar as it increases or decreases the labor. Thus, if anyone asks why the gold found mixed with sand on the banks of many rivers is worth more than the sand, he should note that, if one wishes to fill a bag of sand in a quarter of an hour, he can do so easily, but if he wishes it full of gold, many whole years are required to gather the very rare grains of gold which that sand contains.

In computing labor, we should attend to three things: the number of the people, the time, and the different wages of the workers. I will first discuss the number of people. It is certain that nobody works except to live, nor can he work, if he does not live. Hence, if the labor of fifty persons is required for the manufacture of a roll of cloth, reckoning from the shearing of the wool till it is displayed in the shop, this cloth will be worth more than the wool in it, by an amount equal to the cost of supporting these fifty men for a period equal to that spent on the work: for if twenty are employed for a whole day, ten for half a day, and twenty for three days, the value of the cloth will be equal to the subsistence of a man for eighty-five days; and of these days, the first group earn twenty, the second five, and the third sixty.

This is plain, if we assume that these people all receive the same wages. Let us now take up the question of time.

In the time should be included not only that actually devoted to the work, but also that devoted to rest; for subsistence is also required during a period of rest. This, however, is when the labor is interrupted either by the nature of the work or by law, but not by laziness; unless this laziness is so general in a nation that it has as much force as custom and law. Thus holidays, among those peoples who observe them by not working, render commodities dearer than elsewhere. For, assuming that a man, by working three hundred days a year, finishes a hundred pairs of shoes, the value of these necessarily corresponds to his whole subsistence for a year. But if another, by working three hundred sixty days, finishes a hundred twenty pairs, he will sell his for one fifth less, not having to derive any more gain from the hundred twenty pairs of shoes than the first man derives from his hundred pairs.

Furthermore, there are some kinds of work which by nature cannot be carried on without interruption. Such are the fine arts: for I do not believe there is any sculptor or musician who works more than a hundred days a year; so much time is required for finding work, collecting payment, travelling, and other things, and so their work is justly dearer. Finally we should note the different ages at which a man can begin to earn by his labor in the different trades. Hence those arts and studies which require much time to learn, and involve great expense on the part of parents, bear a higher price; as the wood of pines and nut trees costs more than poplar and elm, on account of the slow growth of these trees.

So much for time. But it is a more abstruse problem, and less understood, to make a just computation of the different values of human talents, from which the different prices of labor are derived. I shall give my views, remaining uncertain whether another would agree with me, since I have found no writer who discusses it. I shall be extremely

pleased to be attacked with reason and honesty by anyone
who has a different and better opinion.

I believe that the value of human talents is determined in
the very same way as that of inanimate things, and that it is
regulated by the same principles of scarcity and utility combined. Men are born endowed by Providence with apti-
tudes for different trades, but in different degrees of scarcity,
and corresponding with marvelous wisdom to human needs.
Thus, of a thousand men, six hundred, for example, are
suited only for agriculture, three hundred adapted to handicrafts of various kinds, fifty to large-scale commerce, and
fifty are fitted to succeed in studies and teaching. Now, on
this assumption, the reward of a man of letters, compared
with a farmer, will be in inverse ratio to this number, that is,
as 600 to 50, or twelve times as great. It is not utility alone,
therefore, which governs prices: for God causes the men
who carry on the trades of greatest utility to be born in large
numbers, and so their value cannot be great, these being, so
to speak, the bread and wine of men; but scholars and
philosophers, who may be called the gems among talents,
deservedly bear a very high price.

Be it noted, however, that scarcity is not to be reckoned
according to the proportion in which talents are produced,
but according to the numbers that reach maturity; hence
the greater the difficulty of developing a talent to a high degree worthy of it, the greater is its price. A general such as
Prince Eugene or Marshal Turenne has an immense price,
in comparison with a common soldier; not because nature
produces so few geniuses like these, but because only a very
few are in such fortunate circumstances that they are able,
by exercising their gifts, to become victorious great captains.
Nature acts in this as in the seeds of plants, where, as if foreseeing the great losses, she produces and drops a good many
more upon the ground than there come plants eventually;
hence a plant is worth more than a seed. When we consider
these sound principles seriously, how marvelously the justice
of human judgments stands out! It will be found that

everything is valued by a standard. It will be realized that the only way riches come to a person is in payment for the just value of his work; although he can give these riches to someone who does not deserve to acquire them. And indeed there is no family or man, that may be called rich, that did not obtain these riches through merit, or as a gift from someone who obtained them through merit. This gift, if made during the giver's life-time, is called a favor; if upon his death, an inheritance. But if we trace back the riches which someone possesses undeservedly, it will always be found that they were originally acquired through merit from the whole body of men. It is true that it is often necessary to go back over a hundred years or persons; but eventually this end is reached, and reason leads us to expect it.

Someone, however, will probably say that merit or virtue goes so often unrewarded that it is folly to deny the frequent and atrocious acts of human injustice. But here let me point out the false reasoning to anyone who does not see it. In the first place, we do not need to apply the names "virtue" and "wisdom" to those professions which, although very scarce and difficult, are not suited to produce true utility or pleasure for the multitude, by whom prices are made, rather than by a few. In the second place, it is to be recalled that since man is made up of virtues and vices, it is impossible to reward the virtues without rewarding the vicious man at the same time; but it will never be found that vice has exalted anyone. It is the useful and good talents a man has which elevate him, and his defects merely fail to obstruct them at times. But it is always true that, if he did not have these defects, he would have gone higher. In the third place, it should always be noted that it is one thing to have skill in obtaining employment, and another to know how to do the work well. The first is merely the art of pleasing the employer, and is always the same, whether it be a position in the toga or in the army that is sought. The talents required for performing one's duties are always different, according to the different positions. Now it is rare that you will find a man who has a position and has not had the skill required to obtain it; but it may well happen that, not knowing how to obtain employment, as well as how to perform his duties, he does badly, is blamed, and is considered undeserving. For men give the name merit only to the knowledge of how to do the work in hand well. For the other they have no concern, as if it were not virtue or did not require labor or skill: hence they call a thing injustice which in a certain way is not. Here also, however, we should not include those who obtain some dignity either through the favor of another, which is a gift between the living, or through descent, which is an inheritance from ancestors. I realize that I have gone outside the limits of my subject; but I have not been able to refrain from doing so, because it seemed to me to be material well worth discussion. Whether my readers pardon me or blame me for it, I shall be satisfied, if I have the pleasure of winning them to my opinion. I fear, however, that few of them will agree with me: so much do men like to accuse others of injustice, in order to defend themselves from blame.

Enough has been said concerning the principles upon which value depends; and we have seen that, since these are certain, constant, universal, and based upon the order and the nature of earthly things, there is nothing arbitrary and accidental among us, but all is order, harmony, and necessity. Values are varied, but not capricious. Their very variation itself is according to order and exact and immutable rules. They are ideal, but our ideas themselves, being founded upon needs and pleasures, that is, upon the inner constitution of man, possess justice and stability.

There seems to be one exception to be made to what I have said; and it is that value and our ideas are sometimes also affected by fashion. After lengthy consideration, I have not been able to devise any definition of this word except the following: an affection of the brain, peculiar to the European nations, as a result of which many things become of small value, simply because they are not new. This is a disease of the mind, which has control over not a few things;

and if we wish to find something reasonable about it, we must say that this diversity of taste is due to a large extent to imitating the customs of the more dominant nations. But since my reasoning has led me to consider the question of fashion, my plan requires me to define the limits of its control; which I will do here, so that I may not have to do it in a less suitable place. The power of fashion applies wholly to the beautiful, not at all to the useful: for when something more useful and convenient becomes the style, I do not call that fashion, but an improvement in the arts or the comforts of life. The beautiful is of two classes: one is based upon certain ideas, which are engraved upon our mind from the beginning; the other, though it does not seem so, is merely an habituation of the senses, which makes a thing appear beautiful. It is only over this second class, which is considerably larger than the first, that the power of fashion extends: hence we may say that the beauty of some gems and of gold and silver is universally based upon the constitution of our mind, never having been subject to fashion anywhere, and being incapable of it; therefore their price is always considered great and exceptional. However, none of my observations are altered by this power of fashion; for this simply causes the utility of things to vary, through variations in the pleasure derived from using them: everything else is the same.

Finally I have to consider the value of objects that are unique, and monopolies, that is, either things for which there is no substitute, such as the Venus de Medici, or those which become unique because there is only one seller. I have often read, even in the wisest authors, that these objects have an infinite value; but of all words none seems to me more improper, in the mouth of one who is reasoning about mortal things. Perhaps they meant indefinite; which is not a proper expression either: for I hold that every human thing possesses order and limits, and that the indefinite is no less foreign to them than the infinite. They have these limits, then: that their price always corresponds to the needs or desires of the buyer and the esteem of the seller combined, and forming a compound ratio. Hence it is that the value of a unique thing may sometimes be equal to nothing; and it is always governed by rule, though it may not be the same under all conditions.

It may seem to many who have followed the observations made thus far, that it would be easy, according to them, to determine the value of everything; but they will abandon this belief, when they have carefully considered what I am about to say. It is very difficult for us, and often impossible, to make this computation on the basis of the principles involved, or as the logicians say, *a priori*: for it is to be noted as a fact that, just as scarcity and value depend on consumption, so consumption varies in conformity with value. As a result of this interrelation, the problem becomes indeterminate, as is always the case when we have two unknown quantities related to each other.

That changes in consumption are caused by price is plain, if we recall that, apart from air to breathe and ground to stand on, man has no other absolute and perpetual needs; having need of eating, but not of any particular food rather than another. Now air and ground have no scarcity or value of any kind: from the others man can abstain more or less; and therefore everyone is desirous of them only in proportion to the inconvenience and labor which it costs to acquire them. Hence whatever is cheaper is more readily taken for consumption; and thus price, which arises from scarcity, regulates consumption.

On the other hand, prices are regulated by consumption: for if fifty thousand casks of wine, for example, are consumed in a country, and the same amount is produced, the unexpected arrival of an army in that country will raise the price of wine, because more is drunk. Now some will find here an inextricable knot and a vicious circle; but they will solve it, if they consider my statement that the scarcity and abundance of many kinds of things changes unexpectedly as a result of external causes, without the work of man, but according to the seasons. In these kinds of things price follows scarcity; and just as men possess unequal wealth, so the purchase of certain commodities corresponds to a certain degree of wealth. If these become cheaper, men of less wealth buy them; if they become dearer, those who formerly used them begin to do without them. This is demonstrated by an excellent example. In the kingdom of Naples about fifteen million *tumoli* of grain are consumed per year, when the harvest is good. Experience shows that, when as much as six or seven million *tumoli* above the ordinary are gathered in years of very great productivity, there is never more than a million and a half exported; and the amount carried over has never been much more. On the other hand, it is certain that in years of low productivity sometimes no more than eight millions are gathered; and yet not more than a million has ever been imported, while that carried over from previous years did not amount to two millions; and yet it sufficed to keep us from suffering from hunger. The reason for this is that in years of plenty very much more grain is eaten, wasted, and sown; in bad years less. Hence the limits of consumption depend more upon price than upon the size of the *tumoli*, so that we ought to say, for example, "The Kingdom consumes thirteen million ducats worth of grain a year," whether fifteen or only ten millions be purchased with this sum makes no difference.

Those kinds of goods which are not subject to changes in harvests, do not change in scarcity for any external reason except fashion. But the precious metals and gems, on account of their sovereign beauty, are not subject to the whims of the latter or to variations in the harvests; hence they have a steadier value than anything else. They would, however, be subject to variations in the amount produced, through the discovery of richer mines, as happened when America was discovered; hence their value fell. Therefore the use of them increased: which use prevented their value from falling as much as their abundance required. And so this interrelation produces the great and very useful effect of the equilibrium of the whole. And this equilibrium fits in wonderfully with the just abundance of the conveniences of life and earthly happiness, although it results, not from human prudence or virtue, but from the base incentive of sordid gain: Providence, out of infinite love for men, having so ordered the relations of things that even our base passions, as if in spite of us, are often arranged for the good of the whole.

Now our plan requires us to explain how this happens. Let us assume that a country entirely Mohammedan in religion and customs suddenly becomes Christian in faith and practice. There are very few vines there, because Mohammedans are forbidden to drink wine; and I assume that they had obeyed this law. Now at a stroke the use of this beverage is permitted, and there being little produced, scarcity will make wine dear, and merchants will begin to have a large supply of wine sent from elsewhere. But soon, since all wish to share in such high profits, so many new vines will be planted, so much foreign wine will be imported, that, as a result of all desiring to make a big profit, everyone will make a fair one. Thus things always come to the same level, such being their intrinsic nature. Often, moreover, so many additional people go into this branch of industry, impetuously but too late, attracted by the first reports and the first examples, that its value falls below what is just; and then all begin to withdraw, each one paying the penalty for his rashness, and the just limit is reached again.

From this two important consequences flow. First, that it is not necessary to consider the first developments in a case, but the permanent and fixed conditions, and in this there is always order and equality; just as water in a vessel, if disturbed, returns to the due level after a confused and irregular fluctuation. Second, that no accident can occur in nature which will carry things to infinite extremity; but a certain moral gravity, existing in everything, always draws them back from the straight line of infinity, turning them in a circle, perpetual indeed, but finite. What I have said I shall apply to money a hundred of times; let my readers therefore fix them in their minds, and be convinced that nothing corresponds more closely to the laws of gravity and of fluids than the laws of commerce. What gravity is in physics, the desire for gain or for happiness is in man; and, this being assumed, all the physical laws of bodies can be verified perfectly in the morality of our life, by anyone who knows how to meditate upon it.

II

From very ancient times rich men have derived an income from money, in contracts of various forms, and at the same time the poor have complained of the greater part of such contracts as unjust and wicked. And as it is characteristic of the fortunate to remain silent and endure the complaints of others, while the sufferer, on the contrary, is loud in his cries and lamentations, all the centuries down to the fifteenth have been filled with a chorus of condemnation and detestation against all income from money. In the sixteenth century, when the discovery of the new Indies, the expansion of the arts, of industry, of commerce, and of money, the institution of interest-bearing public debts, first adopted in monarchies by Francis I, king of France, and imitated by other princes, the destruction of the Jews, most cruel of usurers, and the organization of loan-banks (*monti di pietà*) had practically wiped out usury and pacified the people, keen geniuses appeared, by a marvelous coincidence, to protect and sustain usury after its death, which nobody had defended while it was alive. Claude Salmasius, a man who has perhaps never been surpassed in genius and learning (though he made but slight use of it), was the first to write comprehensively upon usury, with no less erudition than inclination to justify it. After him wrote Nicholas Broedersen, canon of the cathedral of Utrecht, and others; and they are opposed by a very large number of writers of all nations. In recent years the dispute has been revived in Italy, where Scipio Maffei, a gentleman of Verona, wrote *On the Investment of Money;* and as his noble and generous mind, and his reputation for virtue and learning, deservedly established among all, showed that he was not influenced by passion or any consideration, his book made a great stir in the minds of many. He was opposed by Brother Daniel Concina, a Dominican, in two books (the first of which was printed at Naples), full of fervor and incredible fire, and all the less expected, as greater mildness seemed called for between men who were friends, learned, and subject to the same prince. But the disputes were wisely interrupted by the supreme authorities; recognizing that those who have so much to say about the sin of usury have not ordinarily been endowed by Providence with the means for committing it; while those who might do so have not been placed, through defects in their education, in a position to understand the controversy.

It cannot be denied that, although Concina has the better of the argument for the most part, his adversaries have many plausible and specious arguments on their side. Now I am convinced that, when the truth is found apparently divided between two conflicting opinions, and not inclining more to one side than to the other, it is probable that there is some mistake or confusion of words involved; since the true quickly reveals its origin by its own light, as well as its relation to all other truths, and blackens the false so surely that it cannot be missed. Hence, as I reflected on the problem, I noted those things which seem to me to have produced such great disputes, and I will now explain them as well as I can.

During the centuries of ignorance, men had so much dread of the accidents of chance and fortune that, like an unbroken and resisting horse, they fled from it in fear and tried to escape as best they could. The light of the true sciences finally revealed that nothing is less fortuitous than chance, that its vicissitudes have a constant order and a regular cause, and that a proportion can be found between the certain present and the uncertain future. Thus, their fear being gradually quieted, men felt more at home with fortune, and began to bargain about it and make a game of it. Discussion of justice was heard for the first time in connection with games of pure chance; and the art of divination, so much despised, became the daughter of mathematics and truth in the hands of Bernoulli. From games it went to more serious things; and navigation, the lives of men, and the

crops of the country, so long the scorn of chance, were measured, valued, and insured against the whims of fortune, human prudence putting on the bridle and chains. It was then
realized that intrinsic value was always variable according
to the degree of probability which existed that one could or
could not count on enjoying a certain thing; and it was
recognized that a hundred ducats a long way from a man's
hand, when there are ninety chances of not losing them
and ten of losing them, become ninety present ducats, and
are to be valued at ninety in any contract, whether of games
or of exchange. Thus, through mathematics, many contracts were set right, and that justice was recalled which the
shadows of false sciences had driven away. Men's daring in
the face of chance was calculated and restrained within certain and fixed limits.

Hence arose exchange and interest, which are brothers.
One is the equalizing of present money and money distant in
space, made by an apparent premium, which is sometimes
added to the present money, and sometimes to the distant
money, to make the intrinsic value of both equal, diminished by the less convenience or the greater risk. Interest is
the same thing done between present money and money
that is distant in time, time having the same effect as space;
and the basis of the one contract, as of the other, is the
equality of the true intrinsic value. So true is this, that
sometimes in exchange present money is worth less than distant money, and exchange is said to be below par; and the
bills representing money, which really are simply future
money, are often worth more than cash, and this excess is
called *agio*.

Now it is evident how all the error in Nicholas Broedersen's opinions arose from false ideas and from bad use of
words, and all the semblance of verity discernible there is
hidden in badly recognized truth. It was an error to call a
thing *gain* and *for* money, when it is the restitution of what
is missing, included in order to arrive at equality. All gain,
whether great or small, given for money, which is naturally

barren, is blameworthy; nor can it be called the product of labor, since the labor is done by the borrower, not by the lender. But where there is equality there is no profit; and where the intrinsic price is impaired and lessened by risk and inconvenience, the restoration of it cannot be called a profit. It is therefore a false and abominable opinion on the part of him and his followers to make a distinction between the poor man and the rich man, and to confuse justice with compassion. What is just may reasonably be demanded and claimed alike from the richest and most fortunate and from the most unfortunate; what is unjust cannot be claimed from anyone. Nor should any man of sense undertake to correct the dispensations of Providence, and, with his feeble endeavors, to distribute prosperity and misery differently, poverty being more frequently the result of vice than of misfortune.

On the other hand, many theologians, after defining usury and lending very well, have then understood their own definition badly. *Usury is the gain received over and above the principal by virtue of a contract for lending (mutuo).* A very good definition; and anyone wishing to change it (as many non-Catholics have done of late), and say that a loan which is not gratuitous is not a loan, and so its product is not usury, will be playing upon words, no less entirely than uselessly: for God cannot be imposed upon, and there is no need of imposing upon men. So many different formulae have been devised to elude the rigor of human laws against usury, that it is really excessive and intolerable to wish to go so far as to insult and disturb the internal knowledge of what is just. The definition of a loan is likewise very just, namely, *to consign a thing with an agreement to have the equivalent back and no more.* But we need a clearer idea of this equivalent, expressed by the Latin word *tantundem.* Value is the proportion which things bear to our needs. Those things are equal which afford equal satisfaction to the one with respect to whom they are said to be equivalent. Anyone who seeks equality elsewhere, following other principles, and expects to find it in weight or similarity of appearance, will show little understanding of the facts of human life. A sheet of paper is often the equivalent of money, from which it differs both in weight and appearance; on the other hand, two moneys of equal weight and quality, and similar in appearance, are often not equal. When a foreign money is not current in a place, though it is good (like Roman silver money with us), it is not as advantageous to possess a piece of useless metal refused by everyone as to have a similar piece which is good in trade. Therefore the prohibited money costs less, and has to be valued on the basis on which people do accept it, that is, according to the intrinsic value of the metal in it; which is a kind of fairly just and reasonable exchange. Finally it is certain that nothing has a price among men except pleasure, and that only satisfactions are purchased; and just as one cannot obtain pleasure without inconvenience and vexation on the part of somebody else, nothing is paid for but the loss and deprivation of pleasure brought upon another. Keeping someone in anxiety is pain: hence it must be paid for. What is called the product of money, when it is legitimate, is simply the price of anxiety: and whoever thinks it is something different is mistaken.

Now if the teachings of Pope Benedict the fourteenth are considered in the light of the principles I have set forth, they will be found wonderfully full of wisdom and truth: if the human operations not condemned by the people are considered, they will be found to conform to these maxims. Four principal doctrines are taught the faithful in the bull *Vix pervenit*. First that a loan is the restitution of the equivalent; usury, gain above the equivalent; from which the conclusion is drawn: Hence all such gain in excess of the principal is illicit and usurious. A very true teaching. But we should not apply the name gain to the apparent and ideal increase, which appears to be such on account of the mistake in valuing the price of the principal sum.

Secondly, all gain, great or small, is quite properly condemned as sinful and reprehensible, "since human contracts are based upon equality."

Thirdly, it is pointed out that this premium is not inherent in loans: than which nothing can be truer. On the contrary, it is as varied as are the almost infinite degrees of probability of loss, which is very great in some cases (as in maritime usury), sometimes falls to zero (as in the banks and companies of republics), and sometimes even below zero, becoming a negative quantity (as happened in France in the time of Law's System).

Fourthly, it is declared that we cannot find reason for demanding a premium above the equal weight of metal in all loans. This also is an opinion as true as it is obvious; for if the contrary were true, the banks of republics would not have been able to exist; they would not be seen full of unfruitful money; nor, moreover, would anyone be content to keep his money in a bank without profit, and refuse to put it at interest in private hands. Nor does it avail to say that the banks are deposit banks, for it is known that the banks of Holland and Venice have changed from deposit to loan banks, but loans deservedly yielding no interest, because based upon the very best security.

If I should continue this line of reasoning further, I should exceed my due limits. Yet if what I have said should raise doubts and difficulties in anyone's mind, we can continue the discussion elsewhere more conveniently. I only pray those who may wish to oppose me to attack me, and not an imaginary enemy created and armed by them for their pleasure. And to keep to the crux of the argument, it will suffice, above all, to answer the following questions. In any country where restitution of the equivalent was always effected by returning an equal weight of the metal, without other consideration, it is certain that loans would be difficult to obtain and infrequent. Now if, to encourage men to lend, a company of rich merchants should undertake to insure lenders, for a certain percentage paid by the borrowers, would such an insurance be lawful or not? After answering this, there is another question to be answered. If the lender, not desiring outside security, should himself collect the price of the insurance, would the contract change its nature and become sinful?

Now I come to the question of the relation between interest and the art of government. In this connection it is first of all clearly desirable that the interest, just as well as unjust, ordinarily exacted in a community, under whatever name, should be as low and moderate as possible. I have combined the good contracts with the bad; because it is not the business of statesmanship to remedy evils only with the fear of eternal punishment and with the reverence of religion, and it will be ridiculous and foolish for statesmen to rely entirely upon piety. Morality guides men after improving them and making them virtuous; politics has to deal with them as still foul and wrapped in their ordinary passions. Therefore the prince should make such regulations that even the wicked usurer, should he desire it, will be unable to lend at high usury; and he will always be more to be praised for preventing crime than for punishing it.

To make interest low, according to what has been set forth above, it suffices to prevent a monopoly of money and to insure repayment. Hence it has not been merely the abundance of precious metals which has lowered and almost wiped out usury during the last two centuries, but chiefly the excellent government enjoyed in almost all kingdoms. Let law-suits be brief, justice certain, industry and economy wide-spread among the people, and all rich people will be disposed to lend. Where there is a crowd of offerers, the conditions of offering cannot be hard. Thus the poor will be treated without cruelty.

From the same principles it follows that the interest of money cannot always be fixed by law within definite limits. If the return bears the same ratio to the capital as the probability of loss bears to the probability of repayment, the determination of what is called "fruit of money," which might more properly be called "price of insurance," must depend upon very many circumstances. But as John Locke has discussed this at length in one of his treatises, I refer to that; for, although it is still in the original English, I have no doubt that it will sometime be translated into a language more familiar to us.

Finally, it appears that the rate of interest cannot be varied at will by law; but that this must be done by nature itself, and can be obtained by an alteration of the State and of the customs in a kingdom. And, just as the law is broken in the case of contracts, when it is opposed to nature, so the restoration and safety of a country cannot be expected from an ill-timed law to regulate interest.

The best way to lower interest is to make the return on State debts as low as possible. Which I wish to discuss in the next chapter.

XIII

DAVID HUME

POLITICAL DISCOURSES

NOTE

DAVID HUME (1711–1776) was chiefly distinguished as a philosopher, but he also did important work in history, political science, and economics. After finishing his studies at the University of Edinburgh, he tried the law for a time and later business, but found neither to his liking and resolved to devote himself to literature. His *Treatise of Human Nature* (1739) met with a rather disappointing reception, as did his *Essays Moral and Political* (1741), but his *Political Discourses* (1752) were more successful. These contained essays on Commerce, Money, Interest, The Balance of Trade, Taxes, and Public Credit. In 1752 he was appointed librarian of the Faculty of Advocates in Edinburgh, and two years later published the first volume of his *History of Great Britain*, a work now chiefly of literary interest, owing to the marked political bias of the author. In 1763 he was appointed a member of the embassy to France, and in 1767 undersecretary of state, from which position he retired in 1770. He never worked out an economic philosophy, and some aspects of the subject probably had little interest for him, but his essays and correspondence give evidence of remarkable economic insight and judgment.

POLITICAL DISCOURSES

OF INTEREST

NOTHING is esteemed a more certain sign of the flourishing condition of any nation than the lowness of interest: And with reason; though I believe the cause is somewhat different from what is commonly apprehended. Lowness of interest is generally ascribed to plenty of money. But money, however plentiful, has no other effect, *if fixed*, than to raise the price of labour. Silver is more common than gold; and therefore you receive a greater quantity of it for the same commodities. But do you pay less interest for it? Interest in BATAVIA and JAMAICA is at 10 *per cent.*, in PORTUGAL at 6; though these places, as we may learn from the prices of every thing, abound more in gold and silver than either LONDON or AMSTERDAM.

Were all the gold in ENGLAND annihilated at once, and one and twenty shillings substituted in the place of every guinea, would money be more plentiful or interest lower? No, surely: We should only use silver, instead of gold. Were gold rendered as common as silver, and silver as common as copper; would money be more plentiful or interest lower? We may assuredly give the same answer. Our shillings would then be yellow, and our halfpence white; and we should have no guineas. No other difference would ever be observed; no alteration on commerce, manufactures, navigation, or interest; unless we imagine that the colour of the metal is of any consequence.

Now, what is so visible in these greater variations of scarcity or abundance in the precious metals, must hold in all inferior changes. If the multiplying of gold and silver fifteen times makes no difference, much less can the doubling or tripling them. All augmentation has no other effect than to heighten the price of labour and commodities; and even this variation is little more than that of a name. In the progress towards these changes, the augmentation may have some influence, by exciting industry; but after the prices are settled, suitably to the new abundance of gold and silver, it has no manner of influence.

An effect always holds proportion with its cause. Prices have risen near four times since the discovery of the INDIES; and it is probable gold and silver have multiplied much more: But interest has not fallen much above half. The rate of interest, therefore, is not derived from the quantity of the precious metals.

Money having chiefly a fictitious value, the greater or less plenty of it is of no consequence, if we consider a nation within itself; and the quantity of specie, when once fixed, though ever so large, has no other effect than to oblige every one to tell out a greater number of those shining bits of metal for clothes, furniture, or equipage, without encreasing any one convenience of life. If a man borrow money to build a house, he then carries home a greater load; because the stone, timber, lead, glass, &c., with the labour of the masons and carpenters, are represented by a greater quantity of gold and silver. But as these metals are considered chiefly as representations, there can no alteration arise, from their bulk or quantity, their weight or colour, either upon their real value or their interest. The same interest, in all cases, bears the same proportion to the sum. And if you lent me so much labour and so many commodities; by receiving five *per cent.* you always receive proportional labour and commodities, however represented, whether by yellow or white coin, whether by a pound or an ounce. It is in vain, therefore, to look for the cause of the fall or rise of interest in the greater or less quantity of gold and silver, which is fixed in any nation.

High interest arises from *three* circumstances: A great demand for borrowing; little riches to supply that demand; and great profits arising from commerce: And these circumstances are a clear proof of the small advance of commerce and industry, not of the scarcity of gold and silver. Low interest, on the other hand, proceeds from the three opposite circumstances: A small demand for borrowing; great riches to supply that demand; and small profits arising from commerce: And these circumstances are all connected together, and proceed from the increase of industry and commerce, not of gold and silver. We shall endeavour to prove these points; and shall begin with the causes and the effects of a great or small demand for borrowing.

When a people have emerged ever so little from a savage state, and their numbers have encreased beyond the original multitude, there must immediately arise an inequality of property; and while some possess large tracts of land, others are confined within narrow limits, and some are entirely without any landed property. Those who possess more land than they can labour, employ those who possess none, and agree to receive a determinate part of the product. Thus the *landed* interest is immediately established; nor is there any settled government, however rude, in which affairs are not on this footing. Of these proprietors of land, some must presently discover themselves to be of different tempers from others; and while one would willingly store up the produce of his land for futurity, another desires to consume at present what should suffice for many years. But as the spending of a settled revenue is a way of life entirely without occupation; men have so much need of somewhat to fix and engage them, that pleasures, such as they are, will be the pursuit of the greater part of the landholders, and the prodigals among them will always be more numerous than the misers. In a state, therefore, where there is nothing but a landed interest, as there is little frugality, the borrowers must be very numerous, and the rate of interest must hold proportion to it. The difference depends not on the quantity of money, but on the habits and manners which prevail. By this alone the demand for borrowing is encreased or diminished. Were money so plentiful as to make an egg be sold for sixpence; so long as there are only landed gentry and peasants in the state, the borrowers must be numerous, and interest high. The rent for the same farm would be heavier and more bulky: But the same idleness of the landlord, with the higher price of commodities, would dissipate it in the same time, and produce the same necessity and demand for borrowing.

Nor is the case different with regard to the *second* circumstance which we proposed to consider, namely, the great or little riches to supply the demand. This effect also depends on the habits and way of living of the people, not on the quantity of gold and silver. In order to have, in any state, a great number of lenders, it is not sufficient nor requisite that there be great abundance of the precious metals. It is only requisite that the property or command of that quantity, which is in the state, whether great or small, should be collected in particular hands, so as to form considerable sums, or compose a great monied interest. This begets a number of lenders, and sinks the rate of usury; and this, I shall venture to affirm, depends not on the quantity of specie, but on particular manners and customs, which make the specie gather into separate sums or masses of considerable value.

For suppose, that, by miracle, every man in GREAT BRITAIN should have five pounds slipt into his pocket in one night; this would much more than double the whole money that is at present in the kingdom; yet there would not next day, nor for some time, be any more lenders, nor any variation in the interest. And were there nothing but landlords and peasants in the state, this money, however abundant, could never gather into sums, and would only serve to encrease the prices of every thing, without any farther consequence. The prodigal landlord dissipates it, as fast as he receives it; and the beggarly peasant has no means, nor view, nor ambition of obtaining above a bare livelihood. The overplus of borrowers above that of lenders continuing still the same, there will follow no reduction of interest. That de-

pends upon another principle; and must proceed from an encrease of industry and frugality, of arts and commerce.

Every thing useful to the life of man arises from the
ground; but few things arise in that condition which is requisite to render them useful. There must, therefore, beside
the peasant and the proprietors of land, be another rank of
men, who, receiving from the former the rude materials,
work them into their proper form, and retain part for their
own use and subsistence. In the infancy of society, these
contracts between the artisans and the peasants, and between one species of artisans and another, are commonly
entered into immediately by the persons themselves, who,
being neighbours, are easily acquainted with each other's
necessities, and can lend their mutual assistance to supply
them. But when men's industry encreases, and their views
enlarge, it is found, that the most remote parts of the state
can assist each other as well as the more contiguous; and
that this intercourse of good offices may be carried on to the
greatest extent and intricacy. Hence the origin of *merchants*,
one of the most useful races of men, who serve as agents between those parts of the state, that are wholly unacquainted,
and are ignorant of each other's necessities. Here are in a
city fifty workmen in silk and linen, and a thousand customers; and these two ranks of men, so necessary to each
other, can never rightly meet, till one man erects a shop, to
which all the workmen and all the customers repair. In this
province, grass rises in abundance: The inhabitants abound
in cheese, and butter, and cattle; but want bread and corn,
which, in a neighbouring province, are in too great abundance for the use of the inhabitants. One man discovers
this. He brings corn from the one province, and returns
with cattle; and supplying the wants of both, he is, so far,
a common benefactor. As the people encrease in numbers
and industry, the difficulty of their intercourse encreases:
The business of the agency or merchandize becomes more
intricate; and divides, subdivides, compounds, and mixes to
a greater variety. In all these transactions, it is necessary,

and reasonable, that a considerable part of the commodities and labour should belong to the merchant, to whom, in a great measure, they are owing. And these commodities he will sometimes preserve in kind, or more commonly convert into money, which is their common representation. If gold and silver have encreased in the state together with the industry, it will require a great quantity of these metals to represent a great quantity of commodities and labour. If industry alone has encreased, the prices of every thing must sink, and a small quantity of specie will serve as a representation.

There is no craving or demand of the human mind more constant and insatiable than that for exercise and employment; and this desire seems the foundation of most of our passions and pursuits. Deprive a man of all business and serious occupation, he runs restless from one amusement to another; and the weight and oppression, which he feels from idleness, is so great, that he forgets the ruin which must follow him from his immoderate expences. Give him a more harmless way of employing his mind or body, he is satisfied, and feels no longer that insatiable thirst after pleasure. But if the employment you give him be lucrative, especially if the profit be attached to every particular exertion of industry, he has gain so often in his eye, that he acquires, by degrees, a passion for it, and knows no such pleasure as that of seeing the daily encrease of his fortune. And this is the reason why trade encreases frugality, and why, among merchants, there is the same overplus of misers above prodigals, as, among the possessors of land, there is the contrary.

Commerce encreases industry, by conveying it readily from one member of the state to another, and allowing none of it to perish or become useless. It encreases frugality, by giving occupation to men, and employing them in the arts of gain, which soon engage their affection, and remove all relish for pleasure and expence. It is an infallible consequence of all industrious professions, to beget frugality, and make the love of gain prevail over the love of pleasure. Among lawyers and physicians who have any practice, there are many more who live within their income, than who exceed it, or even live up to it. But lawyers and physicians beget no industry; and it is even at the expence of others they acquire their riches; so that they are sure to diminish the possessions of some of their fellow-citizens, as fast as they encrease their own. Merchants, on the contrary, beget industry, by serving as canals to convey it through every corner of the state: And at the same time, by their frugality, they acquire great power over that industry, and collect a large property in the labour and commodities, which they are the chief instruments in producing. There is no other profession, therefore, except merchandize, which can make the monied interest considerable; or, in other words, can encrease industry, and, by also encreasing frugality, give a great command of that industry to particular members of the society. Without commerce, the state must consist chiefly of landed gentry, whose prodigality and expence make a continual demand for borrowing; and of peasants, who have no sums to supply that demand. The money never gathers into large stocks or sums, which can be lent at interest. It is dispersed into numberless hands, who either squander it in idle show and magnificence, or employ it in the purchase of the common necessaries of life. Commerce alone assembles it into considerable sums; and this effect it has merely from the industry which it begets, and the frugality which it inspires, independent of that particular quantity of precious metal which may circulate in the state.

Thus an encrease of commerce, by a necessary consequence, raises a great number of lenders, and by that means produces lowness of interest. We must now consider how far this encrease of commerce diminishes the profits arising from that profession, and gives rise to the *third* circumstance requisite to produce lowness of interest.

It may be proper to observe on this head, that low interest and low profits of merchandize, are two events, that mutually forward each other, and are both originally derived from that extensive commerce, which produces opulent merchants, and renders the monied interest considerable. Where merchants possess great stocks, whether represented by few or many pieces of metal, it must frequently happen, that, when they either become tired of business, or leave heirs unwilling or unfit to engage in commerce, a great proportion of these riches naturally seeks an annual and secure revenue. The plenty diminishes the price, and makes the lenders accept of a low interest. This consideration obliges many to keep their stock employed in trade, and rather be content with low profits than dispose of their money at an under-value. On the other hand, when commerce has become extensive, and employs large stocks, there must arise rivalships among the merchants, which diminish the profits of trade, at the same time that they encrease the trade itself. The low profits of merchandize induce the merchants to accept more willingly of a low interest, when they leave off business, and begin to indulge themselves in ease and indolence. It is needless, therefore, to enquire, which of these circumstances, to wit, *low interest* or *low profits*, is the cause, and which the effect? They both arise from an extensive commerce, and mutually forward each other. No man will accept of low profits where he can have high interest; and no man will accept of low interest, where he can have high profits. An extensive commerce, by producing large stocks, diminishes both interest and profits, and is always assisted, in its diminution of the one, by the proportional sinking of the other. I may add, that, as low profits arise from the encrease of commerce and industry, they serve in their turn to its farther encrease, by rendering the commodities cheaper, encouraging the consumption, and heightening the industry. And thus, if we consider the whole connection of causes and effects, interest is the barometer of the state, and its lowness is a sign almost infallible of the flourishing condition of a people. It proves the encrease of industry, and its prompt circulation through the whole state, little inferior to a demonstration. And though, perhaps, it may not be impossible but a sudden and a great check to commerce may have a momentary effect of the same kind, by throwing so many stocks out of trade; it must be attended with such misery and want of employment in the poor, that, besides its short duration, it will not be possible to mistake the one case for the other.

Those who have asserted, that the plenty of money was the cause of low interest, seem to have taken a collateral effect for a cause; since the same industry, which sinks the interest, commonly acquires great abundance of the precious metals. A variety of fine manufactures, with vigilant enterprising merchants, will soon draw money to a state, if it be any where to be found in the world. The same cause, by multiplying the conveniences of life, and encreasing industry, collects great riches into the hands of persons, who are not proprietors of land, and produces, by that means, a lowness of interest. But though both these effects, plenty of money and low interest, naturally arise from commerce and industry, they are altogether independent of each other. For suppose a nation removed into the *Pacific* ocean, without any foreign commerce, or any knowledge of navigation: Suppose, that this nation possesses always the same stock of coin, but is continually encreasing in its numbers and industry: It is evident, that the price of every commodity must gradually diminish in that kingdom; since it is the proportion between money and any species of goods, which fixes theirmutual value; and, upon the present supposition, the conveniencies of life become every day more abundant, without any alteration in the current specie. A less quantity of money, therefore, among this people, will make a rich man, during the times of industry, than would suffice to that purpose, in ignorant and slothful ages. Less money will build a house, portion a daughter, buy an estate, support a manufactory, or maintain a family and equipage. These are the uses for which men borrow money; and therefore, the greater or less quantity of it in a state has no influence on the interest. But it is evident, that the greater or less stock of labour and commodities must have a great influence; since we really and in effect borrow these, when we take money upon interest. It is true, when commerce is extended all over the globe, the most industrious nations always abound most with the precious metals; So that low interest and plenty of money are in fact almost inseparable. But still it is of consequence to know the principle whence any phenomenon arises, and to distinguish between a cause and a concomitant effect. Besides that the speculation is curious, it may frequently be of use in the conduct of public affairs. At least, it must be owned, that nothing can be of more use than to improve, by practice, the method of reasoning on these subjects, which of all others are the most important; though they are commonly treated in the loosest and most careless manner.

Another reason of this popular mistake with regard to the cause of low interest, seems to be the instance of some nations; where, after a sudden acquisition of money or of the precious metals, by means of foreign conquest, the interest has fallen not only among them, but in all the neighbouring states, as soon as that money was dispersed, and had insinuated itself into every corner. Thus, interest in SPAIN fell near a half immediately after the discovery of the WEST INDIES, as we are informed by GARCILASSO DE LA VEGA: And it has been ever since gradually sinking in every kingdom of EUROPE. Interest in ROME, after the conquest of EGYPT, fell from 6 to 4 *per cent.* as we learn from DION.

The causes of the sinking of interest, upon such an event, seem different in the conquering country and in the neighbouring states; but in neither of them can we justly ascribe that effect merely to the encrease of gold and silver.

In the conquering country, it is natural to imagine, that this new acquisition of money will fall into a few hands, and be gathered into large sums, which seek a secure revenue, either by the purchase of land or by interest; and consequently the same effect follows, for a little time, as if there had been a great accession of industry and commerce. The encrease of lenders above the borrowers sinks the interest;

and so much the faster, if those, who have acquired those large sums, find no industry or commerce in the state, and no method of employing their money but by lending it at interest. But after this new mass of gold and silver has been digested, and has circulated, through the whole state, affairs will soon return to their former situation: while the landlords and new money-holders, living idly, squander above their income; and the former daily contract debt, and the latter encroach on their stock till its final extinction. The whole money may still be in the state, and make itself felt by the encrease of prices: But not being now collected into any large masses or stocks, the disproportion between the borrowers and lenders is the same as formerly, and consequently the high interest returns.

Accordingly we find in ROME, that, so early as TIBERIUS's time, interest had again amounted to 6 *per cent.* though no accident had happened to drain the empire of money. In TRAJAN's time, money lent on mortgages in ITALY bore 6 *per cent.;* on common securities in BITHYNIA, 12: And if interest in SPAIN has not risen to its old pitch; this can be ascribed to nothing but the continuance of the same cause that sunk it, to wit, the large fortunes continually made in the INDIES, which come over to SPAIN from time to time, and supply the demand of the borrowers. By this accidental and extraneous cause, more money is to be lent in SPAIN, that is, more money is collected into large sums than would otherwise be found in a state, where there are so little commerce and industry.

As to the reduction of interest, which has followed in ENGLAND, FRANCE, and other kingdoms of EUROPE, that have no mines, it has been gradual; and has not proceeded from the encrease of money, considered merely in itself; but from that of industry, which is the natural effect of the former encrease, in that interval, before it raises the price of labour and provisions. For to return to the foregoing supposition; if the industry of ENGLAND had risen as much from other causes, (and that rise might easily have happened, though the stock of money had remained the same,) must not all the same consequences have followed, which we observe at present? The same people would, in that case, be found in the kingdom, the same commodities, the same industry, manufactures, and commerce; and consequently the same merchants, with the same stocks, that is, with the same command over labour and commodities, only represented by a smaller number of white or yellow pieces: which being a circumstance of no moment, would only affect the waggoner, porter, and trunk-maker. Luxury, therefore, manufactures, arts, industry, frugality, flourishing equally as at present, it is evident that interest must also have been as low; since that is the necessary result of all these circumstances; so far as they determine the profits of commerce, and the proportion between the borrowers and lenders in any state.

OF THE BALANCE OF TRADE

It is very usual, in nations ignorant of the nature of commerce, to prohibit the exportation of commodities, and to preserve among themselves whatever they think valuable and useful. They do not consider, that, in this prohibition, they act directly contrary to their intention; and that the more is exported of any commodity, the more will be raised at home, of which they themselves will always have the first offer.

It is well known to the learned, that the ancient laws of ATHENS rendered the exportation of figs criminal; that being supposed a species of fruit so excellent in ATTICA, that the ATHENIANS deemed it too delicious for the palate of any foreigner. And in this ridiculous prohibition they were so much in earnest, that informers were thence called *sycophants* among them, from two GREEK words, which signify *figs* and *discoverer*. There are proofs in many old acts of parliament of the same ignorance in the nature of commerce, particularly in the reign of Edward III. And to this day, in FRANCE, the exportation of corn is almost always prohibited; in order, as they say, to prevent famines; though it is evident, that nothing contributes more to the frequent famines, which so much distress that fertile country.

The same jealous fear, with regard to money, has also prevailed among several nations; and it required both reason and experience to convince any people, that these prohibitions serve to no other purpose than to raise the exchange against them, and produce a still greater exportation.

These errors, one may say, are gross and palpable: But there still prevails, even in nations well acquainted with commerce, a strong jealousy with regard to the balance of trade, and a fear that all their gold and silver may be leaving them. This seems to me, almost in every case, a groundless apprehension; and I should as soon dread, that all our springs and rivers should be exhausted, as that money should abandon a kingdom where there are people and industry. Let us carefully preserve these latter advantages; and we need never be apprehensive of losing the former.

It is easy to observe, that all calculations concerning the balance of trade are founded on very uncertain facts and suppositions. The custom-house books are allowed to be an insufficient ground of reasoning; nor is the rate of exchange much better; unless we consider it with all nations, and know also the proportions of the several sums remitted, which one may safely pronounce impossible. Every man, who has ever reasoned on this subject, has always proved his theory, whatever it was, by facts and calculations, and by an enumeration of all the commodities sent to all foreign kingdoms.

The writings of Mr. Gee struck the nation with an universal panic, when they saw it plainly demonstrated, by a detail of particulars, that the balance was against them for so considerable a sum as must leave them without a single shilling in five or six years. But luckily, twenty years have since elapsed, with an expensive foreign war; yet it is commonly supposed, that money is still more plentiful among us than in any former period.

Nothing can be more entertaining on this head than Dr. SWIFT; an author so quick in discerning the mistakes and absurdities of others. He says, in his *short view of the state of* IRELAND, that the whole cash of that kingdom formerly amounted but to 500,000 *l.*; that out of this the Irish remitted every year a neat million to ENGLAND, and had scarcely any other source from which they could compensate themselves, and little other foreign trade than the importation of FRENCH wines, for which they paid ready money. The consequence of this situation, which must be owned to be disadvantageous, was, that, in a course of three years, the current money of IRELAND, from 500,000 *l.*, was reduced to less than two. And at present, I suppose, in a course of 30 years, it is absolutely nothing. Yet I know not how, that opinion of the advance of riches in IRELAND, which gave the Doctor so much indignation, seems still to continue, and gain ground with every body.

In short, this apprehension of the wrong balance of trade, appears of such a nature, that it discovers itself, wherever one is out of humour with the ministry, or is in low spirits; and as it can never be refuted by a particular detail of all the exports, which counterbalance the imports, it may here be proper to form a general argument, that may prove the impossibility of this event, as long as we preserve our people and our industry.

Suppose four-fifths of all the money in GREAT BRITAIN to be annihilated in one night, and the nation reduced to the same condition, with regard to specie, as in the reigns of the HARRYS and EDWARDS, what would be the consequence? Must not the price of all labour and commodities sink in proportion, and every thing be sold as cheap as they were in those ages? What nation could then dispute with us in any foreign market, or pretend to navigate or to sell manufactures at the same price, which to us would afford sufficient profit? In how little time, therefore, must this bring back the money which we had lost, and raise us to the level of all the neighbouring nations? Where, after we have arrived, we immediately lose the advantage of the cheapness of labour and commodities; and the farther flowing in of money is stopped by our fulness and repletion.

Again, suppose that all the money of GREAT BRITAIN were multiplied fivefold in a night, must not the contrary effect follow? Must not all labour and commodities rise to such an exorbitant height, that no neighbouring nations could afford to buy from us; while their commodities, on the other hand, became comparatively so cheap, that, in spite of all the laws which could be formed, they would be run in upon us, and our money flow out; till we fall to a level with foreigners, and lose that great superiority of riches, which had laid us under such disadvantages?

Now, it is evident, that the same causes, which would correct these exorbitant inequalities, were they to happen miraculously, must prevent their happening in the common course of nature, and must forever, in all neighbouring na-

tions, preserve money nearly proportionable to the art and
industry of each nation. All water, wherever it communi-
cates, remains always at a level. Ask naturalists the reason;
they tell you, that, were it to be raised in any one place,
the superior gravity of that part not being balanced, must
depress it, till it meets a counterpoise; and that the same
cause, which redresses the inequality when it happens, must
for ever prevent it, without some violent external operation.[1]

Can one imagine that it had ever been possible, by any
laws, or even by any art or industry, to have kept all the
money in SPAIN, which the galleons have brought from the
INDIES? Or that all commodities could be sold in FRANCE
for a tenth of the price which they would yield on the other
side of the PYRENEES, without finding their way thither, and
draining from that immense treasure? What other reason,
indeed, is there, why all nations at present gain in their
trade with SPAIN and PORTUGAL, but because it is impossible to heap up money, more than any fluid, beyond its
proper level? The sovereigns of these countries have shown,
that they wanted not inclination to keep their gold and silver to themselves, had it been in any degree practicable.

But as any body of water may be raised above the level of
the surrounding element, if the former has no communication with the latter; so in money, if the communication be
cut off, by any material or physical impediment (for all laws
alone are ineffectual), there may, in such a case, be a very
great inequality of money. Thus the immense distance of
CHINA, together with the monopolies of our INDIA companies, obstructing the communication, preserve in EUROPE
the gold and silver, especially the latter, in much greater
plenty than they are found in that kingdom. But, notwithstanding this great obstruction, the force of the causes

[1] There is another cause, though more limited in its operation, which checks
the wrong balance of trade, to every particular nation to which the kingdom
trades. When we import more goods than we export, the exchange turns against
us, and this becomes a new encouragement to export; as much as the charge of
carriage and insurance of the money which becomes due would amount to. For
the exchange can never rise but a little higher than that sum.

abovementioned is still evident. The skill and ingenuity of
EUROPE in general surpasses perhaps that of CHINA, with
regard to manual arts and manufactures; yet are we never
able to trade thither without great disadvantage. And were
it not for the continual recruits which we receive from
AMERICA, money would soon sink in EUROPE, and rise in
CHINA, till it came nearly to a level in both places. Nor can
any reasonable man doubt, but that industrious nation,
were they as near as POLAND or BARBARY, would drain us of
the overplus of our specie, and draw to themselves a larger
share of the WEST-INDIAN treasures. We need not have recourse to a physical attraction, in order to explain the necessity of this operation. There is a moral attraction, arising
from the interests and passions of men, which is full as potent and infallible.

How is the balance kept in the provinces of every kingdom among themselves, but by the force of this principle,
which makes it impossible for money to lose its level, and
either to rise or sink beyond the proportion of the labour and
commodities which are in each province? Did not long experience make people easy on this head, what a fund of
gloomy reflections might calculations afford to a melancholy
YORKSHIREMAN, while he computed and magnified the sums
drawn to LONDON by taxes, absentees, commodities, and
found on comparison the opposite articles so much inferior?
And no doubt, had the *Heptarchy* subsisted in ENGLAND, the
legislature of each state had been continually alarmed by the
fear of a wrong balance; and as it is probable that the mutual hatred of these states would have been extremely violent
on account of their close neighbourhood, they would have
loaded and oppressed all commerce, by a jealous and superfluous caution. Since the union has removed the barriers between SCOTLAND and ENGLAND, which of these nations gains
from the other by this free commerce? Or if the former kingdom has received any encrease of riches, can it reasonably be
accounted for by any thing but the encrease of its art and
industry? It was a common apprehension in ENGLAND, be-

fore the union, as we learn from L'ABBE DU BOS, that SCOT-
LAND would soon drain them of their treasure, were an open
trade allowed; and on the other side of the TWEED a contrary apprehension prevailed: With what justice in both,
time has shown.

What happens in small portions of mankind, must take
place in greater. The provinces of the ROMAN empire, no
doubt, kept their balance with each other, and with ITALY,
independent of the legislature; as much as the several counties of GREAT BRITAIN, or the several parishes of each
county. And any man who travels over EUROPE at this day,
may see, by the prices of commodities, that money, in spite
of the absurd jealousy of princes and states, has brought itself nearly to a level; and that the difference between one
kingdom and another is not greater in this respect, than it is
often between different provinces of the same kingdom.
Men naturally flock to capital cities, sea-ports, and navigable rivers. There we find more men, more industry, more
commodities, and consequently more money; but still the
latter difference holds proportion with the former, and the
level is preserved.[1]

Our jealousy and our hatred of FRANCE are without
bounds; and the former sentiment, at least, must be ac-
knowledged, reasonable and well-grounded. These passions
have occasioned innumerable barriers and obstructions
upon commerce, where we are accused of being commonly
the aggressors. But what have we gained by the bargain?

---

[1] It must carefully be remarked, that throughout this discourse, wherever I
speak of the level of money, I mean always its proportional level to the commodities, labour, industry, and skill, which is in the several states. And I assert, that
where these advantages are double, triple, quadruple, to what they are in the
neighbouring states, the money infallibly will also be double, triple, quadruple.
The only circumstance that can obstruct the exactness of these proportions, is the
expence of transporting the commodities from one place to another; and this expense is sometimes unequal. Thus the corn, cattle, cheese, butter, of DERBY-
SHIRE, cannot draw the money of LONDON, so much as the manufactures of LON-
DON draw the money of DERBYSHIRE. But this objection is only a seeming one.
For so far as the transport of commodities is expensive, so far is the communica-
tion between the places obstructed and imperfect.

We lost the FRENCH market for our woollen manufactures, and transferred the commerce of wine to SPAIN and PORTUGAL, where we buy worse liquor at a higher price. There are few Englishmen who would not think their country absolutely ruined, were FRENCH wines sold in ENGLAND so cheap and in such abundance as to supplant, in some measure, all ale, and home-brewed liquors: But would we lay aside prejudice, it would not be difficult to prove, that nothing could be more innocent, perhaps advantageous. Each new acre of vineyard planted in FRANCE, in order to supply ENGLAND with wine, would make it requisite for the FRENCH to take the produce of an ENGLISH acre, sown in wheat or barley, in order to subsist themselves; and it is evident that we should thereby get command of the better commodity.

There are many edicts of the FRENCH king, prohibiting the planting of new vineyards, and ordering all those which are lately planted to be grubbed up; So sensible are they, in that country, of the superior value of corn, above every other product.

Mareschal VAUBAN complains often, and with reason, of the absurd duties which load the entry of those wines of LANGUEDOC, GUIENNE, and other southern provinces, that are imported into BRITTANY and NORMANDY. He entertained no doubt but these latter provinces could preserve their balance, notwithstanding the open commerce which he recommends. And it is evident, that a few leagues more navigation to ENGLAND would make no difference; or if it did, that it must operate alike on the commodities of both kingdoms.

There is indeed one expedient by which it is possible to sink, and another by which we may raise money beyond its natural level in any kingdom; but these cases, when examined, will be found to resolve into our general theory, and to bring additional authority to it.

I scarcely know any method of sinking money below its level, but those institutions of banks, funds, and paper credit, which are so much practised in this kingdom. These render paper equivalent to money, circulate it throughout the whole state, make it supply the place of gold and silver, raise proportionably the price of labour and commodities, and by that means either banish a great part of those precious metals, or prevent their farther encrease. What can be more short-sighted than our reasonings on this head? We fancy, because an individual would be much richer, were his stock of money doubled, that the same good effect would follow, were the money of every one encreased; not considering, that this would raise as much the price of every commodity, and reduce every man, in time, to the same condition as before. It is only in our public negociations and transactions with foreigners, that a greater stock of money is advantageous; and as our paper is there absolutely insignificant, we feel, by its means, all the ill effects arising from a great abundance of money, without reaping any of the advantages.[1]

Suppose that there are 12 millions of paper, which circulate in the kingdom as money (for we are not to imagine, that all our enormous funds are employed in that shape), and suppose the real cash of the kingdom to be 18 millions: Here is a state which is found by experience to be able to hold a stock of 30 millions. I say, if it be able to hold it, it must of necessity have acquired it in gold and silver, had we not obstructed the entrance of these metals by this new invention of paper. *Whence would it have acquired that sum?* From all the kingdoms of the world. *But why?* Because, if you remove these 12 millions, money in this state is below its level, compared with our neighbours; and we must immediately draw from all of them, till we be full and saturate, so to speak, and can hold no more. By our present politics, we are as careful to stuff the nation with this fine commodity

---

[1] We observed in Essay III. that money, when encreasing, gives encouragement to industry, during the interval between the encrease of money and rise of the prices. A good effect of this nature may follow too from paper-credit; but it is dangerous to precipitate matters, at the risk of losing all by the failing of that credit, as must happen upon any violent shock in public affairs.

of bank-bills and chequer-notes, as if we were afraid of being overburthened with the precious metals.

It is not to be doubted, but the great plenty of bullion in FRANCE is, in a great measure, owing to the want of paper-credit. The FRENCH have no banks: Merchants bills do not circulate as with us: Usury or lending on interest is not directly permitted; so that many have large sums in their coffers: Great quantities of plate are used in private houses; and all the churches are full of it. By this means, provisions and labour still remain cheaper among them, than in nations that are not half so rich in gold and silver. The advantages of this situation, in point of trade as well as in great public emergencies, are too evident to be disputed.

The same fashion a few years ago prevailed in GENOA, which still has place in ENGLAND and HOLLAND, of using services of CHINA-ware instead of plate; but the senate, foreseeing the consequence, prohibited the use of that brittle commodity beyond a certain extent; while the use of silver-plate was left unlimited. And I suppose, in their late distresses, they felt the good effect of this ordinance. Our tax on plate is, perhaps, in this view, somewhat impolitic.

Before the introduction of paper-money into our colonies, they had gold and silver sufficient for their circulation. Since the introduction of that commodity, the least inconveniency that has followed is the total banishment of the precious metals. And after the abolition of paper, can it be doubted but money will return, while those colonies possess manufactures and commodities, the only thing valuable in commerce, and for whose sake alone all men desire money?

What pity LYCURGUS did not think of paper-credit, when he wanted to banish gold and silver from SPARTA! It would have served his purpose better than the lumps of iron he made use of as money; and would also have prevented more effectually all commerce with strangers, as being of so much real and intrinsic value.

It must, however, be confessed, that, as all these questions of trade and money are extremely complicated, there are

certain lights in which this subject may be placed, so as to
represent the advantages of paper-credit and banks to be
superior to their disadvantages. That they banish specie
and bullion from a state is undoubtedly true; and whoever
looks no farther than this circumstance does well to condemn them; but specie and bullion are not of so great consequence as not to admit of a compensation, and even an
overbalance from the encrease of industry and of credit,
which may be promoted by the right use of paper-money. It
is well known of what advantage it is to a merchant to be
able to discount his bills upon occasion; and every thing
that facilitates this species of traffic is favourable to the general commerce of a state. But private bankers are enabled
to give such credit by the credit they receive from the depositing of money in their shops; and the Bank of ENGLAND,
in the same manner, from the liberty it has to issue its notes
in all payments. There was an invention of this kind, which
was fallen upon some years ago by the banks of EDINBURGH;
and which, as it is one of the most ingenious ideas that has
been executed in commerce, has also been thought advantageous to SCOTLAND. It is there called a BANK-CREDIT; and
is of this nature. A man goes to the bank and finds surety to
the amount, we shall suppose, of a thousand pounds. This
money, or any part of it, he has the liberty of drawing out
whenever he pleases, and he pays only the ordinary interest
for it, while it is in his hands. He may, when he pleases, repay any sum so small as twenty pounds, and the interest is
discounted from the very day of the repayment. The advantages, resulting from this contrivance, are manifold. As
a man may find surety nearly to the amount of his substance, and his bank-credit is equivalent to ready money, a
merchant does hereby in a manner coin his houses, his
household furniture, the goods in his warehouse, the foreign
debts due to him, his ships at sea; and can, upon occasion,
employ them in all payments, as if they were the current
money of the country. If a man borrow a thousand pounds
from a private hand, besides that it is not always to be found

when required, he pays interest for it whether he be using it or not: His bank-credit costs him nothing except during the very moment in which it is of service to him: And this circumstance is of equal advantage as if he had borrowed money at much lower interest. Merchants likewise, from this invention, acquire a great facility in supporting each other's credit, which is a considerable security against bankruptcies. A man, when his own bank-credit is exhausted, goes to any of his neighbours who is not in the same condition; and he gets the money, which he replaces at his convenience.

After this practice had taken place during some years at EDINBURGH, several companies of merchants at GLASGOW carried the matter farther. They associated themselves into different banks, and issued notes so low as ten shillings, which they used in all payments for goods, manufactures, tradesmen's labour of all kinds; and these notes, from the established credit of the companies, passed as money in all payments throughout the country. By this means, a stock of five thousand pounds was able to perform the same operations as if it were six or seven; and merchants were thereby enabled to trade to a greater extent, and to require less profit in all their transactions. But whatever other advantages result from these inventions, it must still be allowed that, besides giving too great facility to credit, which is dangerous, they banish the precious metals: and nothing can be a more evident proof of it than a comparison of the past and present condition of SCOTLAND in that particular. It was found, upon the recoinage made after the union, that there was near a million of specie in that country: But notwithstanding the great encrease of riches, commerce and manufactures of all kinds, it is thought, that, even where there is no extraordinary drain made by ENGLAND, the current specie will not now amount to a third of that sum.

But as our projects of paper-credit are almost the only expedient, by which we can sink money below its level; so, in my opinion, the only expedient, by which we can raise money above it, is a practice which we should all exclaim against as destructive, namely, the gathering of large sums into a public treasure, locking them up, and absolutely preventing their circulation. The fluid, not communicating with the neighbouring element, may, by such an artifice, be raised to what height we please. To prove this, we need only return to our first supposition, of annihilating the half or any part of our cash; where we found, that the immediate consequence of such an event would be the attraction of an equal sum from all the neighbouring kingdoms. Nor does there seem to be any necessary bounds set, by the nature of things, to this practice of hoarding. A small city like GENEVA, continuing this policy for ages, might engross nine tenths of the money of EUROPE. There seems, indeed, in the nature of man, an invincible obstacle to that immense growth or riches. A weak state, with an enormous treasure, will soon become a prey to some of its poorer, but more powerful neighbours. A great state would dissipate its wealth in dangerous and ill-concerted projects; and probably destroy, with it, what is much more valuable, the industry, morals, and numbers of its people. The fluid, in this case, raised to too great a height, bursts and destroys the vessel that contains it; and, mixing itself with the surrounding element, soon falls to its proper level.

So little are we commonly acquainted with this principle, that, though all historians agree in relating uniformly so recent an event as the immense treasure amassed by HARRY VII. (which they make amount to 2,700,000 pounds), we rather reject their concurring testimony, than admit of a fact, which agrees so ill with our inveterate prejudices. It is indeed probable, that this sum might be three-fourths of all the money in ENGLAND. But where is the difficulty in conceiving, that such a sum might be amassed in twenty years, by a cunning, rapacious, frugal, and almost absolute monarch? Nor is it probable, that the diminution of circulating money was ever sensibly felt by the people, or ever did them any prejudice. The sinking of the prices of all commodities would immediately replace it, by giving ENGLAND the advantage in its commerce with the neighbouring kingdoms.

Have we not an instance in the small republic of ATHENS with its allies, who, in about fifty years between the MEDIAN and PELOPONNESIAN wars, amassed a sum not much inferior to that of HARRY VII? For all the GREEK historians and orators agree, that the ATHENIANS collected in the citadel more than 10,000 talents, which they afterwards dissipated to their own ruin, in rash and imprudent enterprises. But when this money was set a running, and began to communicate with the surrounding fluid; what was the consequence? Did it remain in the state? No. For we find, by the memorable *census* mentioned by DEMOSTHENES and POLYBIUS, that, in about fifty years afterwards, the whole value of the republic, comprehending lands, houses, commodities, slaves, and money, was less than 6,000 talents.

What an ambitious high-spirited people was this, to collect and keep in their treasury, with a view to conquests, a sum, which it was every day in the power of the citizens, by a single vote, to distribute among themselves, and which would have gone near to triple the riches of every individual! For we must observe, that the numbers and private riches of the ATHENIANS are said, by ancient writers, to have been no greater at the beginning of the PELOPONNESIAN war, than at the beginning of the MACEDONIAN.

Money was little more plentiful in GREECE during the age of PHILIP and PERSEUS, than in ENGLAND during that of HARRY VII: Yet those two monarchs in thirty years collected from the small kingdom of MACEDON, a larger treasure than that of the ENGLISH monarch. PAULUS ÆMILIUS brought to Rome about 1,700,000 pounds *Sterling*. PLINY says 2,400,000. And that was but a part of the MACEDONIAN treasure. The rest was dissipated by the resistance and flight of PERSEUS.

We may learn from STANIAN, that the canton of BERNE had 300,000 pounds lent at interest, and had above six times as much in their treasury. Here then is a sum hoarded of

1,800,000 pounds *Sterling*, which is at least quadruple what should naturally circulate in such a petty state; and yet no one, who travels in the PAIS DE VAUX, or any part of that canton, observes any want of money more than could be supposed in a country of that extent, soil, and situation. On the contrary, there are scarce any inland provinces in the continent of FRANCE or GERMANY, where the inhabitants are at this time so opulent, though that canton has vastly encreased its treasure since 1714, the time when STANIAN wrote his judicious account of SWITZERLAND.

The account given by APPIAN of the treasure of the PTOLEMIES, is so prodigious, that one cannot admit of it; and so much the less, because the historian says, that the other successors of ALEXANDER were also frugal, and had many of them treasures not much inferior. For this saving humour of the neighbouring princes must necessarily have checked the frugality of the EGYPTIAN monarchs, according to the foregoing theory. The sum he mentions is 740,000 talents, or 191,166,666 pounds 13 shillings and 4 pence, according to Dr. ARBUTHNOT'S computation. And yet APPIAN says, that he extracted his account from the public records; and he was himself a native of ALEXANDRIA.

From these principles we may learn what judgment we ought to form of those numberless bars, obstructions, and imposts, which all nations of Europe, and none more than ENGLAND, have put upon trade; from an exorbitant desire of amassing money, which never will heap up beyond its level, while it circulates; or from an ill-grounded apprehension of losing their specie, which never will sink below it. Could any thing scatter our riches, it would be such impolitic contrivances. But this general ill effect, however, results from them, that they deprive neighbouring nations of that free communication and exchange which the Author of the world has intended, by giving them soils, climates, and geniuses, so different from each other.

Our modern politics embrace the only method of banishing money, the using of paper-credit; they reject the only method of amassing it, the practice of hoarding; and they adopt a hundred contrivances, which serve to no purpose but to check industry, and rob ourselves and our neighbours of the common benefits of art and nature.

All taxes, however, upon foreign commodities, are not to be regarded as prejudicial or useless, but those only which are founded on the jealousy abovementioned. A tax on German linen encourages home manufactures, and thereby multiplies our people and industry. A tax on brandy encreases the sale of rum, and supports our southern colonies. And as it is necessary, that imposts should be levied, for the support of government, it may be thought more convenient to lay them on foreign commodities, which can easily be intercepted at the port, and subjected to the impost. We ought, however, always to remember the maxim of Dr. SWIFT, That, in the arithmetic of the customs, two and two make not four, but often make only one. It can scarcely be doubted, but if the duties on wine were lowered to a third, they would yield much more to the government than at present: Our people might thereby afford to drink commonly a better and more wholesome liquor; and no prejudice would ensue to the balance of trade, of which we are so jealous. The manufacture of ale beyond the agriculture is but inconsiderable, and gives employment to few hands. The transport of wine and corn would not be much inferior.

But are there not frequent instances, you will say, of states and kingdoms, which were formerly rich and opulent, and are now poor and beggarly? Has not the money left them, with which they formerly abounded? I answer, If they lose their trade, industry, and people, they cannot expect to keep their gold and silver; For these precious metals will not hold proportion to the former advantages. When LISBON and AMSTERDAM got the EAST-INDIA trade from VENICE and GENOA, they also got the profits and money which arose from it. Where the seat of government is transferred, where expensive armies are maintained at a distance, where great funds are possessed by foreigners; there naturally follows from these causes a diminution of the specie. But these, we may observe, are violent and forcible methods of carrying away money, and are in time commonly attended with the transport of people and industry. But where these remain, and the drain is not continued, the money always finds its way back again, by a hundred canals, of which we have no notion or suspicion. What immense treasures have been spent, by so many nations, in FLANDERS, since the revolution, in the course of three long wars! More money perhaps than the half of what is at present in EUROPE. But what has now become of it? Is it in the narrow compass of the AUSTRIAN provinces? No, surely: It has most of it returned to the several countries whence it came, and has followed that art and industry, by which at first it was acquired. For above a thousand years, the money of EUROPE has been flowing to ROME, by an open and sensible current; but it has been emptied by many secret and insensible canals: And the want of industry and commerce renders at present the papal dominions the poorest territory in all ITALY.

In short, a government has great reason to preserve with care its people and its manufactures. Its money, it may safely trust to the course of human affairs, without fear or jealousy. Or if it ever give attention to this latter circumstance, it ought only to be so far as it affects the former.

XIV

FRANÇOIS QUESNAY

TABLEAU ÉCONOMIQUE

NOTE

FRANÇOIS QUESNAY (1694–1774) was the son of a distinguished lawyer, but his early education appears to have been completely neglected. By dint of his own efforts, however, he became a master surgeon at the age of twenty-four. In 1730 he published an able paper on the practice of bleeding, which led to his appointment as secretary of the academy of surgery in Paris. Other essays on medical subjects followed, and in 1749 he became physician to Mme. de Pompadour. The remainder of his life was spent at Versailles. It was not till late in life that he became interested in economic questions, his first work being an article on *Farmers* for the *Encyclopédie* in 1757. In this and a subsequent article on *Grains* he advocated more intensive methods of farming and the abolition of vexatious taxes and restrictions. These and his *Tableau Économique*, which was privately printed at Versailles in 1758, attracted a small but able circle of disciples, who regarded him with the greatest admiration and zealously spread his doctrines. It is to the activities of this group — les Économistes, as they called themselves — that his fame is chiefly due, for he himself wrote little else on economics. Adam Smith came in contact with them during his stay in France, and was much influenced by some of their ideas.

EXPLANATION
OF THE ECONOMIC TABLE[1]

THE *productive Expenditures* are employed in agriculture, meadows, pastures, forests, mines, fishing, &c. to perpetuate riches in the form of grain, beverages, wood, cattle, raw materials for the handicrafts, &c.

The *sterile Expenses* are made upon handicraft products, housing, clothing, interest on money, servants, commercial expenses, foreign commodities, &c.

The sale of the net product which the Cultivator has produced during the preceding year, by means of the *annual Advances* of 600 livres employed in agriculture by the Farmer, furnishes the proprietor a *revenue* of 600 livres.

The *annual advances* of 300 livres in sterile expenses are employed for the capital & the expenses of commerce, for the purchase of raw materials for the handicrafts, & for the subsistence & other needs of the artisan until he has finished & sold his product.

Of the 600 livres of *revenue*, one half is spent by the Proprietor on purchases from the productive class, such as bread, wine, meat, &c., & the other half on purchases from the sterile class, such as clothing, furnishings, implements, &c.

These expenditures may incline more or less to one side or the other, as the spender goes in more or less for luxury in the way of subsistence or luxury in the form of ornamentation. Here the average situation is taken, where the reproductive expenditures renew the same revenue from year to year. But it is easy to see what changes would be caused in the annual reproduction of revenue, as the sterile expend-

---

[1] To save space, the diagram on the next page is simplified slightly, but not so as to require any modification of Quesnay's *Explication*.

ECONOMIC TABLE

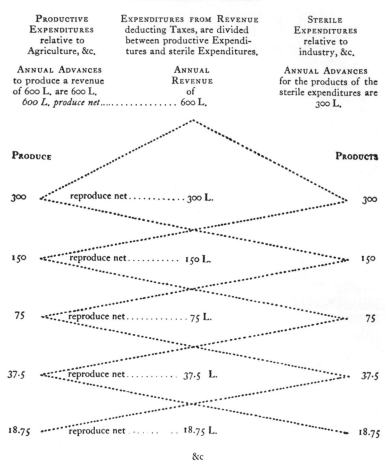

PRODUCTIVE EXPENDITURES relative to Agriculture, &c.	EXPENDITURES FROM REVENUE deducting Taxes, are divided between productive Expenditures and sterile Expenditures.	STERILE EXPENDITURES relative to industry, &c.
ANNUAL ADVANCES to produce a revenue of 600 L. are 600 L. *600 L. produce net*	ANNUAL REVENUE of .... 600 L.	ANNUAL ADVANCES for the products of the sterile expenditures are 300 L.

PRODUCE   PRODUCTS

300   reproduce net.............300 L.   300

150   reproduce net..........150 L.   150

75   reproduce net...........75 L.   75

37.5   reproduce net...........37.5 L.   37.5

18.75   reproduce net ....18.75 L.   18.75

&c

TOTAL REPRODUCTION.........600 L. of revenue; besides the annual expenditures of 600 L. and the interest on the original advances of the Husbandman, amounting to 300 L., which the land restores. Thus the reproduction is 1500 L., including the revenue of 600 L. which is the basis of the calculation, apart from taxes deducted, and the advances required for its annual reproduction, &c.

itures or the productive expenditures became more or less important than the other: it is easy, I say, to tell this from the very changes which would take place in the table. For, suppose that luxury in the form of ornamentation should increase by a sixth in the case of the Proprietor, by a sixth in the case of the Artisan, & by a sixth in the case of the Cultivator, the reproduction of revenue would fall from 600 livres to 500 livres. If, on the contrary, an increase of expenditure of the same extent occurred in the consumption or the exportation of raw materials, the reproduction of revenue would rise from 600 livres to 700 livres, & so on. Thus we see that an excess of luxury in the way of decoration may quickly ruin with magnificence an opulent Nation.

The 300 livres of revenue which were devoted to productive expenditures in the table bring back to this class, in money, *advances* which reproduce 300 livres net, which make up a part of the reproduction of the Proprietor's revenue; And by the distribution of the remaining sums which return to this same class, the total revenue is reproduced yearly. These 300 livres I say, which return to the productive class at first through the sale of the products which the Proprietor buys of them, are spent by the Farmer, half upon the consumption of products furnished by this same class, & the other half upon clothing, implements, tools, &c. which he buys of the sterile class. And they arise again with the net product.

The 300 livres of the Proprietor's revenue which were devoted to sterile expenditures are spent by the artisan, half on productive expenditures in the purchase of subsistence, raw materials, & for foreign commerce; the other half is distributed among the sterile class itself for living expenses, & to restore the *advances*. This circulation & this reciprocal distribution continues by subdivisions in the same order, down to the last penny of the sums which pass reciprocally from one class of expenditures to the other class of expenditures.

Circulation brings 600 livres to the sterile class, from which it is necessary to deduct 300 livres for the *annual ad-*

vances, leaving 300 livres for wages. These wages are equal to the 300 livres which this class receives from the productive class, & the advances are equal to the 300 livres of revenue which go to this same sterile class.

The productions of the other class amount to 1200 livres, after deducting taxes, tithes, & interest on the advances of the Husbandman, which will be considered separately, in order to avoid undue complications in analyzing the expenditures. In the expenditure of the 1200 livres of production, the Proprietor of the revenue buys 300 livres of them. Another 300 livres goes to the sterile class, of which a half, or 150 livres, is consumed for subsistence by this class; the other half, or 150 livres, being taken for foreign commerce, which comes under this same class. Finally, 300 livres are consumed in the productive class, by the men who produce them, & 300 livres for feeding & care of the cattle. Thus of the 1200 livres of product this class expends 600 livres, & its *advances* of 600 livres are returned to it in money through the sales which it makes to the Proprietor & to the sterile class. An eighth of the total product enters into foreign commerce, either as exports or for raw materials & subsistence for the workers of the country who sell their products to the other Nations. The sales of the Merchant balance the purchases of merchandise & of gold & silver which are obtained from abroad.

Such is the distributive order of the consumption of the native products among the different classes of citizens, & such is the idea we should have of the practice & the extent of the foreign commerce of a flourishing agricultural Nation.

The reciprocal traffic of one class with the other distributes the revenue of 600 livres from one side to the other; giving 300 livres to each side, over & above the advances which are conserved. The Proprietor subsists by means of the 600 livres which he spends. The 300 livres distributed to each class, added to the product of the taxes, the tithe, &c., which are added to them, can support a man in one or the other class: thus 600 livres of revenue & the supplementary sums can furnish subsistence to three heads of families. On this basis, 600 millions of revenue can furnish subsistence to three million families of four persons of all ages each.

The expenses furnished by the *annual advances* of the productive class, which also are renewed each year, & of which about a half is spent on food for the cattle & the other half in paying wages to the men engaged in the work of this class, add 300 millions of expenditures which can, with the part of the other products which are added to them, furnish subsistence for another million heads of families.

Thus these 900 millions, which, not counting taxes, tithes, & the interest on the annual advances & on the original advances of the Husbandman, would be renewed annually from the landed property, could furnish subsistence to sixteen million persons of all ages, according to this order of circulation & distribution of the annual revenues.

By circulation we mean here the purchases at first hand, paid for out of the revenue which is distributed among all the classes of men, excepting commerce, which multiplies purchases & sales without multiplying things, & which is only an increase of sterile expenditures.

The *riches of the productive class* of a Nation where the Proprietors of the land have constantly 600 millions of revenue may be evaluated as follows.

A revenue of 600 millions for the Proprietors assumes in addition 300 millions in taxes, & 150 millions for the tithe of the annual product, including all the charges, levied on those subject to the tithe: This makes a total of 1 billion 50 millions, including the revenue: In addition there are the reproduction of 1 billion 50 millions of annual advances, & 110 millions of interest on these advances at 10 per 100: making a grand total of 2,210,000,000 livres.

In a kingdom having many vineyards, forests, meadows, &c. there would be only about two-thirds of these 2 billions 210 millions which would be obtained by the labor of the plow. This part would require, in a good State of large-scale cultivation carried on by horses, the employment of three hundred thirty-three thousand three hundred thirty-four plows at 120 acres of land per plow, three hundred thirty-three thousand three hundred thirty-four men to direct them, & 40 million acres of land.

This culture may, with 5 or 6 billions of advances, be extended in France to more than 60 million acres.

We are not speaking here of small-scale cultivation carried on with oxen, in which more than a million plows would be needed, & about 2,000,000 men to exploit 40 million acres of land, which would yield only two-fifths as much as large-scale cultivation does. This small-scale cultivation to which the Cultivators are reduced, from lack of riches to make the original advances, is carried on at the expense of the landed property itself, employed to a great extent for the expenses, & by excessive annual expenditures for the subsistence of the multitude of men occupied in this form of cultivation, which absorb almost all the product. This ungrateful cultivation, which reveals the poverty & the ruin of the Nations where it prevails, has nothing to do with the order of the Table, which is arranged on the basis of half of the employment of a plow, where the annual advances can, in conjunction with the fund of original advances, produce one hundred per cent.

The total original advances required for the establishment of a plow in large-scale cultivation, for the first fund for the purchase of cattle, tools, seed, food, up-keep, wages, &c. in the course of two years' work before the first harvest, are estimated at 10,000 livres; thus the total for three hundred thirty-three thousand three hundred thirty-four plows is 3,333,340,000 livres. (See the articles *Farms, Farmers, Grains,* in the *Encyclopédie.*)

The interest on these advances should amount to at least 10 per 100, for the products of agriculture are exposed to ruinous accidents, which in ten years destroy the value of at least one year's crop. These advances demand, moreover, much up-keep & renewals; hence the total of interest on the original advances for establishing the Husbandmen is 333,-322,000 livres.

The meadows, vineyards, ponds, forests, &c. require slight original advances on the part of the Farmers. The value of these advances may be reduced, including the original expenses for plantings & other work done at the expense of the Proprietors, to 1,000,000,000 livres.

But vineyards & gardens require large annual advances, which, taken in connection with those of the other parts, may on the average be included in the total of annual advances set forth above.

The total annual reproduction in net product, in annual advances with the interest thereon, & in interest on the original advances, reckoned in conformity with the order of the table, is 2,543,322,000 livres.

The territory of France could produce as much & even much more.

Of this sum of 2,543,322,000 livres, 525 millions constitute half of the reproduction of the annual advances employed in feeding the cattle: leaving (if all taxes go back into circulation, & if they do not encroach upon the advances of the Husbandmen) 2,018,322,000 livres.

This makes, For the Expenditure of Men, *on the average 504,580,500 livres for each million heads of families, or for each head of a family 562 livres, which accidents reduce to about 530 livres.* On this footing a State is rich, & men live comfortably there.

. . . .

We are speaking of an opulent Nation which possesses a territory & advances which yield annually, & without wasting away, 1 billion 50 millions of net product; but all these riches kept up successively by this annual product may be destroyed or lose their value, in the decadence of an agricultural Nation, by the mere wasting away of the productive advances, which may make great headway in a short time as a result of eight principal causes.

    1. A bad system of taxation, encroaching upon the advances of the Cultivators. *Noli me tangere* is the motto of these advances.

2. Increase of taxes through expenses of collection.
3. Excess of luxurious expenditure on decoration.
4. Excess of expenses for litigation.
5. Lack of foreign trade in the produce of the land.
6. Lack of freedom in domestic trade in native commodities & in agriculture.
7. Personal vexations of the inhabitants of the rural districts.
8. Failure of the annual net product to return to the productive class.

XV

ANNE ROBERT JACQUES TURGOT

REFLEXIONS SUR LA FORMATION ET LA DISTRIBUTION DES RICHESSES

NOTE

ANNE ROBERT JACQUES TURGOT (1727–1781) was the son of a government official of distinction, and born and educated in Paris. Being destined by his family for the church, he obtained the degree of bachelor of theology, and entered the Sorbonne, of which he was later elected Prior. After about three years, however, he decided to enter government service, his first appointment being a judicial one. In 1761 he was appointed Intendant of Limoges, where he remained for thirteen years and instituted many important reforms. He was then appointed Controller General of Finance. During his two years in this office he established free trade in grain within France, abolished the burdensome *corvée*, and suppressed the guilds. These drastic measures aroused much opposition from those whose privileges were attacked, and the king was persuaded to dismiss him. The *Réflexions* were written in 1766 for two Chinese students, to help them in sending him information concerning economic conditions in their country, to which they were about to return. Turgot also wrote the articles *Fairs and Markets* and *Foundations* for the *Encyclopédie*, and numerous able letters and memoirs on economic questions, most of which were not published till after his death.

ON THE FORMATION AND DISTRIBUTION OF RICHES

§ XLIX

On the reserve of annual products accumulated to form capitals

A S soon as there were men whose ownership of land assured them an annual revenue more than sufficient to satisfy all their needs, there must have been some, anxious about the future or merely prudent, who laid aside a portion of what they garnered every year, either to provide for possible emergencies or to increase their comfort. When the commodities which they garnered were difficult to keep for any length of time, they must have sought to exchange them for things of a more durable character, which would not lose their value with the passing of time, or which could be utilized in ways which would yield a profit to more than make up for the loss.

§ L

Moveable riches. Accumulation of money

This class of property, resulting from the accumulation of unconsumed annual products, is known as *moveable Riches*. Furniture, plate, merchandise in warehouses, the tools of the various trades, and cattle belong to this class of riches. It is obvious that people had made vigorous efforts to acquire as much as possible of these riches before they knew about money; but it is no less evident that after money became known, after it was established that it was the most stable of all articles of commerce, and the easiest to preserve without inconvenience, it must have been the principal thing sought by people desirous of accumulating. It was not only the owners of lands who saved some of their surplus in this way.

Although the profits of industry are not, like the revenue from land, a gift of nature, and the worker in industry derives from his labor only the price given him by the one who pays his wages; although the latter economizes as much as possible on these wages, and competition compels the worker in industry to accept a lower price than he would like, still it is certain that this competition has never been extensive enough or keen enough in all branches of industry to prevent a man who was more skillful, more industrious, and especially more economical about his living expenses than other men from being able in all periods to earn a little more than what was needed for the support of himself and his family, and to lay aside this surplus in order to accumulate a little property.

§ LI

Moveable riches are an indispensable prerequisite for all lucrative occupations

It is even necessary that, in each trade, the Workers or the Entrepreneurs who employ them should have a certain fund of moveable riches accumulated in advance. Here we have to retrace our steps again and recall several things which were only briefly referred to, when we discussed the different classes of professions and the various means available to Proprietors for exploiting their land, because at that time it would have been impossible to explain them without breaking the continuity of ideas.

§ LII

Necessity of advances for agriculture

All classes of work in agriculture, industry, or commerce require advances. Even if the earth were cultivated by hand, it would be necessary to sow before reaping; it would be necessary to live until after the harvest. The more elaborate and vigorous cultivation becomes, the larger the advances are. Cattle, farm implements, buildings to shelter the cattle and to store the crops are needed; a number of people in proportion to the extent of the operations must be paid and supported until the harvest. It is only by means of large advances, that a large product is obtained, and that lands yield a large revenue. Whatever the trade, the artisan must have tools in advance, and a sufficient supply of the raw materials upon which he works; he has to live while looking forward to the sale of his products.

§ LIII

First advances furnished by land even before cultivation

Land is always the first and sole source of all riches; it is land which, as a result of cultivation, yields all revenue; it is land also which furnished the first fund of advances prior to all cultivation. The first cultivator took the seed which he sowed from plants which were the spontaneous product of land; while waiting for the harvest, he lived by hunting, fishing, wild fruits; his tools were branches of trees broken off in the forests and fashioned by means of sharp stones edged upon other stones; he captured with his hands or in his snares the animals wandering in the woods; he domesticated them; he used them at first for food, later to help him in his work. This first fund increased little by little; cattle were at first the most sought after kind of moveable riches, and the easiest to accumulate: they perish, but they reproduce, and wealth in this form is in a sense imperishable: this fund even grows as a result of mere natural increase, and yields an annual product, either in the form of milk, or wool, hides, and other things, which, with the wood gathered in the forests, constituted the first fund for industrial operations.

§ LIV

Cattle, moveable riches even prior to the cultivation of land

In an age when there was still a large supply of uncultivated land belonging to no one, it was possible to own cattle without being a Proprietor of land. It is even probable that men almost everywhere began to collect herds and to live on their product before devoting themselves to the more arduous labor of tillage.

The Nations that cultivated the soil in earliest times appear to have been the ones that found in their territory those species of animals which are most readily domesticated, and that were turned in this way from the wandering, troubled life of Peoples who live by hunting and fishing to the more tranquil life of pastoral Peoples.

Pastoral life makes people remain longer in the same place; it gives more leisure, more occasions for studying the difference between districts, and for observing the course of Nature in producing the plants which provide food for cattle. This may be the reason why the Asiatic Nations were the first to cultivate the soil, and the peoples of America remained so long in a savage state.

§ LV

Another kind of moveable riches, and of advances in agriculture: slaves

Slaves were another kind of moveable riches, obtained at first by violence, and later by means of trade and exchange.

Those who had a good many employed them not only in agriculture but also in the different branches of industry. The possibility of accumulating and utilizing these two kinds of riches in almost unlimited amounts, even independently of land, made it possible to evaluate lands themselves and to compare their value with that of moveable riches.

§ LVI

Moveable riches have a value in exchange like land itself

A man owning a large amount of land and no cattle or slaves would certainly make a good bargain by relinquishing a part of his land to some one who would give him in exchange cattle and slaves to cultivate the remainder. It is chiefly in this way that lands themselves came to be traded in and to have a value comparable with that of all other commodities. If *four bushels* of wheat, the net produce of an acre of land, were worth *six sheep*, the acre itself which produced them might have been given for a certain price, greater, to be sure, but always easy to determine in the same way as the prices of all other merchandise, that is, at first by discussion between the two parties concerned, and later according to the current price established by the intercourse of those who wish to exchange land for cattle and those who wish to give cattle for land. It is according to this current price that lands are valued when a debtor, sued by his creditor, is compelled to turn over his property to him.

§ LVII

Valuation of lands by the proportion between the revenue and the amount of moveable riches, or the value, for which they are exchanged: this proportion is what is called the PENNY *in the price of land*

It is evident that if a piece of land which yields a revenue equal to *six sheep* can be sold for a certain value which can always be expressed by a number of sheep equal to this value, this number will bear a definite ratio to *six*, and will contain it a certain number of times. The price of a piece of land will therefore be simply a certain number times its revenue; twenty times, if the price is *a hundred twenty* sheep; thirty times, if it is *a hundred eighty* sheep. The current price of land depends, therefore, upon the ratio between the value of the land and the value of the revenue; and the number of times which the price of land contains the revenue is called *the penny in the price of land*. Land is sold for the *twentieth penny*, the *thirtieth penny*, etc., when twenty, thirty, etc. times its revenue is paid for it. It is also evident that this price or *penny* must vary according to the greater or smaller number of people who wish to sell or buy land, just as the price of all other merchandise varies according to the different relation between supply and demand.

§ LVIII

Every capital in money, or every sum of value of any kind, is the equivalent of a tract of land yielding a revenue equal to a definite fraction of this sum. First employment of capitals. Purchase of landed property

Let us come back now to the period subsequent to the introduction of money: the ease with which it may be accumulated soon made it the most desired of moveable riches, and provided the means of increasing them unceasingly through the simple process of saving. Anyone receiving more income per year than he needs to spend, whether from the revenue of his land, or from the recompense of his labor or his industry, can lay aside this surplus and let it accumulate: these accumulated values are what is called *a capital*. The timid miser who accumulates money merely to free his imagination from the fear of being in need of the necessaries of life in an indefinite future, keeps his money together. If the dangers he had foreseen came to pass, and he were reduced by poverty to living every year upon his treasure, or if it chanced that a prodigal heir spent it piecemeal, this treasure would soon be used up, and the capital entirely lost to the possessor: the latter can make a much better use of it. Since a landed property yielding a given revenue is simply the equivalent of a sum of value equal to a certain multiple of this revenue, it follows that any sum of values is the equivalent of a property yielding a revenue equal to a definite fraction of this sum: it makes absolutely no difference whether this sum of values or this capital consists of a mass of metal or of anything else, since money represents every kind of value, just as every kind of value represents money. The possessor of a *capital* can therefore, in the first place, employ it to buy land; but he has still other opportunities.

§ LIX

Another employment of money in advances for manufacturing and industry

I have already remarked that all kinds of work, whether in agriculture or in industry, require advances, and I have shown how land, through the fruits and plants which it produces spontaneously for the support of men and animals, and through the trees from which men made their first tools, had furnished the first advances for agriculture, and even for the first objects wrought by individuals for their own use. For example, it is land which furnished the stone, the clay, and wood from which the first houses were built, and before the division of labor, when the man who tilled the soil provided for his other needs by his own labor, no other advances were needed: but when a large part of society depended on the labor of their hands for a livelihood, those who lived on wages in this way had to begin by having something in advance, either to procure the materials upon which they worked, or to live on while awaiting the payment of their wages.

§ LX

Analysis of the practice of making advances of capital in industrial enterprises, of their return, and of the profit they ought to yield

In early times an employer used to furnish materials himself, and pay the workman his wages from day to day. The Farmer or Proprietor himself gave the spinner the hemp he had gathered, and supported her while she was working; he then turned the thread over to the weaver, to whom he gave every day the wages agreed upon; but these small daily advances can suffice only for coarse handicraft operations. A great many trades, even among those followed by the poorest members of Society, require that the same material should pass through a great many different hands, and undergo very long, difficult, and varied preparation. — I have already referred to the preparation of leather for shoes: anyone who has seen a tanner's shop realizes how utterly impossible it is for one man, or even several poor men, to lay in a stock of hides, lime, tanbark, tools, etc., erect the buildings required for establishing a tannery, and live for several months until the leather is sold. In this industry and in many others, do not the workmen have to learn the trade before venturing to touch the materials, which they would spoil in their first attempts? This makes another advance necessary. Who, then, will bring together the materials for the work, the ingredients and tools required for their preparation? Who will have canals, markets, and buildings of all kinds erected? Who will support, until the leather has been sold, this large number of workmen, no one of whom could prepare a single hide by himself, and no one of whom could live on the profit from the sale of a single finished piece? Who will pay the expenses of learners and apprentices? Who will provide them with subsistence until they are trained by having worked up by degrees from simple tasks suited to their age to work requiring the greatest strength and skill? It will be one of these owners of *capitals* or accumulated moveable values (*valeurs mobiliaires*) who will employ them, partly in advances for construction and the purchase of material, partly for the daily wages of the workmen engaged in preparing them. It is he who will wait until the sale of the leather returns him not only all his advances, but also a profit sufficient to recompense him for what he could have earned on his money, if he had used it to buy land; and, in addition, for the wages due him for his labor, his oversight, his risk, and even his skill; for, at the same profit, he would doubtless have preferred to live without any trouble on the revenue from the land he might have acquired with the same capital. As this capital returns to him through the sale of the products, he employs it in new purchases to supply and maintain his manufacture by this continual circulation: he lives on his profits, and lays aside what he can spare to increase his capital and put it into his business by increasing the amount of his advances, in order to increase his profits still more.

§ LXI

Subdivision of the stipendiary industrial class into capitalist Entrepreneurs and simple Workmen

The whole class engaged in supplying the immense variety of industrial products required to satisfy the different needs of Society, is therefore subdivided, so to speak, into two categories: that of the manufacturing Entrepreneurs, Master craftsmen, all owners of large capitals, which they turn to account by employing people by means of their advances; and the second, which is composed of simple Artisans, who have no property but their hands, who advance nothing but their daily work and receive no profit except their wages.

§ LXII

Another employment of capitals in advances for agricultural enterprises. Analysis of the use, the return, and the necessary profits of capitals in agricultural enterprises

In speaking first of the employment of capitals in manufacturing enterprises, my object was to present a more obvious example of the necessity and the effect of large advances and of their regular circulation; but I reversed the natural order somewhat, which would have required me to begin by speaking of agricultural enterprises, which likewise are carried on, extended, and made profitable only by means of large advances. It is the owners of large capitals who, in order to employ them to advantage in agricultural enterprises, lease estates and pay the Proprietors big rentals for them, undertaking to make all the advances for cultivation. — Their position must be the same as that of the manufacturing Entrepreneurs: like them they have to make the first advances for the enterprise, to provide themselves with cattle, horses, agricultural implements, and to buy the first seed; like them they have to support and provide subsistence for the ploughmen, reapers, threshers, servants, and workmen of all kinds, who have only their hands, advance only their labor, and earn only their wages; like them they have to take in, besides the recovery of their capitals, that is, of all their original and annual advances, (1) a profit equal to the revenue they might have made on their capital without any work; (2) the wages and price of their labor, their risk, and their industry; (3) the means of replacing annually the wasting away of the equipment used in their enterprise, the cattle that die, the tools that wear out, etc.

All this must be deducted from the price of the produce of the land; the surplus enables the Cultivator to pay the Proprietor for the permission given him by the latter to use his land for the establishing of his enterprise. It is the price of the lease, the revenue of the Proprietor, the *net product*, for what the land produces up to the amount required to cover the advances of all kinds, and the profits of the one who makes them, cannot be considered a *revenue*, but only as *recovery of the expenses of cultivation*, inasmuch as, if the Cultivator did not obtain them, he would be careful not to employ his riches and his trouble in cultivating somebody else's land.

§ LXIII

The competition of Capitalist entrepreneurs engaged in agriculture establishes the current price of leases and large-scale farming

The competition of rich entrepreneurs engaged in agriculture establishes the current price of leases in proportion to the fertility of the land and the price at which its produce sells, always according to the estimates which the farmers make of all their expenses and the profit they should make on their advances: they can pay the Proprietor only the surplus.

But when the competition between them is very keen, they pay him all this surplus, the Proprietor leasing his land only to the one who offers the highest rent.

§ LXIV

The lack of Capitalist entrepreneurs in agriculture limits the
exploitation of land to small-scale cultivation

When, on the contrary, there are no rich men with large
capitals to invest in agricultural enterprises, when, as a result of the low price of agricultural products, or any other
cause, the harvests do not suffice to assure the Entrepreneurs, in addition to the recovery of their investment, profits
at least equal to what they would earn on their money by
employing it in any other way, there are no Farmers desirous of leasing land.

The Proprietors are compelled to have them cultivated by
Tenants or Metayers who are unable to make any advances
and to cultivate efficiently.

The Proprietor in this case makes small advances himself,
which yield him a very small revenue: if the land belongs
to a Proprietor who is poor, or in debt, or careless, or to
a Widow or a Minor, it remains uncultivated.

This is the real basis of the difference which I have already
pointed out between the Provinces where the land is cultivated by rich Farmers, such as Normandy and the Isle of
France, and those where it is cultivated only by poor Metayers, such as Limousin, Angoumois, Bourbonnais and
many others.

§ LXV

Subdivision of the class of Cultivators into Entrepreneurs or
Farmers, and simple Wage-earners, Servants or Day-laborers

It follows from the foregoing that the class of Cultivators is
divided, like the manufacturing class, into two categories of
men — the Entrepreneurs or Capitalists, who make all the
advances, and the simple Wage-earners. It is also evident
that it is the capitals alone which develop and sustain great
agricultural enterprises; which give lands a constant rental
value, if I may so express myself; which assure the Proprietors a steady revenue as large as possible.

§ LXVI

Fourth employment of capitals in advances for commercial enterprises. Necessity of the intervention of Merchants, properly so called, between the Producers of the commodity and the Consumers

The Entrepreneurs, whether in agriculture or in manufacturing, obtain their advances and their profits only by the sale of the produce of the land or the manufactured articles.

It is always the needs and the means of the consumer that determine selling prices; but the consumer does not always need the goods manufactured or produced, at the time of the harvest or when the products are finished.

The Entrepreneurs, however, need to get their funds back immediately and regularly, in order to put them into their business again. Plowing and sowing must follow the harvest without interruption, the workmen in a manufactory must be kept busy, new production must be started as the earlier is finished, materials must be replaced as they are used up. The operations of a going enterprise are not to be interrupted with impunity, and they are not to be resumed whenever one wishes.

The Entrepreneur, therefore, has the greatest interest in getting his funds back promptly, through the sale of his crops and his products. On the other hand, the consumer is interested in finding the things he needs, when he wishes them, and where he wishes them; it would be very inconvenient for him to have to buy his supply for the whole year at the time of the harvest.

Among the articles of common consumption there are many which require long and expensive labor, labor which cannot be undertaken with profit except upon a very large quantity of material, so large that the consumption of a small number of people, or of a small district, could not provide a market for the products of a single plant.

Enterprises of this sort are therefore necessarily limited in number, at a considerable distance from each other, and consequently very far from the homes of most of the consumers; there is no one, above the level of extreme misery, who is not in a position to consume several things not produced or made except at a great distance from his home, and equally distant from each other. A man who could procure what he consumes only by purchasing directly from producer or maker would do without many things or would spend his life in travelling.

This double interest on the part of the producer and the consumer, the first in finding a sale, and the second in finding what he wishes to buy, without losing valuable time waiting for a buyer or looking for a seller, must have given some third parties the idea of intervening between them. — This is the purpose of the profession of Merchants, who buy commodities from the producer to get together a stock or store, where the consumer comes to supply his needs.

In this way, the entrepreneur, assured of a sale and of the return of his funds, devotes himself to new production without anxiety and without interruption, and the consumer finds what he needs available at all times.

§ LXVII

Different classes of Merchants. All have this in common, that they buy to sell again, and that their operations are carried on by means of advances which have to be recovered with a profit in order to be put back into the enterprise

From the Huckster who displays her herbs in the market, to the Merchant of Nantes or Cadiz, who extends his purchases and sales as far as India and America, the profession of Merchant, or commerce properly so called, is divided into an infinite number of branches, and, so to speak, of grades. One Merchant confines himself to carrying a stock of one or several kinds of goods, which he sells in his shop to all who come there. Another goes to sell certain commodities where they are lacking, bringing back in exchange the commodities which are produced there and which are lacking in the place from which he came. One does his trading in the vicinity, acting for himself; another by means of Correspondents and with the assistance of Carriers whom he pays, sends, and orders from one Province to another, from one Kingdom to another, from Europe to Asia, from Asia to Europe. One sells his merchandise in small lots to the individual consumers; the other sells only large quantities at a time to other Merchants, who resell them piecemeal to the Consumers; but all have this in common that they *buy to sell again*, and that their first purchases are an advance which comes back to them only after a time. It must come back to them, like that of the Entrepreneurs in agriculture and manufacturing, not only entire within a certain period, in order to be put back into new purchases, but also (1) with a profit equal to the revenue they might make on their capital without any work; and (2) with the wages and price of their labor, their risks, and their skill. Without the assurance of this return and these indispensable profits, no Merchant would go into commerce; none could keep on with it; it is on this basis that he regulates his purchases, estimating the amount and the price of the things he can expect to sell in a certain time. The Retailer learns by experience, by the success of limited experiments made cautiously, about how great are the needs of the consumers he is in a position to supply. The Merchant obtains information through Correspondents concerning the abundance or scarcity and the price of merchandise in the different countries to which he extends his trading; he directs his speculations accordingly; he sends commodities from places where they are cheap to places where they are dearer; with the understanding, of course, that the expenses of transportation enter into the calculation of the advances which have to come back to him.

Since commerce is necessary, and it is impossible to undertake any kind of commerce without advances in proportion to its extent, this makes another employment for moveable riches, a further use which the owner of a mass of saved and accumulated values, of a sum of money, in a word, of a capital, can make of it to earn a profit, to procure his subsistence, and to increase his riches if possible.

§ LXVIII

True idea of the circulation of money

It is evident from what has just been said how agriculture, manufacturing of all kinds, and all the branches of commerce are carried on by means of a mass of *capitals* or accumulated moveable riches, which, having been at first advanced by the Entrepreneurs in each of these different classes of work, must return to them every year with a regular profit: the capital, in order to be put back and advanced anew in continuing the same enterprises; the profit, for the more or less comfortable support of the Entrepreneurs. It is this continual advance and return of capitals which constitutes *what ought to be called the circulation of money*, that useful and fruitful circulation which enlivens all the works of Society, which sustains movement and life in the body politic, and which may well be compared to the circulation of the blood in animal bodies. For if, through any derangement in the scale of expenses of the different classes of Society, the Entrepreneurs cease recovering their advances with the profit they have a right to expect, it is evident that they will be obliged to cut down their operations; that the sum of labor, of consumption of agricultural products, of production, and of revenue will be proportionately diminished; that poverty will take the place of riches, and that Wage-earners, failing to find work, will sink into deepest misery.

§ LXIX

All industrial enterprises, especially in manufacturing and commerce, could only have been very limited before the introduction of gold and silver in commerce

It is hardly necessary to remark that enterprises of all kinds, but especially in manufacturing, and still more in commerce, could only have been very limited before the introduction of gold and silver in commerce, since it was almost impossible to accumulate considerable capitals, and even more difficult to multiply and divide payments as much as is necessary to facilitate and multiply exchanges to the extent required by a vigorous commerce and circulation. Only agriculture could maintain itself to some extent, since cattle are the principal object of the advances it requires; it is even probable that there were then no entrepreneurs in agriculture except the Proprietors. As for the arts of all kinds, they could only have been in a most sluggish state before the introduction of money. They were confined to the coarsest kinds of work, for which the proprietors furnished the advances by supporting the Workmen and supplying them with materials, or which they had done in their households by their servants.

§ LXX

Capitals being as necessary for all enterprises as labor and skill, the man in industry willingly shares the profits of his enterprise with the Capitalist who provides him with the funds he needs

Since capitals are the indispensable basis of all enterprises, since money is a principal means for saving small gains, accumulating profits, and becoming rich, those who along with skill and diligence have no capitals, or not enough for the enterprises they wish to establish, do not find it hard to resolve to give the owners of capitals or money, who are willing to trust them with it, a share of the profits they expect to obtain in addition to recovering their advances.

§ LXXI

Fifth employment of capitals: lending at interest. Nature of lending

The owners of money weigh the risk which their capital may run, if the enterprise does not succeed, against the advantage of enjoying a steady profit without working, and determine on this basis whether to demand more or less profit or interest on their money, or to consent to lend it for the interest offered them by the borrower. This makes another outlet for the owner of money, lending at interest or trading in money. For we should make no mistake about it; lending at interest is simply a kind of trading, in which the Lender is a man who sells the *use* of his money, and the Borrower a man who buys it, just as the Proprietor of an estate and his Farmer sell and buy respectively the *use* of leased property.

This was expressed perfectly by the name the Romans gave to interest on money loans, *usura pecuniæ*, a word whose French translation has become odious as a result of the false ideas which people have had about interest on money.

§ LXXIX

The rate of interest depends proximately upon the relation between the demand by borrowers and the offer by lenders; and this relation depends principally upon the amount of moveable riches accumulated by saving revenues and annual products to form capitals, whether these capitals exist in money or any other kind of property having a value in commerce

The value of silver in the market depends only on the quantity of this metal employed in current trade; but the rate of interest depends on the amount of values accumulated and laid aside to form capitals. It makes no difference whether these values are in metal or in some other kind of property, provided they may easily be converted into money.

The mass of metal in a State is far from being as large as the sum of values lent at interest in the course of a year; but all these capitals, in furnishings, merchandise, tools, cattle, take the place of this money and represent it. A note signed by a man known to own property worth *a hundred thousand francs,* and who promises to pay *a hundred thousand francs* at the end of a certain period, passes during this period for *a hundred thousand francs.* All the capitals of the man who signed this note are security for its payment, whatever the nature of the property he possesses, provided they have a value of *a hundred thousand francs.*

It is therefore not the quantity of money in the form of metal which causes interest on money to rise or fall, or which causes more money to be offered for lending; it is solely the sum of capitals in commerce, that is to say, the actual sum of moveable values of all kinds, accumulated, saved by degrees from revenues and profits, to be employed in obtaining further revenues and further profits for the owner. It is these accumulated savings that are offered to borrowers, and the more there are of them, the lower the interest on money is, unless the number of borrowers be increased in proportion.

§ LXXX

The spirit of economy in a Nation continually increases the sum of capitals; luxury continually tends to destroy them

The spirit of economy in a Nation tends to increase continually the sum of its capitals, to increase the number of lenders, to diminish the number of borrowers. Luxurious habits have precisely the opposite effect; and from what has already been said about the use of capitals in all agricultural, industrial, or commercial enterprises, one can judge whether luxury enriches a Nation or impoverishes it.

§ LXXXI

The fall in the rate of interest proves that in general economy has prevailed over luxury in Europe

Since interest on money has been falling steadily in Europe for several centuries, we must conclude that the spirit of economy has been more general than the spirit of luxury. It is only rich people who indulge in luxuries, and among the rich all those who are reasonable limit themselves to spending their revenue, and are careful not to trench upon their capitals. Those who wish to become rich are much more numerous in a Nation than the rich; now in the present state of things, when all land is occupied, there is only one means of becoming rich: To have or to obtain, in some way, an annual revenue or profit in excess of what is absolutely necessary for subsistence, to lay aside this surplus every year to form a capital, by means of which an increase of annual revenue or profit may be obtained, which may in turn be saved and converted into capital. There are therefore many men interested and occupied in accumulating capitals.

. . . .

§ LXXXIII

Influence of the different employments of money upon each other

It is evident that the annual products which can be derived from capitals invested in these different ways are mutually limited, and are all dependent upon the current rate of interest on money.

§ LXXXIV

Money invested in land should yield less

A man who invests his money by buying an estate leased to a Farmer of good credit obtains a revenue which involves very little trouble on his part, and which he can spend in the most agreeable manner, indulging all his tastes. He has the further advantage that land is, of all possessions, the one that is most secure against accidents of all kinds.

§ LXXXV

Money loans should yield a little more than the revenue of land purchased with an equal capital

A man who lends his money at interest enjoys his income with even less trouble and restraint than the owner of land; but the insolvency of his debtor may cause him to lose his capital.

He will therefore not be satisfied with an interest equal to the revenue from the land he could buy with the same capital.

The interest on money loans should therefore be higher than the revenue of land purchased for the same capital; for if the lender had an opportunity to buy an estate yielding an equal revenue, he would prefer this investment.

§ LXXXVI

Money invested in agricultural, manufacturing, or commercial enterprises should yield more than the interest on money loans

For similar reasons, money invested in agriculture, industry, or commerce should yield a profit greater than the revenue from the same capital invested in land, or the interest on the same money loaned; for these investments require, in addition to the capital advanced, much care and labor, and if they were not lucrative, it would be much better to procure an equal revenue, which could be enjoyed without doing anything. Besides the interest on his capital, therefore, the entrepreneur must obtain every year a profit to recompense him for his trouble, his labor, his skill, and his risks, and to provide him, moreover, with the wherewithal to replace the annual wasting away of the advances, which he has to convert from the beginning into things subject to change and exposed to all kinds of accidents.

§ LXXXVII

Nevertheless, the returns from these different employments are mutually limited, and, despite their inequality, maintain a kind of equilibrium

The different employments of capitals, then, yield very unequal returns; but this inequality does not prevent them from exercising a mutual influence upon each other, and from establishing a kind of equilibrium among themselves, as between two liquids of different densities, communicating with each other through the arm of an inverted siphon of which they occupy the two branches; they would not come to the same level, but the height of one could not increase without the other also rising in the opposite branch.

Suppose a great many owners of estates suddenly desire to sell them: It is evident that the price of land will fall, and that a smaller sum will buy a greater revenue. That cannot come about without the interest on money becoming higher; for the owners of money will prefer to buy estates rather than to lend at an interest no higher than the revenue from the estates they might buy. If, therefore, the borrowers wish to obtain money, they will be obliged to pay a higher rental for it. If the interest on money becomes higher, people will prefer to lend it, rather than utilize it, at greater trouble and risk, in agricultural, industrial, or commercial enterprises; and only those enterprises will be carried on which yield, in addition to the wages of labor, a profit much greater than the rate of interest on money loans. In short, when the profits yielded by any employment of money increase or diminish, capitals flow into them from other employments, or are withdrawn to be put into the other employments; which necessarily changes the relation between the capital and the annual return in each of these employments. In general, money invested in land yields less than money loans, and money loans yield less than money employed in industrial enterprises; but the return on money employed in any way whatever cannot increase or diminish, without causing all the other employments to experience a proportionate increase or diminution.

§ LXXXVIII

The current rate of interest on money is the thermometer by which we can form an opinion as to the abundance or scarcity of capitals; it is the measure of the degree to which a Nation can extend its agricultural, manufacturing, and commercial enterprises

The current interest on money loans may therefore be regarded as a kind of thermometer of the abundance or scarcity of capitals in a Nation, and of the extent of the enterprises of all kinds to which it can devote itself: it is evident that the lower the rate of interest is, the greater the value of land is. A man with rents amounting to fifty thousand livres has property worth only a million, if land sells for only the twentieth penny; he has two millions, if land sells for the fortieth penny.

If interest is five per cent, all uncleared land which will not yield five per cent, over and above replacing the advances and recompensing the Farmer for his trouble, will be left idle; all forms of manufacturing or commerce which will not yield five per cent, over and above wages for the trouble and risk of the Entrepreneur, will not exist.

If there is a neighboring Nation where interest on money is only two per cent, it will not only carry on all the commerce from which the Nation where interest is five per cent is excluded, but its Manufacturers and its Merchants, being able to get along with less profit, will offer their commodities at lower prices in all markets, and will get control of almost all the trade in everything not preserved to the Nation where money is worth five per cent by special circumstances or excessive costs of transportation.

§ LXXXIX

Influence of the rate of interest on money upon all profit-yielding enterprises

The rate of interest may be regarded as a kind of level below which all labor, all cultivation, all industry, all commerce cease. It is like a sea spread over a vast territory: the summits of the mountains rise above the waters, forming fertile and cultivated islands. If this sea happens to be drained away, the hillsides, then the plains and the valleys, appear as the water subsides, and become covered with vegetation of all kinds. The water only has to rise or fall a foot to flood immense stretches of shore or return them to cultivation. — It is the abundance of capitals which enlivens all enterprises, and low interest on money is at once the effect and the index of the abundance of capitals.

.   .   .   .

§ XCII

In which of the three classes of Society should the Capitalist lenders of money be placed?

Let us now consider how what we have just set forth concerning the different ways of employing capitals fits in with what we laid down earlier concerning the division of all the members of Society into three classes, the productive class or those engaged in Agriculture, the industrial or commercial class, and the disposable [1] class or the Proprietors.

§ XCIII

The Capitalist lender of money belongs, with respect to his person, to the disposable class

We have seen that every rich man is necessarily the owner of a capital in moveable riches, or of an estate equivalent to a capital. Every landed estate is equivalent to a capital; and so every Proprietor is a capitalist, but not every Capitalist is proprietor of a landed estate; and the owner of a moveable capital has a choice of employing it to acquire land or of investing it in enterprises of the agricultural class or of the industrial class. The capitalist who has become an entrepreneur in agriculture or industry is no more disposable, either himself or his profits, than the mere laborer in these two classes; both are bound up with the continuation of their enterprises. The Capitalist who becomes a mere money-lender makes loans to a Proprietor or to an Entrepreneur. If he lends to a Proprietor, he seems to belong to the class of Proprietors; he becomes a joint owner of the property; the revenue from the land is pledged to pay the interest on his loan; the value of the property is pledged to secure his capital as far as required. If the lender of money has lent to an entrepreneur, it is certain that his person belongs to the dis-

---

[1] In the earlier passage referred to, this class was characterized as "the only one which, not being bound to a particular task by the necessity of earning a living, may be employed for the general needs of society, . . . either by personal service or by the payment of a part of their revenues." — ED.

posable class; but his capital remains involved in the advances for the enterprise, and cannot be withdrawn without injuring the enterprise, unless replaced by a capital of equal value.

§ XCIV

The interest received by the lender of money is disposable, with respect to the use he can make of it

It is true that the interest which he receives on this capital appears to be disposable, since the entrepreneur and the enterprise can do without it; and it also seems as if we might conclude that in the profits of the two classes engaged in labor, whether agricultural or industrial, there is a disposable portion, namely, what corresponds to the interest on the advances, calculated at the current rate on money loans; and it also seems that this conclusion conflicts with our statement that only the class of Proprietors had a revenue properly so called, a disposable revenue, and that all the members of the two other classes had only wages or profits. — This deserves some explanation.

If we consider the thousand crowns received every year by a man who has lent sixty thousand francs to a Merchant, from the point of view of what he can do with them, there is no doubt that they are perfectly disposable, since the enterprise can get along without them.

§ XCV

The interest on money is not disposable in the sense that the State may, without bad effects, appropriate a part thereof for its own needs

But it does not follow that they are disposable in the sense that the State can with impunity appropriate a part of them for public needs. These thousand crowns are not a return made gratuitously by agriculture or commerce to the man who made the advances; it is the price and the condition of this advance, without which the enterprise could not continue. — If this return is diminished, the capitalist will withdraw his money, and the enterprise will come to an end. This return should therefore be inviolate and enjoy complete immunity, since it is the price of an advance made to the enterprise without which the enterprise could not continue. To touch it would mean raising the price of the advances for all enterprises, and consequently diminishing the enterprises themselves, that is to say, agriculture, industry and commerce.

This answer should lead us to conclude that if we said that the capitalist who had lent to a Proprietor *seemed* to belong to the proprietary class, this *appearance* had something equivocal about it which needed to be cleared up.

As a matter of fact, it is perfectly true that the interest on his money is no more disposable, that is to say, no more fit to be trenched upon, than the interest on money lent to Entrepreneurs in agriculture and commerce. This interest is equally a price freely agreed upon, and it can no more be trenched upon without changing the rate of interest: it makes little difference to whom the loan was made; if the rate of interest changes and increases for the Proprietor, it will change and increase for the Cultivator, the Manufacturer, and the Merchant. In short, the Capitalist lender of money should be regarded as a dealer in a commodity absolutely necessary for the production of riches, and which cannot bear too low a price. It is as foolish to burden his trade with a tax as to levy a tax on the manure used to fertilize land. Let us conclude from this that the lender of money belongs indeed to the disposable class, with respect to his person, because he does not have to work; but not with respect to the character of his riches, whether the interest on his money be paid by the Proprietor of land from a part of his revenue, or by an Entrepreneur from a part of his profits pledged to pay the interest on advances.

XVI

JONANN H. G. VON JUSTI

SYSTEM DES FINANZWESENS

NOTE

JOHANN HEINRICH GOTTLOB VON JUSTI (1720–1771), the greatest of the German Cameralists, was born in Thuringia and studied jurisprudence at several of the German universities. In 1750 he was made professor of cameral sciences in the new Ritter Akademie in Vienna, where he remained three years. After leaving the Austrian service he spent two years in Göttingen, as a member of the council of mines and commissioner of police. In 1757 he went to Berlin, where he became director of mines and superintendent of glass and steel work. He was removed because of irregularities in his accounts and died in prison. The list of bulky volumes from his hand, notably his *Staatswirtschaft oder systematische Abhandlung aller ökonomischen- und Cameralwissenschaften* (1755), *Ausführliche Vorstellung der gesamten Policeywissenschaften* (1760), and *System des Finanzwesens* (1766) is evidence of his great industry. Though he drew heavily on his predecessors, he showed much sound judgment of his own, and considerable genius for organization. In his *Finanzwesen* we have the ablest product of one of the most important aspects of cameral science.

PUBLIC FINANCE

BOOK IV

GENERAL PRINCIPLES OF TAXES AND CONTRIBUTIONS

A STATE—a society of men who occupy a considerable portion of the surface of our earth, who have united with a view to their common welfare, and who have placed a supreme authority over themselves for this purpose — requires great expenditures and outlays for its own support and for the achievement of this purpose. It must put its prince, or those who exercise the supreme authority, in a position to live in a style befitting their dignity. It must support those whom the supreme authority employs for the administration of justice and other functions. The establishments and institutions for the protection of the state, as well as those for the common advantage and convenience of all citizens, which are ordinarily called police (*Policey*) establishments, likewise require large outlays; and the maintenance of relations and intercourse with other states similarly cannot go on without expenditures. It is therefore impossible for a civil society to exist that does not have to spend a good deal for its maintenance and welfare.

The principle that no state can exist without expenses is therefore an undeniable truth. A civil society, which constitutes a moral body, can no more maintain its condition without support than a natural body can live without subsistence. But that a state which makes large expenditures is therefore more fortunate than another which spends but little, can no more be claimed than that an individual is happier because he spends a great deal. A man living in all possible splendor and plenty may be exceedingly unhappy and miserable, on account of the slavery in which he is held, and many other circumstances. States are in the same position in this respect as men. Vanity and luxury lead them to imagine a thousand needs, without being any happier for having all these imaginary wants satisfied. The true necessities and conveniences of Nature, in the case of both states and men, have no great extent; and the needs of states mentioned in the preceding paragraph can all be provided for at very moderate expense, if the fundamentals of a civil society are properly established. States, it is true, must look after their welfare as well as individuals; and therefore they cannot avoid the expenditures which the morality, the manners, and customs of their century have introduced; unless they wish to live in a sort of separation and suspension of all intercourse with other states. But even without ignoring welfare, and in the midst of a luxurious and extravagant century, the support of the state can be provided for at very moderate expense. We see this plainly in the case of the present Swiss republics, where the expenses of the state are met with very moderate sums. However, it must be confessed that these expenses depend very much upon the nature of the political organization. A republic which employs the surest and most natural mode of defence, namely, the citizens themselves bearing arms for the protection of their fatherland, which knows how to keep the motives of love for the fatherland and zeal for the common welfare strong and tense, which knows no other basis of honor and privilege except service rendered the fatherland and the common good; such a republic, I say, will require only moderate expenses for its support. The establishments for the defence of the state will require no great sums; and all officials and servants of the state will be actuated, not by a salary, but by the honor of furthering the general welfare. Such political organizations are not mere ideal republics, which have never really existed or could exist. Rome and many republics of Greece — where nobody asked a salary for services rendered the state, while in the early and virtuous days people did not try to recompense and enrich themselves through the misuse of public offices — are too convincing evidence that such political organizations are not mere images of the understanding: and if such arrangements seem impossible to us, that is an indication of the corruption of our times. But it is not to be denied that monarchies always require much greater expenditures, both on account of the maintenance of the prince and his family, which must be in keeping with his great dignity, and because it is less consistent with the nature of a monarchy to leave the defence of the state to the citizens themselves; partly because monarchs always prefer to trust their own safety and that of the state to enlisted and paid soldiers; principally, however, because self-interest is the chief motive in monarchies, and love for the fatherland and zeal for the general welfare are never found there in their true and real extent and effect. Consequently nobody can and will perform services for the state without a salary. Nevertheless, it is the duty of monarchs to make nothing but necessary expenditures for the support of the state; and wise and upright monarchs will always keep this in mind as a principle. The purpose of all these considerations is that we believe they demonstrate that it should be laid down here as a fundamental rule that the expenses for the support of the state should not be increased by merely imaginary wants, and that no expenditures should be made which are not really necessary and useful.

The writers who deal with the present subject, after showing the necessity and unavoidableness of the expenditures which a state must make, by the same arguments which we have used above, at once draw the conclusion that therefore the subjects must pay taxes and contributions. But that is a big leap in logic. The fact that the state cannot support itself without expense does not prove that the subjects must pay these expenses out of their private means. It is clear that two other conditions must be assumed; first, that no other means are available for the maintenance of the state, or if there are any, they are not adequate for the necessary outlays. For contributions from the private means of the subjects must, according to all sound ideas, be the last resort. When men organize into civil societies, they unite all their individual powers into one, and consequently all their individual property as well; and there is no doubt that the state can make use of this general property for the general welfare. But, in addition to this general property, the state also has special property of its own, which consists of the estates belonging to it specifically, and the exercise of the prerogatives (*Regalien*), which by their very nature cannot be private property, because the things involved must remain available for the use of all the inhabitants. This special property of the state may also be called its direct property, while its general property is given the name of indirect property. It is natural and reasonable, however, that the state should first pay the expenses of its maintenance out of its direct and special property, before having recourse to its indirect and general property. From the necessity and un-avoidability of the expenses which a state has to meet for its maintenance, it does not follow directly, therefore, that the subjects must contribute the necessary funds from their private means; but this follows only in the case where a state has no direct and special property, or where this is in-adequate for the state's necessary expenses.

The direct and special property of the state consists principally of domains, or crown estates, and prerogatives. We cannot imagine a state without a people, or a people without a considerable area of land inhabited by this people, and belonging to it exclusively. This is one of the principal bases required for the existence of a state, and without it men can organize societies for this or that special purpose, but no general civil society devoted to the general welfare, that is, a state. When a state comes into being, it is either formally set up all at once, or it attains its form only gradually. When a society of men takes possession of a territory by conquest, or chooses an unoccupied area for its home, and with mature consideration sets a supreme authority over it-self, in order to found a nation and a state, they see the necessity of the expenditures which a state has to make too plainly to fail to make provision for this point in their fundamental laws. Since the supreme authority can be established only by the free consent of all the individual members of the society, we know the sentiments of men too well to imagine that these individual members would be inclined to burden their private property with a contribution to the expenses of the state. When they establish property, therefore, they will also set aside a special property for the state, from which the expenses of its maintenance shall be met; and this special property of the state is what is called crown estates or domains. The same thing takes place in a different way when individual families, which have been living in a condition of natural freedom on a certain territory, gradually unite into a civil society, and set a supreme authority over themselves. Each family then receives the land which it previously possessed as its property. But all that part of the territory which was not the property of individuals belongs in common to these families, who have now united to form a nation; and from the time a supreme authority is recognized, everything that is not the property of individuals is subject to the supreme authority, which represents the whole nation and acts in its name. This supreme authority will also not fail to employ everything useful which does not belong to individuals, for itself and to meet the expenses of the state. Here we have, therefore, another origin of domains; and this double origin actually occurs in history, so far as we find any traces and information concerning the first institutions of the earliest nations.

Upon and under the surface of every country there are always things which are not suitable for private property, either because their use must remain common to all citizens, and no one can be excluded from them, which is an essential characteristic of property, or because their extent is too great to enable them to be in the exclusive use and custody of an individual. In this class are rivers, lakes and seas, highways, great forests, and the metals under the earth, whose lodes and veins extend too far to enable them to be included in the division of property on the surface, and which require to be worked as a unit; which would be difficult to manage without much contention among the neighbors owning the surface. All such things, therefore, are best left a direct and special property of the state. Now since the state requires large expenditures for its support, this is a very suitable source of revenue for it; moreover, the use of these things could hardly be regulated in a more equitable way for all the subjects. This double reason makes it necessary to require those who wish to use these things to pay a certain charge, according to definite laws and conditions: in this way the needs of the state are met, and the difficulty of apportioning the use among the citizens is solved.

It is certain that the oldest states made these two chief sources of funds suffice for all the expenses of the state; and only gradually did the corruption of the times and of governments introduce contributions from the private property of the subjects. The abuse of these was carried so far in the later period of the Roman empire, through bad administration and the greed of public officials, that all free men lived in unspeakable misery, and therefore either gave themselves as serfs to anyone who would have them, or fled to the barbarians. This was also the principal cause of the collapse of the Roman empire, since all the provinces received the barbarians with open arms, regarding them as rescuers from their unspeakable afflictions. Nor were they deceived in this hope. Among the German nations, which destroyed the Roman empire, contributions were very moderate; and in Germany princes confined themselves so completely to the income from their crown estates and prerogatives, that they did not even consider it justified to demand special contributions from the private property of their subjects. When they could not get along with these incomes, in very unfortunate and urgent situations, it was only as a request that they turned to their subjects for a special contribution. Hence the first name given to taxes in Germany was *Bät*,

which means the same as request. It would, indeed, be very
desirable if rulers had always limited themselves to these
two sources of revenue, domains and prerogatives, and had
never opened up the third source, taxes and contributions.
Nothing is so subject to abuse, and can so weaken the state,
as this source; and it is also human nature to abuse it. Men
are seldom prudent managers of their own property; they
are either spendthrifts or misers, and the difference is simply
a question of more or less. How can we feel assured, therefore, that they will be good and prudent managers of property not their own, namely, the property of the state? How
can we expect that they will restrain their natural tendencies
to extravagance or avarice when managing the property of
a stranger, when they never hold these tendencies within
bounds in the case of their own property, although they
easily foresee that these tendencies will always be accom-
panied by inconveniences and harmful consequences for
themselves? Once contributions have been resorted to, they
have not the slightest compunctions about abusing them. It
costs them nothing, they can simply take it out of some
other man's property; and one would have to have no
knowledge of men whatever, not to admit that when a man
only has to take what he needs out of the property of others,
his needs will always soon multiply enormously. Men are
very ingenious in thinking up new needs, when they have
such an easy prospect of obtaining what they want. The
natural result of once resorting to contributions is therefore
bound to be that these taxes are steadily increased, and
finally become an intolerable burden to the subjects, resulting in the ruin of both the subjects and the state itself. For
such a steady bleeding must eventually reduce the body
politic to a consumptive, wasted frame. This natural result
is also in complete accord with the whole course of history.
Contributions have never been introduced without gradually attaining a height injurious to the state itself, until
finally a general revolution converted the fundamentally
corrupted state into an entirely different form. What should

be well noted here, however, is that almost every inclination of rulers furnishes ways to increase the contributions. The inclination toward splendor wastes the property of the subjects; avarice gathers it into huge treasures, which is just as bad for the subjects, and in some respects even worse. Ambition for honor and fame dissipates it in unnecessary wars; and great benevolence on the part of the sovereign exposes it to the plundering of his favorites. How fortunate, therefore, it would have been for the subjects in all times and all countries, if this source of revenue had never been opened; if men had always adopted the fixed principle that the private property of the subjects was not a source to draw upon for the expenses of the state; then expenditures would have been so regulated that the two previously mentioned sources of revenue would have sufficed.

I believe that the foregoing remarks demonstrate amply that contributions from the subjects can be resorted to only when the domains and prerogatives do not suffice for the necessary expenditures of the state. I readily admit, however, that this is only a vain limitation; since under present conditions in states these two sources as a matter of fact do not suffice; and it would be an equally futile endeavor to inquire whether these conditions could not be changed. Therefore we shall rather turn to the question whether it is more natural and more conducive to the convenience and welfare of the state and of the citizens to have this contribution from the private property of the subjects take the form of money, or produce, or services and labor. Here the rule must certainly be that it should be arranged in whatever way is least burdensome to the subjects. For the state, having so many servants and soldiers to look after, can always use produce as well as cash. It is chiefly a question of the amount of money in circulation in the country. If there is little money available, the produce of the farmer is very cheap, and he cannot even always sell it whenever he wishes. Under such circumstances, it is sometimes a great hardship to collect all contributions in money, which embarrasses the farmer greatly. A few centuries ago, therefore, it was very customary in Germany to collect a part of the contributions in grain and other farm produce; and the states used this produce, being in the habit of giving all their servants allowances of grain and other things needed in their households. Since money has become much more plentiful in Germany in the last hundred years, and the farmers seldom have any difficulty about selling their produce, it is more convenient in most places, both for the government and for the farmer, to have the contributions collected in money. Even to-day, however, this rule is sometimes applied. In Denmark a large part of the contributions are payable in grain; and in great states there are sometimes provinces, distant from the capital, having little trade, sparsely populated, and therefore often in difficulty about selling their produce, where this rule might very well be applied even to-day; since the payment of contributions in money is too burdensome for them. At least I know this is true of Carinthia, Carniola, and some other Austrian provinces.

It has even been held that a certain share of all produce, work, and earnings would be the best regulation for all contributions. This was the object of the well-known proposal of Marshal Vauban for a royal tithe, which he advocated as the most just form of contribution, providing for complete equality among the subjects, and which attracted much attention in his time. But not to mention the fact, which would be easy to demonstrate, that this complete equality would in many cases by no means be attained in this way, this proposal also has the defect that it gives no encouragement to diligence, since those who are diligent and cultivate their farms better, will as a result have to pay a much larger contribution than the lazy and careless. In any case, however, this royal tithe, as the only form of contribution, by no means suffices for the enormous expenditures made by states nowadays. Most governments collect a fourth of all earnings and profits from their subjects in contributions, some as much as a third of earnings. How could they, then,

meet their expenses with a tenth of all produce and earnings
This proportion — taking a fourth of all earnings in con
tributions — seems enormous to all those who have no ade
quate acquaintance with public finance. Where Baron vor
Bielefeld wrote in his *Outline of Political Science* (Part I
chap. 12) that it was in accord with sound political science
to collect 25 per cent of every income in contributions, Professor Gottsched, on page 401 of the German translation,
remarks, "This seems to be a terrible proportion. If I borrow someone else's capital, I pay only five per cent interest.
Now if the state levied five per cent on all my income, it
would be the same as if I borrowed all my income from the
state and paid interest to the state. Anyone who asked ten
per cent would surely be the hardest Jew or worse. Shall the
state, then, demand twenty-five per cent? What sort of
interest would this be?" If Baron von Bielefeld had written
that most states do collect twenty-five per cent of all incomes in contributions, he would have been quite right,
despite all the astonishment shown by Professor Gottsched.
That is, unfortunately, the rate of contribution in most
states, and no cameralist can and will deny it. To such
enormous heights have contributions mounted. But Baron
von Bielefeld's error lies in saying that it is in accord with
sound political science to collect that much. That I should
be careful never to say. What happens in the world is not
always in accord with sound political science. But we must
excuse the Baron, since the chief object of his work is to approve all principles which he finds introduced in modern
states.

After these preliminary considerations we come to the
principles which should be adopted and assumed in questions of taxes and contributions. For this purpose we must
first get a correct idea of what taxes and contributions are.
This idea is plain from the foregoing considerations. Taxes
and contributions are the payments by the subjects from
their private property, which they have to make for the
necessary expenses of the state in a certain proportion to

their property and earnings, when the revenues from the domains and prerogatives are inadequate. The method of raising these sums is one of the most important subjects of public finance, and, in a certain sense, of political science as well; and the arrangements and activities concerned with it are called the country's tax and contribution system.

The first and chief principle which must continually be kept in mind in questions of taxes and contributions is that the subjects must be in a position to be able to pay them. They are in such a position, however, only when they can bear the contributions without depriving themselves of necessaries, and without trenching upon their capital. Contributions which exceed these limits do not deserve this name; they are tyrannical exactions and a violent theft of the property of the subjects. And every state expenditure requiring contributions in excess of these limits is anything but a necessary expenditure. For no expenditure can be necessary which defeats the very purpose for which men live in civil societies. They live thus in order that they may, under the protection of a supreme authority, enjoy the necessaries, and, according to their position, the comforts of life, and keep their property in safety. A supreme authority, therefore, which deprives the subjects of the necessaries of life by contributions, and compels them to trench upon their capital, acts directly contrary to the purpose of civil societies; it overturns civil societies at their foundation, and it ceases, therefore, to be a legitimate supreme authority, and becomes tyranny. It is clear that no expenditure of the state can be so necessary as to justify going to such lengths. Necessity can never demand the impossible. It is always morally impossible, however, that is, it is impossible according to the purpose of civil societies and according to the rules of justice and wisdom, that contributions should be carried that far. We may even boldly assert that there is never a real necessity for it. This necessity is always merely imaginary, and if you examine the expenditures of such a state, you will always find hundreds of outlays which are either quite unnecessary or are not required in such amounts. The institutions of the state should be completely reorganized, before the contributions are raised to any such height. For example, if an adequate standing army could not be maintained without increasing the contributions beyond all proper limits, the army should be put on an entirely different basis, using the citizens themselves, without distinction, for the protection of the state. We may even assert that under a well-organized and wise government there cannot even be an emergency which would make it necessary to raise contributions so high. For such a government can borrow the sums which this distress requires; and then only the interest thereon will have to be paid out of contributions; and who would doubt that this is the way to choose? There are governments, it is true, which would find it impossible in emergencies to raise the necessary sums on credit, because they have no credit. But that is no argument against my proposition. A government that has no credit is not a well-organized and wise government, and I am speaking only of such.

From this principle it follows, therefore, that contributions can never be increased unless there is assurance that the subjects can pay them without depriving themselves of necessaries and without trenching upon their capital. Indeed, still another conclusion should be drawn and kept in mind as a permanent rule, namely, that contributions should never be increased without first putting the subjects in a position to bear this increase; that is, the conditions of the working class must be raised before an increase of contributions is thought of. That is the only way in which the increase can be just, and which is not injurious to the subjects, and consequently proper for a wise government. On this alone should the increase be based. But I need hardly say how little this rule is considered in the world.

The second principle of the tax and contribution system is that the contributions must be levied upon the subjects with complete equality and just proportions. Since all subjects have an equal share in the purpose of civil societies, the general welfare, and since they all enjoy equal protection, they must contribute equally to the great expenses of the state. But since, according to the preceding principle, the subjects must be in a position to be able to pay the contributions, and since the one who possesses more property also enjoys more protection, this just equality is simply a question of each subject contributing to the expense of the state in proportion to his property. Thus the more property a man has, the greater contribution he must bear; and this all the more justly, since it must be assumed that his earnings are always proportionately much larger. The point may be illustrated by an example. Martin, a merchant, has property amounting to twenty thousand dollars, and makes a profit of three thousand dollars. Christopher, another merchant, has property amounting to sixty thousand dollars, and makes at this rate nine thousand dollars a year. Let us assume that each of these merchants needs two thousand dollars a year for the support of his household, family, and servants; Martin, therefore, has only one thousand net earnings, while Christopher has seven thousand. Now if contributions are collected in exact proportion to property, and Martin pays two hundred dollars, while Christopher, having three times as much property, pays six hundred dollars a year, it is evident that Christopher nevertheless has to pay a much more moderate contribution than Martin; for the latter has only eight hundred dollars·left to increase his property, while Christopher has six thousand four hundred dollars, that is, eight times as much, though he pays only three times as great contributions. There have, indeed, been states which have taken this circumstance into account, and increased the contributions proportionately, when the property exceeded a certain amount. But nowadays there is so little thought of this increasing in proportion to increases in property, that the system of contributions is so arranged in all states that the richest subjects always contribute least to the expenses of the state; and since nothing can be collected from the poor, all the burden of contributions falls upon the middle class. However, it is by no means easy to arrange taxes exactly in proportion to property. There are almost insuperable difficulties in the way of such an arrangement.

Before we can explain these difficulties, we must consider the objects upon which contributions can be levied, and their various subdivisions. These objects are either things or persons. Things may be taxed for two reasons: first, because industry is carried on with them and profit made thereby, or because the use of them is general, and consequently, if this use is taxed, everyone contributes; second, they may be made the basis of contributions because they are included in property. These last things, included in property, are again to be divided into moveable and immoveable property. In moveable property belongs money, and since in most states there are now negotiable instruments in the form of bank-paper, shares of trading companies, government bonds, and the like, which are representatives of money, just as money is a representative sign of wealth, we have to make another subdivision and divide moveable wealth into actual moveable property and representative moveable property. As for persons, they may be assessed for contributions either according to their number and heads or according to their class, rank, and merit. Let us now see whether in all these objects, considered from various points of view, equality of contributions with respect to property can be attained in the case of all citizens.

There is not one of all these objects in which insurmountable difficulties are not encountered, when we try to levy contributions with just equality in proportion to the property of the citizens. If we wish to levy contributions on those things with which industries are carried on, this is not really a contribution that falls upon those who carry on the business. If their products are in demand, they always add the contribution to the price of their wares, and so the buyers have to bear it, upon whom the burden is by no means in proportion to property; if they are not in demand, they have to dispose of them at a loss anyway, and so the contribution hits them all the harder. This is a result of bad conditions in the laboring class; and it is plain that the burden is not in proportion to the property or the earnings of either the buyer or the seller.

If the contribution is levied upon things in common use, which nobody can do without, this is equally unsuccessful in imposing a contribution upon all the subjects in proportion to their property. A citizen possessing two thousand dollars' worth of property does not therefore eat more bread and salt than the wage-earner who has no property, and lives simply on his hard work; indeed, the citizen will eat much less bread, because he can have all sorts of palatable vegetables on his table. If it be objected that the citizen will support more servants and employees, and consequently will consume more bread and salt and other necessaries, this is probably true in barely half the cases. The wage-earner may have more children, and since he is unable to buy much of any other food, he and his family will eat more bread. If we consider the question solely with respect to distinguished and wealthy persons who are not engaged in business, we find not the least proportionality to property in these contributions; and, in my opinion, no more unfair and unjust form of contribution can be devised than this.

Among things included in property, immoveable wealth affords the best basis for a levy in proportion to property; provided all immoveable wealth is levied upon without regard to the rank of the owner, without granting any exemptions or privileges, which are quite contrary to the nature and purpose of civil societies. But fundamentally the equality which can be attained here rests more upon the value and yield of the lands than upon the property of the subjects. For a man may possess lands worth ten thousand dollars, and yet have scarcely a thousand dollars worth of property, since he owes nine thousand dollars. Moreover, since there are always many men in a country who possess no immoveable wealth, this can never be a general basis of contribution, forcing all the subjects to pay in just equality with respect to their property.

With respect to moveable property, just equality and proportionality of contributions is even less possible. This kind of property can be concealed so easily that it is especially difficult to levy contributions on it. Even if ways and means could be devised for that, however, good principles of government do not sanction it; because it is very prejudicial to merchants, traders, and manufacturers to compel them to reveal their property; whereby the progress of the working class itself is consequently hindered. It is true, there are various ways of levying on capital put out at interest, which are not harmful to the working class. But there are no means of imposing contributions in just proportion upon bankers and big traders, those whose property consists of bank-paper, shares, and the like. These, however, are the people who make most in a state, often with no effort, without contributing anything to the general welfare, simply battening on the industry of their fellow-citizens. For that part of the citizens who have to bear the burden of the contributions, this is a very hard situation which works to their great disadvantage; and in many states, where the public debt is large, as in England and Holland, and where an exceedingly large number of people consequently own the bonds of the state, live comfortably on the interest, and become richer and richer, which the industrious and laboring part of the nation have to bear in contributions, it is a great and real injustice. However, as conditions are now with states, no remedy is in sight.

Perhaps it may occur to some of my readers to ask whether no organization of civil societies is possible in which all subjects have perfectly equal property, and in which equality of contributions therefore presents no difficulty. This thought, which is very proper for noble and sympathetic souls who see the great majority of men living an exceedingly hard and miserable life, and are touched by the sight, has occurred to many in ancient and modern times, and in various republics of antiquity has caused great disturbances and unrest, when the poor citizens demanded that the rich and property-owning classes should consent to a new and equal distribution of all immoveable property. The demands of these poor citizens are completely justified in the eyes of anyone who considers the matter without prejudice. For what dictate of reason or of natural law can prescribe or approve that the great majority of creatures, of the same nature and origin, should languish in the greatest want and misery, at a time when the smallest part of them, not a whit better, batten on the sweat and blood of their poor fellow-citizens, and revel in every luxury? When the first Americans came to France, and noted the astonishing inequality in European civil societies, this, according to the statement of Monsieur de Montaigne, was what most surprised them. They could not understand how this greatest part of men could bear their woes so patiently, and why they did not fall upon their rich fellow-citizens and set fire to their houses. But however fair and just complete equality of property among all the members of a civil society may be in itself, it is impossible in all states where the use of money and full property rights have been introduced. Even if a state wished to undertake a new and complete equal distribution of immoveable wealth among all the citizens and inhabitants, this complete equality would not last long under a money régime, and where everyone is free to dispose of his property. Since families neither have the same diligence and skill nor make the same expenditures, there would always be families who accumulated money, and others in need, who would have to sell their property. But whether the invention of money and the adoption of gold and silver as a general equivalent of all things has really been good for the human race, is a very big question, which I shall never venture to answer in the affirmative. This invention may rather be regarded as the source of all evil and all misfortune in the world. It is really the evil first principle which the Manichæans considered necessary in order to justify a good God. And in fact, if we imagine a state which does not make use of money, where all citizens have an equal portion of land for their support, which they cannot alienate, as the Peruvian state was organized, all doubts concerning the providence and justice of God will disappear, which the condition of men in states infected with the plague of money arouses, and which reason is unable entirely to remove. But it would involve too great a digression to go into the question more fully here.

We come now to the third fundamental rule which must always be kept in mind in organizing a system of taxes and contributions. This is that the methods of raising the contributions must be of such a character that the welfare of the state and of the subjects and civil freedom suffer no harm. The importance and necessity of this rule is obvious to everyone. The general welfare of the state and of the subjects is the great purpose of all civil societies. All special purposes, organizations, and institutions of the state must therefore be derived from this first and general purpose, as from their great source; and a state which has any institution or organization that conflicts with this great purpose, is monstrous in form and structure. It is therefore clear that the tax and contribution system must contain nothing prejudicial to the welfare of the state and of the subjects. There may, however, be many features of a contribution system which work harm to commerce, manufactures, the whole working class, and the population in general, and hinder their progress and increase. This fundamental rule therefore deserves to be given careful consideration at all times in levying and organizing taxes and contributions. The civil liberty of the subjects deserves to be given just as great consideration. This freedom is certainly included in the welfare and happiness of the citizens; and without it we cannot imagine them happy. To disregard this liberty is likewise prejudicial to the welfare of the state. A state which impairs this freedom by its contribution system has slight chance of developing a flourishing working class or a large population; for not only will strangers show little desire to settle there, but the natives will seize every opportunity to leave their fatherland to settle in some other country, where civil liberty is given more consideration. The best and wisest system of contributions would doubtless be one that not only worked no harm to their civil liberty and welfare, but was also such that they paid willingly with a glad heart, and almost of their own accord. But this last is hardly possible as states are now organized, although the thing would be quite feasible under a different organization of republics.

The fourth fundamental rule is that contributions should be organized according to the nature of the state and of the form of government; and the justice of this rule is easily demonstrated. There are important reasons inherent in the nature of the government why a particular state can function in this and no other way. Hence if a financial system were to be set up in a state at variance with its political institutions, not only would its efficiency be weakened, by giving it a direction not in harmony with the other conditions in the state, but the necessary connection and agreement between all parts of the body politic, which combine to make a whole, and should all be directed toward a common purpose, would be interrupted. If the farming out of the customs, excises, and contributions, which in general is not to be approved, is ever suitable in a certain measure for any form of government, it is in unlimited monarchies. But it is quite unsuitable for aristocratic and democratic republics. It was no wonder, therefore, that the masses rebelled against these tax farmers in Holland about 16 years ago. It was more surprising that they had not done it long ago. Thus there are many circumstances which require a different financial organization under each form of government, but which cannot be dealt with in this chapter on general considerations. It is also necessary in all questions of taxes and contributions to consider the nature, situation, fertility, standard of living, and other characteristics of the country;

and due regard must be had for the genius, inclinations, sentiments, and spirit of the people. A form of contribution paid by one people without opposition would sometimes arouse much dislike for the government in another people.

The fifth fundamental rule to be kept in mind in organizing a system of taxes and contributions is that they must be given a certain and honest basis, fixing the contributions definitely and making them clear to all. The necessity of this rule is evident in more than one respect. From the point of view of the state it is necessary to be able to feel confident that the contributions will bring the required sums into the treasury. For the expenditures of the state cannot be postponed, without disorganizing and confusing everything. Consequently the contributions cannot be levied on any objects which yield very uncertain revenues, and where fraud on the part of the collecting staff and silence and deception on the part of the subjects may considerably decrease the sum expected. From the point of view of the subjects it is just as necessary that the contributions should be definite and certain. Everyone must know both the reason for the contributions and their amount, so that he may not be exposed to the whims and oppressions of the collecting staff. This is a great defect of the financial system in France, and one of the chief causes which expose this unhappy nation to the plundering of the tax farmers, as to so many insatiable harpies.

The sixth and last fundamental rule is that contributions should be so arranged that they can be collected in the easiest and most convenient way, and with as little expense as possible, both on the part of the state and of the subjects. The necessity of this rule is so obvious that it scarcely requires any elucidation. The advantage of both the state and the subjects depends upon it; and there is no doubt that it should be considered from both these points of view, since according to sensible and genuine principles they are inseparable. The state makes contributions convenient and easy for the subjects, if it makes them payable in small installments, such as monthly, and *in loco*, so that they may not have to lose time making long journeys to pay them. From the point of view of the government, convenience and ease of collecting contributions depends upon properly establishing and coördinating the collecting agencies, in short, in a very careful organization of the financial system. That it is an advantage both to the government and to the subjects to have the contributions collected with as little expense as possible requires no proof. The larger the expenses of collection, the less revenue does the state enjoy, or the more must the subjects be burdened with contributions unnecessarily. In this connection every care must be taken to avoid a multiplicity of collectors and offices, and to arrange that there shall be only one collecting office in each place.

These are the six fundamental rules which must always be kept in mind in dealing with taxes and contributions. They are all equally necessary; none is dispensable; and none is implied in the others, as many writers have imagined, who have tried to reduce them to two or three, but in doing so have lost sight of the most essential qualities of contributions.

BIBLIOGRAPHICAL NOTES

ST. THOMAS AQUINAS. The translation follows the text of the Fiaccadori edition (Parma, 1852–73).

ORESME. In general the translation follows the French version, as published by Wolowski (Paris, 1864), but in a few passages the Latin version seems clearer and I have followed that.

MOLINAEUS. The translation follows the first edition (Paris, 1546), nos. 9, 10, 11, 75, 528, 529, 530, 534, 535, 536, omitting some of the references to authorities.

BODIN. The *Response* was combined with a tract on debasement and printed as a sort of supplement to some of the later editions of the *Republic*. The translation follows one of these reprints (Cologne, 1608).

SERRA. The translation follows the reprint of the original edition, published by Graziani (Bari, 1913).

MUN. The text here printed is that of the edition of 1664.

HORNICK. The translation follows the edition of 1727 (Regenspurg).

CANTILLON. The translation follows the reprint of the first edition, published by Harvard University (1892).

GALIANI. The translation follows the reprint of the second edition (1780), published by Nicolini (Bari, 1915).

HUME. Hume revised his essays several times and slight changes were made by his literary executors. The text here printed is the final version, omitting the references to authorities.

QUESNAY. The translation follows the facsimile of the first edition, published by the British Economic Association (1894).

TURGOT. The translation follows Turgot's original version, as published by Robineau (Paris, 1889).

JUSTI. The translation follows the first edition (Halle, 1766).